RE-ROOTED LIVES:

inter-disciplinary work within the
Family Justice System

RE-ROOTED LIVES:

inter-disciplinary work within the
Family Justice System

Edited by Carola Thorpe and Judith Trowell

Foreword by the Rt Hon Lord Justice Thorpe

Family Law

Published by
Jordan Publishing Limited
21 St Thomas Street
Bristol BS1 6JS

British Library Cataloguing-in-Publication Data

A catalogue record for this book is available from the British Library.

ISBN 978 1 84661 047 9

Typeset by Letterpart Ltd, Reigate, Surrey

Printed in Great Britain by Antony Rowe Limited

Contributors

Dr Clifford Yorke

The Rt Hon Lord Justice Wall

Dr Judith Freedman

Beverley Tydeman

Dr Eia Asen

Jenifer Wakelyn

Dr Janine Sternberg

Professor Jo Sibert

The Hon Mr Justice Hedley

Stephen Cobb, QC

Dr Anne Zachary

Khatun Sapnara

Katherine Gieve

Henry Brown

Christopher Richards

Michael Leadbetter

Professors Cowan

Dr Stephen Cretney, QC

Foreword

Contested Children Act proceedings are dominated by the search for the welfare of the child. Government policy makers pursue the same goal. The United Nations Convention has the same declared central theme. So judges, legislators, and nations are united in their work. But is the welfare of the child a concept that permits of generalisation or are individual cases so fact dependent to defeat the formulation of a general rule, or even of any presumption? Certainly the formulation of a rule must be limited to the century or even the generation in which it is to be applied. The acceptability of corporal punishment of children in past generations contrasts with our acceptance today of homosexual relationships between 16-year-olds. What one generation accepts another generation condemns.

Let me take two examples in the more specific context of parenting. First it used to be a presumption, if not a rule, that mothers were naturally better endowed. Recently, fathers have entered the field with ever increasing confidence. Dual residence orders are now much more frequently made. Across the channel in 2002 France legislated Residence Alternée as an available norm. Second, what about contact between the child and the absent parent? In modern times it has generally been presumed to be beneficial. That presumption is reinforced by the advent of the Human Rights Act 1998; the Article 8 rights of child and absent parent point to the need to ensure post separation contact.

But to what extent are judges and policy makers listening to the voices of other disciplines, particularly mental health practitioners and researchers? In 1979 Goldstein Freud and Solnit in Beyond the Best Interests of the Child (Free Press 1973) advised, on the foundation of psychoanalytic theory, that conflicted contact was contrary to the welfare of the child and that the child's relationship with the absent parent should be determined by the custodial parent. That conclusion now seems quaint, particularly with the advent of the Children and Adoption Act 2006. However, recent research which focuses on the views and feelings of the children themselves is ambiguous over the benefits of contact: it suggests that we cannot presume that contact is always in the child's best interests, see Young Adults Perceptions of Court-Ordered Contact: Fortin Ritchie Buchanan: Child and Family Law Quarterly (2006) Vol. 18.211. Further a more recent article ('Contact/Shared Residence and Child Well-Being: Research Evidence and its Implications for Legal Decision-Making' Gilmore International Journal of Law Policy and the Family 20 (2006) 344) summarises a large volume of international research and also suggests that no presumptions should be adopted over the benefits or otherwise of contact. The reader of these articles may wonder whether the advice of Goldstein Freud and Solnit had not some validity.

If I narrow the focus to contested legal proceedings, and in settling the post separation regime less than 10% of families choose that route, it is surely obvious that judges who decide and practitioners who advise need to be informed of current research and broad mental health consensus. The work of Professors Murch and Hooper, in demonstrating the emergence of a distinct family justice system and its essentially inter-disciplinary character, has helped free lawyers from over-reliance on purely legal thinking. But lawyers are generally cautious of dialogue with other learnings and perhaps particularly of psychoanalytic thinking. That brings me to my theme, *Rooted Sorrows* and *Re-Rooted Lives*.

Rooted Sorrows was the product of a residential conference to consider the contribution of the psychodynamic mental health approach to work in the family justice system. How did it come about? The Portman Clinic had launched a course in Forensic Psychotherapy and had established an advisory body to meet once a year to discuss the utility and development of the course. Lord Lloyd of Berwick spoke for criminal justice and I for family justice. He saw the value of the courses for sentencing judges and persuaded the Home Office to fund a residential conference for judges and forensic psychotherapists who were assessing for the trial process or who were treating the convicted. I, following in his wake, persuaded the Lord Chancellor's Department to fund a family justice conference. Influenced by what I had learned from Mervyn Murch I proposed an interdisciplinary gathering and Dartington as the venue. The reaction of those who attended illustrates the caution that I have suggested. Some were unenthusiastic in their response. I remember one mental health professional in particular who was vehement in the conclusion that there had been insufficient acknowledgment of other approaches to forensic work in family proceedings.

However, the conference has had its enduring legacies, which is more than can be said for most conferences that generate only transient enthusiasm. First, it led immediately to the creation of the President's Interdisciplinary Committee. Second, it justified the publication of the conference papers, skilfully edited by Nicholas Wall. But the principal credit for the publication must go to Richard Hudson, then Managing Director of Jordan's. Richard had a huge influence on the expansion of the library now available to the specialist family lawyer. He was brave in publishing what was not certainly, or even probably, profitable. He and then his successor, Caroline Vandridge-Ames, have published the papers from each succeeding Dartington Conference, allowing comparison of the respective popularity and influence of each. *Rooted Sorrows* has outstripped all its successors. It has long been out of print and library copies do not sit forlorn and unread on their shelves.

So it was that in 2002 Richard suggested to me his idea of a second edition, not a reprint but a new work that would catch developments in the intervening seven years. My efforts to recruit an editor with the time and expertise proved frustrating. I tried the recently retired, but expertise was easier to locate than enthusiasm for the partial return to work. Time passed and Richard made the courageous move from publishing to teaching English to the sixth form at his old school. Fortunately, Caroline endorsed the plan and the search for an editor resolved with not one but two.

The editors have conjured papers from leading practitioners and thinkers in the family justice field of today. Here are papers that will better inform judges and legal practitioners of the experience and convictions of other disciplines. Here too are papers by judges and legal practitioners that view the same territory from a different vantage point. Just as lawyers need to broaden their understanding of child welfare and development, so other disciplines need to have sufficient comprehension of the law and the practice of the courts to enable them to communicate comfortably as reporters or witnesses of fact or opinion.

My hope is that *Re-Rooted Lives* will prove as influential and enduring as its predecessor. It will, undoubtedly, offer judges, practitioners and policy makers the opportunity to think more profoundly about the issues that confront them in their working lives.

The Rt Hon Lord Justice Thorpe
June 2007

Introduction by Dr Judith Trowell[1]

We think this book comes at a timely moment. The legal profession and senior practitioners from the health services have been alarmed that so few practitioners of any discipline in Children's Services (paediatrics and child mental health) have been developing their skills in court work, and that many have conveyed clearly their reluctance to undertake this work. Concern about the situation and subsequent representations to the Department of Health and the National Service Framework have lead the Chief Medical Officer, Professor Sir Liam Donaldson, to suggest that court work is a core and essential part of work with children and families, (*Bearing Good Witness*, 2006) and that therefore it needs to be included in the contracts Primary Care Trusts have with provider agencies. We hope this book will demonstrate how the inter-disciplinary work in the Family Courts has grown and will provide professionals with encouragement to discover that the work can be rewarding. The desire to achieve the best outcomes for the children and their families is a common concern.

WHY THE RELUCTANCE?

A number of factors have lead to the clinicians' reluctance to take on court work.

Since the new NHS contractual arrangements have been in place, service managers like to specify the work commitments individuals must undertake in each half-day session. Service demands and the pressure of waiting lists at the place of employment, means that clinical time is precious. Clinical assessment sessions can be absorbed into the work pattern, especially if they are cases from the locality and are therefore part of the contractual task. But the additional requirements such as reading the documents, writing reports and court attendance consume a great deal of time. If there are several children involved in the case, then reading the documents may take six to eight hours, and writing the report often takes a similar amount of time. Courts try to accommodate NHS practitioners, but a day away from the workplace is usually needed and more may be required. Sometimes the day and time may be changed at short notice. These demands cannot usually be managed comfortably in a busy NHS post, therefore the reading and writing are frequently done in the practitioner's own time. The court attendance may necessitate the cancellation of regular commitments, in turn causing disruption and risking poor service delivery. Retaining a time slot to be used flexibly offers the possibility of incorporating this work, although under the new contracts there is little leeway available. If this work does become established as a core task as proposed, then it will bring badly needed change and relief to the stress levels in the management of this work.

Another reason for practitioners' reluctance is the alien language of the courtroom and the different discourse that is undertaken there. Solicitors, barristers, judges, and court officers all have their own language and perspective. Whilst the language and approach of mental health

---

[1]   Professor Judith Trowell worked for many years as a Consultant child and adolescent psychiatrist at the Tavistock Clinic and is now Professor of Child Mental Health West Midlands NIMHE/CSIP. She is also a psychoanalyst and child analyst. Other previous appointments include psychiatric advisor NSPCC, chair of Young Minds, vice-chair Camden area child protection committee, founder and past director Tavistock Monroe young family centre. She was a member of the President's Interdisciplinary Committee and frequently acts as an expert witness in the family division.

practitioners is likewise alien to the legal profession, it is the former who have to move into the latter's domain. Barristers are self employed and insecure in an intensely competitive field; they are therefore heavily personally invested in their client 'winning'. This is so starkly at variance with the conditions under which most clinicians work. Many solicitors do try hard to reduce the adversarial nature of the process, particularly when on the Children's Panel or working in accordance with Resolution's code of practice, but their task is nevertheless still focussed on the current situation, the making of a case and the correct administration of the law.

The clinicians' approach to cases is different. They consider all aspects of the lives of the children and their parents and try to predict which intervention, if any, will be helpful. They then review the case in a few days, a week, or a few weeks and revise and refine their diagnosis in response to the changes in the child and family, allowing for the intervention to be modified according to the new situation. Therefore court work involves a different focus and means of proceeding from that with which the clinicians are familiar and comfortable.

When working therapeutically the clinical work is completely confidential; departure from this usual relationship with patients can feel antipathetic to the practitioner. Clinicians working with individuals or families have reasonable anxieties that any trust and confidence in the therapeutic relationship can be damaged or completely lost by a court attendance. Work that is based on the use of the relationship between patient and practitioner (transference and counter-transference) will be altered by a court attendance, and is likely to impact on it in an unhelpful way. There may be disagreements over the methodology being used: for instance, if the practitioner works psycho-dynamically, the issue of what weight is given to dreams, fantasies and drawings becomes significant.

Some cases require a definite decision that carries the weight of the law: this can be helpful in those cases that are intractable, or where there has been evasion or pseudo compliance. Clinicians recognise that such cases need a legal intervention, but many cases that come to court are not in this category. This is particularly so where marital breakdown has lead to allegations against a previous partner and the case comes to the attention of the Child and Adolescent Mental Health Services. Further reasons for the reluctance to take on court work are based on perceptions and hierarchies within the clinical multidisciplinary teams. It is a common perception that doctors are treated with more respect and their time constraints are given more weight than other practitioners with the result that nurses, psychologists and therapists prefer to leave the report and court attendance to the medical profession. The hierarchy is well established particularly in terms of pay scales. Nevertheless this is something the multi-disciplinary teams need to address if others outside the medical profession are going to be well-respected contributors.

Two processes that have become more prevalent recently deter clinicians from embracing this work.

(a)   An individual's professionalism or judgement may be besmirched, either in the witness box or during the discussions prior to the hearing. Insinuations about the clinician's judgement can be made, his/her private life noted and implications may be made that s/he is not reliable.

(b)   The other discouraging process is referral to the General Medical Council, which is a protracted and unpleasant experience that many senior medical practitioners have had to go through, with the complaint usually brought by one or other party to the proceedings. Given that litigation has become more prevalent this may be inevitable, but is a rare experience in work restricted to clinical practice.

OTHER ISSUES AND IMPLICATIONS

Clinical work is changing and evolving largely due to social changes that are happening at a considerable pace, bringing with it the need for the provision of more legal work of diverse kinds. Therefore the loss or lack of development of skills that are needed is potentially serious across a broad area of work.

Childcare work remains the core of Public Family Law. When child abuse and neglect first began to be recognised, Child and Adolescent Mental Health were often involved early on in the assessment work. Now that Social Services and Accident and Emergency personnel have become much better trained in this area, they work directly with paediatricians. This change was appropriate, but the consequence is that Child and Adolescent Mental Health services are called upon later in the cases when they are asked to assist in the assessment of the more subtle and difficult areas of emotional abuse, or in complex cases where there are questions of sexual abuse or neglect. The experience gained previously in more straightforward cases is seldom available, leaving clinicians anxious when confronted with the multi-faceted, serious issues to be considered. Vulnerable children and 'Looked after Children' frequently have complex mental health needs whilst simultaneously being the centre of legal, policy and social concerns (see references). Such complicated situations cause professionals to be fearful of complaints and blame for subsequent problems, and deter clinicians from taking on this demanding work. When obliged to do so, some resort to communicating in jargon rather than plain English as a means of misguided self-protection.

The breakdown of relationships, whether manifested in divorce or cohabitation dissolution, has lead to an increase in requests for legal work (private family law). Where domestic violence has been involved, it is now recognised that decisions about the children need to consider the impact on them of continuing to witness violence. As well as the possible danger of being caught up in the physical exchanges, their emotional and psychological development may become impaired as a result.

Relationship breakdown also frequently leads to allegations against previous partners of inappropriate sexual behaviour or abuse involving the children. Both these newer areas are complex and challenging, requiring clinicians to make careful, thorough assessments. The court hearing can involve a rigorous cross-examination needing confidence and mental agility to manage, which is achieved through experience and practice.

A major growth area that had not been anticipated is the legal work needed by refugees and asylum seekers, which may be to consider mental health requirements but the fundamental issue is often 'leave to remain'. A treatable mental health disorder may help to justify leave to remain. Whether the refugee is an unaccompanied minor who will therefore be considered under the Children Act, or a family member to be considered by a tribunal, skill and sensitivity are necessary to elicit the required evidence.

Work in the criminal court on behalf of young offenders or victims is not considered in this book. Nevertheless, issues such as criminal injuries compensation assessments and reports also need a capacity to use skill and sensitivity in the face of complexity, and to communicate in a straightforward way.

CONCLUSION

All these areas of work are demanding, exciting and very worthwhile. It is a result of many people's hard work that the impact of adult behaviour on children and young people is now recognised. Professionals need to develop the skills to be able to speak and write lucidly on behalf of children and their families. They need to have confidence and believe they have an important contribution to make and trust that their views make a difference. This contribution has been acknowledged by the recent document from Professor Sir Liam Donaldson (*Bearing Good Witness*, 2006). It is currently a consultation document but in principle is likely to be confirmed. It recognises that public family law court work is an essential part of CAMHS work and therefore needs to be included in the contractual arrangements made by the commissioners (PCT and LA). Teams in each geographical area will be expected to specialise in this work. The role of solicitors and others requesting the work remains to be clarified, as does the procedure by which the work will be allocated.

We should remind colleagues and the Department of Health that the implementation of 'Bearing Good Witness' is going to take time. Sufficient skilled and interested practitioners will have to be trained and in the interim retired colleagues, who presently undertake a considerable amount of this work, will still be needed. London and the South East are currently fortunate in having many trained and experienced practitioners, whereas the rest of England and Wales is not so well supplied, which will make implementation across the rest of the country less straightforward. Also, a problem may arise in a case where a local authority commissions a service and there is a disagreement over the approach to the resolution of the problem. The practitioner could feel pressurised by management to agree to the views of the purchasers and an outside expert may still be needed in such a situation.

Nevertheless, public law family work is likely to be part of the core CAMHS services, thereby recognising its value and importance. We hope this book will make a helpful contribution to this evolution.

References

Chief Medical Officer (2006) Bearing Good Witness: proposals for reforming the delivery of medical evidence in family law cases (Consultation, DoH)

Children Act 1989 (London, HMSO)

Children Act 2004 (London, HMSO. http://www.opsi.gov)

Every Child Matters: change for children (2004) (London, DfES. http://www.everychildmatters.gov.uk)

National Service Framework for Children, Young People and Maternity Services: (2004) *Standards 9. The mental health and psychological well being of Children and Young People, and 11* (DoH and DfES. http://www.dh.gov.uk)

Introduction by Carola Thorpe[1]

THE TRAGEDY OF MACBETH, ROOTED SORROWS, AND RE-ROOTED LIVES

We chose the title, 'Re-rooted Lives', to link with a previous publication 'Rooted Sorrows', the first volume in the series from the inter-disciplinary Dartington Conferences. Our title is idealistic and therefore unrealistic in the context of the family justice system, yet those working in and contributing to family justice, however diverse their roles, are joined by a common aim of attempting to prevent and/or remove the effects of 'rooted sorrows'. There is an inevitable tension between the aspiration to 're-root lives' and the difficulty of providing that ideal in most cases.

The title 'Rooted Sorrows' was drawn from Macbeth's consultation with the doctor about Lady Macbeth's well-being. He asks:

M   How does your patient, Doctor?

D   Not sick, my Lord

As she is troubled with thick-coming fancies

That keep her from her rest.

M   Cure her of that: Canst thou not minister to a mind diseas'd,

Pluck from the mind a rooted sorrow,

Raze out the written troubles of the brain,

And with some sweet oblivious antidote

Cleanse the stuffed bosom of that perilous stuff

Which weighs upon the heart?

D   Therein the patient must minister to himself.

The doctor's reply angers Macbeth and it indicates how helpless we can feel in the face of deep-rooted psychological distress in others, especially when it touches a distress of our own that we do not wish to know about. This seems to be so for Macbeth who fights to deny how disturbed he is by the crime he has committed, and intensifies his efforts to achieve his goal by arranging for further homicides to be carried out.

---

[1]   Carola Thorpe worked in the mental health field as an occupational therapist and in hospitals she experienced the value and the difficulties of multi-disciplinary work. She undertook further training as a psychoanalytic psychotherapist at the British Association of Psychotherapy and now works in private practice in London.

Whilst on the face of it there may appear to be little similarity between the lives of those who come into contact with the family courts today and the Tragedy of Macbeth, yet the story centres on a crime committed against a defenceless victim. That sadly is a very familiar story within the family courts, with children as trapped victims, helpless within disturbed families until someone notices their plight. The perpetrator's acts often disgust us, but we have learnt to understand that such acts are born of attempts by the perpetrator to manage his/her own troubled interior life. These attempts are usually futile psychologically in that they circumvent the core distress that is too painful to admit into consciousness. And because the hoped for relief is not achieved, except perhaps briefly, it has to be repeated. 'The violent act is, in phantasy, life preserving. It seeks equilibrium. This is a violent and cruel state of mind and, at the extreme is murderous.' (S Ruszczynski, 2006). These situations are indeed tragic for all involved.

It is not clear what drives Macbeth and his wife's shared ambition to be monarchs, but we have a hint that it may be their helplessness in the face of a childless union. (A 'babe' mentioned by Lady Macbeth must have died). Progeny help to protect us from facing the ultimate finality of death, as something of the parents lives on in the next generation. We can speculate that Macbeth hoped to reverse this narcissistic wound of childlessness and his powerlessness in the face of death, by achieving a phantasised immortality through becoming king. He does not seem prepared to give up and mourn that unfulfilled ambition to be a father and distracts himself from the pain, by seeking power. 'Hyatt-Williams too suggests that a state of murderousness is derived from a failure to work through emotional disturbances engendered by experiences, thoughts, feelings and phantasies to do with loss, life-threatening situations and death'. (S Ruszczynski, 2006 and Hyatt-Williams, 1995).[2]

We know nothing of Macbeth's early life, but it seems safe to imagine that some failure to cope with frustration and disappointment and loss in his maturational journey, left him ill equipped to tolerate a lack of omnipotence in adult life. When working with and learning about aggressive patients today, we frequently find that they experienced a failure of containment, usually maternal, very early in their lives.

> 'Without the experience of containment, no development of a psychological self can take place, a self that can process and think about experiences and psychic states. This cannot happen because such development requires the primary experience and perception of oneself, in another person's mind as thinking and feeling . . .Without this experience, the sense of self is **rooted** not in the mind, but in the **body**, The incapacity to psychologically reflect on and integrate mental experiences results in the person having only the body and bodily experiences through which to provide a sense of relief, release or consolidation'. (S Ruszczynski, 2006)

Again we can speculate that Macbeth's physical successes on the battlefields helped to protect him and shore up his vulnerable sense of self, but it seems that the comfort he found there was waning, possibly due to his ageing, and it was necessary for him to find an alternative, yet dishonourable way of maintaining his psychic equilibrium.

If Macbeth had been captured he would have found himself tried as a criminal, for in the external world, that is in reality, he had murdered. Those who come before the family courts are not usually criminals, yet in those cases where cruelty is present, be it psychological or physical, it can help our understanding of abuse to think of the relationship the perpetrator has to the object of his/her attack, as partial murder. Whilst 'partial murder' is impossible in the straightforward external world of realities, it is possible in the internal world of phantasy. Psychoanalysis introduced the term 'part- object relating' to refer to relationships where it does not seem that the perpetrator treats the victim (chosen object) as a whole person; the parts of the

---

[2]   Hyatt-Williams worked with prisoners in Wormwood Scrubs for many years.

victim that are incompatible with the required object are killed off. The 'other' then represents something to the perpetrator that needs to be punished or destroyed, deprived or hurt and sometimes this may be the perpetrator him/herself through identification with the object. 'Part-objects' may also be highly esteemed, as for instance in fetishes and other perversions, but this comes at the cost of not relating to the object as a whole and is therefore, at base, a denial of reality and denigrating of the other.

It is almost impossible for the mental health services or the family justice system to prevent a 'rooted sorrow': the very fact that the family has come into contact with these services indicates that something has gone seriously wrong with one or more of the individual's ability to negotiate their lives in a constructive way, and the root of that mal-function will already be embedded in the psyche(s). But these institutions may be able to intervene and ameliorate situations; for example through a legal order that alters the physical environment and, in some cases given time and treatment it may also be possible to help willing patients alter their internal states. By removing young children from a harmful situation, an opportunity is introduced for them to have experiences that contradict those they have lived thus far. This will not eliminate the negative experiences but will stop their repetition from external sources, and it is repetition that fixes experiences in memory. Even the very earliest experiences are recorded, and although not available to conscious thought in later life, ie explicit memory, they are stored as implicit memory and show up in bodily responses to certain stimuli. (Mancia, M 2006).

Macbeth seems to know that the events have been recorded through a physical process, 'the *written* troubles', alternately expressed as '*rooted* sorrows', and he makes the link between that process and Lady Macbeth's feeling state, as in 'troubles' and 'sorrows'.

Until recently we had to make do with theories of the mind based on observation and surmise, but technological advances have given us new instruments which allow for research into the development and function of the brain (Glaser, D 2003), bringing with it a wealth of fresh information about how the *brain* shapes experiences to become the *mind*, but also confirming much of the understanding that had been gained through clinical practice, particularly the significance of the part played by maternal emotional engagement with the infant as instanced by the work of Winnicott (1960) and Stern (1973).

The brain is made of physical matter which exists at birth and controls vital involuntary functions, but it also awaits the experiences of life gathered by the various sensory receptors, which create the connections (Solms, M & Turnbull, O 2002) that give us our own personal view of what we can expect, what we should fear, what makes us happy and all the various attitudes about our experiences that construct each of us into a unique individual. The connections in the brain, which are created by experience, cannot be removed, 'neurons that fire together, wire together' (Courchesne, Chisum, Townsend, 1994). This development is at its most active from birth to 3 years and is vitally dependent on the emotional participation of the carer(s).

Therefore positive responses to an infant's requirements are essential in the first years if the child is not to develop defensive reactions in intimate relationships and form a poorly rooted, confused sense of him/herself, with an unconscious tendency to repeat in later life, patterns of care that s/he have received that may range from the inadequate to grossly abusive. The connections made by early negative experiences are indelible, 'Once an object has been cathected as a fear object it is never de-cathected, it is never changed: and the only change that can occur is in the executive control mechanisms (pre-frontal lobes), which modulate and regulate and inhibit those basic drive states' (Solms, M 2006). By the time children are subjects in court proceedings they will inevitably have had experiences of varying intensity that are not conducive to healthy emotional development, resulting in degrees of disturbance that impoverish their subsequent lives. Re-rooting lives in more nutritious soil requires that the immature mind implants itself in the new environment, and allows the nourishing situation to grow and dominate in the mind. The roots that already exist will remain, and those roots seek to interpret the new situation to fit with what is already known, making the task of developing an altered internal view a struggle for the individual and difficult for those carers offering to facilitate change.

Facilitating change in disturbed families is an extremely difficult task, and frequently it requires the efforts of the family justice system and the mental health services working in conjunction. Inter-disciplinary work has developed due to the acknowledgement that understanding the inter-relationship between the external and internal world of individuals gives professionals the best chance in their attempts to help families amend damaging situations. If thought necessary, the courts can introduce changes in the external world and willing individuals and families may benefit from therapeutic work. There is far too little provision of the latter to reflect the needs of this population and insufficient recognition of treatment potential. It is as if society notices the needs, then, by providing inadequate resources, re-enacts the early deprivation making this group victims again. Thereby an unconscious collective abuse is committed.

In the following chapters you will find examples of the diversity of work undertaken by those contributing to the family justice system. The dedicated efforts by many practitioners leave the impression that their work should be considered more as vocations than professions. We hope that papers by practitioners from fields other than your own will be of particular interest to you. It is time, 10 years after the publication of 'Rooted Sorrows', that we return to confront the tragedy of disfigured internal lives and the sorrows that tend to repeat abusive behaviour in the following generation.

The editors and publishers have made every endeavour to ensure confidentiality throughout this book.

References

Courchesne, E, Chisum, H, & Townsend, J, (1994) 'Neural activity-dependent brain changes in development: implications for psychopathology' *Development and Psychopathology, 6: 697-722*

Glaser, D (2003) 'Early experience, attachment and the brain' in: Jenny Corrigall & Heward Wilkinson (eds) *Revolutionary Connections* (London: H. Karnac Books)

Hyatt-Williams, A (1995) 'Murderousness in relation to psychotic breakdown (madness)' in: J Elwood (ed) *Psychosis – Understanding and Treatment* (London and Bristol, PA: Jessica Kingsley)

Mancia, M (2006) 'Implicit memory and early-unrepressed unconscious: Their role in the therapeutic process (How the neurosciences can contribute to psychoanalysis)' *International Journal of Psychoanalysis 87: 83–103*

Ruszczynski, S (2006) 'The problem of certain psychic realities: aggression and violence as perverse solutions' in: Celia Harding (ed) *Aggression and Destructiveness* (London: Routledge)

Solms, M & Turnbull, O (2002) The Brain and The Inner World: An Introduction to the Neuroscience of Subjective Experience (London: Karnac Books)

Solms, M. (2006) *Sigmund Freud Today – lecture on the occasion of Freud's 150th Birthday 6th May 2006* The Arnold Pfeffer Center for Neuro-Psychoanalysis, New York (available from www. neuro-psa.org)

Stern, D (1973) *The Interpersonal World of the Infant* (New York: Basic Books)

Winnicott, DW (1960) The Theory of the Parent–Infant Relationship. *The Maturational Processes and the Facilitating Environment* (The Hogarth Press and the Institute of Psycho-analysis)

Contents

SECTION 1

We introduce this collection of papers with the only essay we are reprinting from the publication 'Rooted Sorrows' by **Dr Clifford Yorke**. We do so because it is a timeless and touching description of the start of the journey from the child's omnipotent world to that of a socialised citizen.

We then focus on the work of expert witnesses. **Lord Justice Wall** gives a legal perspective of the role of the expert in the family courts and **Dr Judith Freedman** of the Portman Clinic responds to this (the papers are based on the Glover Lecture 2005). These two papers are followed by descriptions of different ways of exploring the family dynamics, or the individual child's mind, in order to form views that could provide useful evidence to the courts. Whilst the settings may be different, the common factor is that the work is informed by psycho-dynamic theory: that is a view of mental life dominated by unconscious thoughts and ideas.

Beverley Tydeman, a child psychotherapist and **Dr Eia Asen,** a psychiatrist, describe how they undertake their assessments in a day unit. **Jenifer Wakelyn** raises important issues that require consideration when the placement of siblings is being decided and **Janine Sternberg,** also a child psychotherapist, explains the tools she and her discipline bring to assessments for the courts.

We recognize the important contribution offered by paediatricians with a paper by **Professor Jo Sibert.** He raises concerns about the role of the expert in the light of the Meadows case (amongst others), and the impact this has had on paediatricians. He emphasises the importance of Systematic Review studies.

Childhood and Social Order: the Emergence of Internal Law

Dr Clifford Yorke*

I want to say at once that I am not a forensic psychiatrist. I cannot even claim any special knowledge of the law, the courts or court procedure. Like any other psychiatrist, I have, from time to time, written reports or given evidence, and, on rare but unhappy occasions, done so to coroners' courts. So I thought it might be helpful to write on matters about which I am rather better informed, and to look briefly at some of those stages in the development of a child that may have a bearing on behaviour that, later on, may get people into trouble or help to keep them out. That means saying something about *conflict* in relation to childhood, and conflict that lies *within the self* and not simply between the child and the earliest society – the family or its substitute – in which he grows up. In particular, it may be useful to try to understand a little about the way conscience develops, and how an *internal* law giver may stand in relation to an *external* one. Whether that is of any practical use or not, it may, I suggest, be something that neither the lawyer nor the professionals who advise him should altogether neglect.[1]

Freud did not invent the notion of conflict within the self, nor was he the first to speak of it. Montaigne was hardly breaking new ground when he wrote:

> 'We are, I know not how, somewhat double in ourselves, so that what we believe we disbelieve, and cannot rid ourselves of what we condemn.'

Every rediscoverer of conscience knows, on the basis of simple introspection, something about discord within the mind. Most people are easily, or perhaps uneasily, aware of guilt and the conflict within themselves when they want to carry out some particular action but feel at one and the same time that they ought not to do it. But this easy familiarity with an internal arbiter may not be a decisive influence on our behaviour. For although, as Shakespeare pointed out, conscience *can* make cowards of us all, and 'enterprises of great pith and moment lose the name of action', it can also vary greatly in its effectiveness. Indeed, it is perfectly possible to feel guilty about something one is in the act of doing while still continuing to carry it out. So Shakespeare's statement is certainly no rule, though it is sometimes strikingly true of those who suffer from a conscience of such severity that it borders on, and sometimes even amounts to, the pathological. It is not too difficult to think of people whose sense of right and wrong effectively interferes with their everyday lives and makes the most trivial of decisions a matter of earnest and unending internal debate.

For all that we regard conscience, however imperfect, as a major guide to human behaviour. But it is important to understand how its role as internal watchdog stands in relation to the external forces of social enterprise and censure. An issue of this complexity is easily shirked, or

---

*   Formerly psychiatrist-in-charge, the Anna Freud Centre and Consultant Psychotherapist to the Psychiatric Unit at Watford General Hospital.
1   I have in places drawn on a Radio 3 talk delivered in January 1986, the text of which was reprinted in *The Listener*. It was called 'Conscience and The Divided Self'.

sidestepped altogether, by excessively simple formulations. Of these, the doctrine of total conditioning had, for long, a clamorous appeal. From this standpoint, human development is quite uncomplicated: our views, opinions, and sense of right and wrong are simply the results of *social* forces. People are purely the products of their upbringing. Changes in society will radically alter the way they view themselves, and decisively change their social behaviour. This view is avidly propagated by various types of liberationist, but it colours a good deal of current political thinking.

Freud was as interested in conscience as he was in social psychology. His reflections on large groups hold good, in many respects, for small groups too, especially if there is a charismatic leader with which the group identifies. He was particularly concerned about the disappearance of *individual* conscience in a group organisation that seeks to become a powerful social force, and one that *knows* it is always right. But the phenomenon is not restricted to the many kinds of social activists who are so intolerant of disagreement. And conscience can certainly be suspended in crowds: today we would perhaps first think of the seemingly mindless violence of some football team supporters; but the behaviour of some animal rights proselytisers is not always very different. When Freud once stated that 'social anxiety' is the essence of what we call conscience, he had similar matters in mind; but in emphasising the *historical* link between them (with the family or its substitute as the first society) he never confused the two.

The fact is that internal and external arbiters of conscience may be much more at odds with each other than some fashionable viewpoints allow. This was vividly brought home to me by a friend who works in a student health service. Some years ago, he told me that the permissive society might well have a lot to recommend it, but that it occasioned him more than a few problems. He repeatedly came across students who felt obliged to take part in sexual activity for which they felt unprepared and who could not understand why something everyone said was a joy brought, for them, so much inner anguish. He added that he spent some time with people who, intellectually, welcomed the principle of communal living in rebelling against the 'nuclear family' but who were surprised and dismayed when they discovered that the new social setting did nothing to subdue the pain of jealousy.

Not all the suffering endured by students like these springs from the rebukes of conscience. Feelings of inadequacy, inferiority, ignorance, or the fear of the loss of a partner through a failure to comply with expectations, are among the more obvious examples of personal misery that readily spring to mind. But, for all the disparities between them, each one has some connection with what might loosely be called self-regard, and involves some degree of self-comparison with others. Once again, the states of feeling involved appear to have both internal and external points of reference. They are not to be equated with conscience, to be sure; but they may be sufficiently related to it to suggest a common ancestry.

Everyday experience, whether of ourselves or others, tells us that it is perfectly possible to have a strong sense of right and wrong, but that inner controls over impulse may be frail. Something snaps; restraint is lost; impulse spills over into action without further thought; and the result becomes a cause for profound regret. Conscience may be strong, but the power to respond to it less than adequate. So it cannot be that conscience alone, however great its strength, controls our actions. There must be something else – an internal system that keeps our impulses under control and makes our responses to conscience effective.

Children are not born with a ready-made conscience, with a sense of guilt, of shame, and other internal deterrents; nor are they born with inner controls. They are, of course, born with needs, and very strong needs at that; and the satisfaction for which those needs cry out may feel far too imperative to wait on events without protest. So it seems worth looking at the way in which internal deterrents, internal controls, and for that matter internal guides, standards, aims and *ideals* may come into being, and to try to see how they become effective or sometimes fail to do so. For though it may be said that *internal* discipline is the only discipline really worth having, and perhaps the only one to be respected by its proprietor, no one can pretend it is easily acquired. And since human beings are enormously complex, what I write about these matters today will be limited by knowledge as well as the constraints of space.

Even the most casual observer of children, is bound to be impressed by the changes brought about in the first five years of life. (They may not add up to a miracle, but they come remarkably close to it.) In that short space of time, the infant is transformed. Helplessly dependent at the start, all need and *want*, his[2] existence is largely measured by rocketing need, satiation, and oblivion. By the time he starts school, he has embarked on an articulate social life, able to respond to, and relate with, teachers and schoolmates, able to work and play, to join in group activities, to undertake new tasks and obligations, able to leave the family behind for substantial periods, and, if all goes well, to get true pleasure from becoming part of this wider world outside. En route, complexities multiply in a developing world of emotional ups and downs, of fresh fears, frustrations, satisfactions and changing demands. If memory sprang from the drama of events, recall of these tempestuous times would indeed be vivid.

And yet ... that is exactly what it is not. Few people can bring to mind more than a hazy recollection of what is arguably the most formative part of their past. Childhood amnesia of this magnitude calls for explanation, and nothing as naïve as mere remoteness in time will do by way of it.

Montaigne does not help much here. Something more is needed than the notion that the mind is divided against itself. The mind indeed is *divided against its own past*. Only an internal division of a very special kind could make those vivid early years so inaccessible to consciousness. Nor can this be a simple matter of a mental divide, which permanently shuts off one part of the mind from another. That would mean that those first eventful years had no influence or bearing on those that followed.

Freud's early awareness of this apparent anomaly – that much that defies the memory maintains a significant influence on early life and its subsequent development – had an important bearing on many of his further formulations. The notion of a divide between events that *can* be recalled – albeit sometimes with difficulty – and events that, unlike the pangs of conscience, defy recollection – has long since passed into common currency under the term *repression*. But this is a term that is often misunderstood. It has nothing whatever to do with repression in a political sense. Nor does it mean *suppression*. We often suppress thoughts and feelings – or try to – but that is a conscious process. Repression, in contrast, is a process of which we remain unaware. It is of particular interest, in the present context, that Nietzsche, in one of his aphorisms, had already portrayed the process in terms that Freud found singularly impressive. The quotation may speak for itself. '"I have done that," says my Memory. "I could not have done that", says my Pride, and remains inexorable. Finally, my Memory yields.'

It's surely worth noting that what Freud later called repression was, for Nietzsche, no mere matter of entertaining a memory in consciousness and then deliberately discarding it. 'Finally', he says, 'my Memory yields'. Awareness is now denied, but not as a matter of choice. It is no longer accessible to introspection. And it is striking that he invokes *Pride* as a motivator of very considerable power. Pride is the antithesis of shame. So Nietzsche's construction suggests that it is the preservation of self-esteem that can play a major part when memory is so decisively jettisoned.

But close observation of small children suggests that the role of pride and shame in the maintenance of self-esteem is operative long before childhood amnesia sets in. The capacity to feel disgust, for example, and so to feel ashamed of whatever it is in oneself that gives rise to it,

---

[2]   'His' is used generically throughout, unless the context suggests otherwise, and can equally be read as 'hers'.

is generally acquired some time during the third year of life when an impressive interest in excreta and all things lavatorial gives way to feelings of aversion. But if shame springs from such humble origins, it later extends, as everyday experience confirms, to very different and diverse thoughts, fantasies and actions. And it is perhaps the *fear of shame* that is such a powerful motivator, which brings with it a fear of exposure and the wish to hide.

To start with, the child wants to hide from others, through fear of disapproval. Anna Freud – Freud's youngest daughter and the only one of his children to follow him into his profession – used to tell a story about Lisa, a little girl of two-and-a-half in a nursery school. The nurse was in the habit of offering the children fruit juice and chocolate by way of elevenses. Wisely, she kept the chocolates on a shelf out of the children's reach. One day she had occasion to leave the room unattended. The little girl at once seized a stool, dragged it to the wall, climbed onto it, reached for the shelf, and was just about to close her fingers on the chocolates when the nurse reappeared. With great presence of mind Lisa moved her hand to a more neutral object and climbed down with it. The nurse left the room again and the child climbed on the stool once more. This time, when the nurse reappeared, Lisa's hand had closed on a chocolate and seized it. Unruffled, she climbed down and graciously offered it to a somewhat surprised but appreciative little boy. The third time the process was repeated, the nurse returned in time to see the little girl stuffing the chocolate into her mouth.

Lisa is clearly at the moment of transition: she is approaching a point where a fear of shame is about to preside over actions with increasing effectiveness. But her behaviour is still, for the most part, a fear of disapproval, and not a fear of disapproval by her peers but by an adult authority. For all that, the child is on the road that leads from *external* to *internal* disapproval, to disapproval of herself. But she is not there *yet*.

Perhaps this little story will remind us that this discussion needs to be set in the context of the steps that lead from external to internal controls, and from external to internal *law*. And bearing in mind what has been said about Nietzsche and Freud, about shame and guilt, we have to try to trace the steps from external to internal *conflict*.

At the beginning of life the infant's needs and wishes are met by the mother's facilitation or restraint.[3] Within this interaction, *affective* (emotional) bonds are mutually established which open up new areas of gratification and well-being for the child and mark a departure from purely biological to psychological needs. In due course this interaction will modify the peremptory quality and urgency of the infant's demands, to that extent marking the beginning of a capacity to tolerate frustration. The way in which the mother exercises her functions as guardian and caretaker, the way she recognises and responds to her baby's needs, how she provides satisfaction and substitute satisfactions, and the ways in which she makes frustration more bearable – all these have a part to play in building up of child's inner world. Those experiences which enable the infant to tolerate delay in the face of mounting need, and which themselves become increasingly pleasurable in terms of the child's well-being, enable him to lay the foundations for inner controls, though it is axiomatic that for some time to come these measures will intermittently yield to the pressure of internal demands. In all these matters the influence of endowment, maturational factors, and of course experience itself, will together determine the individual variations in the way the mind develops in each child.

As the child becomes less dependent on his mother's body, as he grows more aware of the world around them both, and as he starts to explore it, learning to crawl and then to walk, his wishes and pursuits are increasingly interfered with by the mother or others in charge of him. The toddler is repeatedly frustrated by limitations imposed by what, to him, is an incomprehensible

---

[3]　For 'mother' read 'mother or her substitute'. Some of this material appeared in a more academic form in a paper by my colleague Hansi Kennedy and myself published in 1982 in the Psychoanalytic Study of the Child (New Haven: Yale University Press).

series of maternal interventions designed (unknown to him) to protect him from danger. He is driven by wishes that cannot always be granted and demands that cannot be met.

In order to adapt to these conditions the child has to develop new capacities. He has to learn to *remember* these experiences of wishes and activities that are tolerated (and often enjoyed) and those that are frustrated or forbidden (and often no less enjoyed). He has to learn to classify them in terms of the mother's approval or disapproval. But these new abilities do no more than reflect his mother's view of these different situations. He simply apprehends the models of 'goodness' or 'badness' which his mother holds up to him.

These models do not as a rule reflect his own wishes. Indeed they create formidable struggles that persist for some time and which can appropriately be called *external conflicts* – conflicts, that is, between himself and others. For example, a 3-year-old who particularly wanted to get her mother's approval repeatedly asked, 'Am I good?' As soon as she was reassured of this, however, she would add, with a certain immediacy: 'But I don't *like* doing what I'm told!' Another little girl, aged 4 at the time, clashed with her mother whenever she couldn't get her own way. In these circumstances the child would say, 'You don't love me or you wouldn't say "no". I don't love *you*'. Elements of these primitive barter systems can, of course, be detected much later in life. It is one thing to *understand* a prohibition and quite another to *accept* it. And without acceptance there is no possibility of making adaptations and modifying behaviour on the strength of *internal* resources alone. (Perhaps that is why we sometimes say that a law that no one obeys is bad law.)

There is, then, a line of development that leads from dependence on the mother as controller, through physical restraints, verbal restraints, interdiction or forbidding glance, to internal impulse control. External controls originally operate against a multitude of childhood wishes, not all of which are simple representatives of wishful impulses,[4] but nevertheless endanger the child or, for that matter, the security of a brother or sister, the cat, or objects around the home.

While burgeoning achievements contribute to the child's capacity for inner control and self-regulation, the wishes that remain closest to these basic impulses are still the hardest to give up. It is these wishes that continue to mobilise anger with the restraining adult. Toilet training often provides some of the most striking examples. Tony, who at the age of 3 was excessively messy in his water-play and required repeated physical restraint, became very angry with his therapist when she interfered with his wishes. On such occasions he called her 'a bloody cow' and defined her in fantasy by pretending to be a fireman and dousing her with hoses. All the same, he was careful to emphasise that this was for her own protection! Another young patient repeatedly called his therapist 'naughty' whenever his own aggression was aroused and he anticipated her disapproval and retaliation.

Children have at their disposal a number of ways of dealing with these inner struggles. Some of these are still recognisable in the adult. It is easy to attribute something you do not like in yourself to someone else – to say *he* is mean, *she* is nasty, but not to indict yourself. If you want

---

4　Freud referred to these basic impulses as instinctual drives, intrinsic to the organism, of which there were two main groups – libidinal and aggressive. In childhood the sexual drives are not to be equated with later genitality (of adolescence or adulthood) though genital wishes are recognisable very much earlier, normally passing into latency somewhere around the age of five. The drives go through various stages, rooted in bodily areas – to begin with the lips, mouth and skin. Pleasure derived from these various bodily areas can be recognised in the sexual foreplay of adults. The drives have various mental representation in the form of fantasies and wishes; many of these succumb to childhood amnesia, but others deriving and developing from them will find acceptable outlets. Others remain permanently unconscious. In adolescence there is a remodelling of drive derivatives as aggression and sexuality become capable of forceful expression, but the first five years or so of life, though for the most part inaccessible to memory, have profound influences on adolescent development. Man appears to be the only animal in which sexuality is bi-phasic. No one, I think, would dispute the reality of childhood aggression, though the force of it is limited by physical capability.

to hit somebody, but fail to recognise the fact, you may feel that this same person wants to hit *you*. And lots of people rationalise actions that they would otherwise find difficult to justify, and *for which they do not know the real reasons*. These defences against unwanted impulses are generally unconscious, though they are rather more accessible in children under five than they are in later life.

Nursery observations have furnished us with lots of examples of how children begin to internalise prohibitions. A first step is to deflect the adult's prohibitions by directing them against other children. Many a child who has not yet acquired bladder control points with indignation at puddles on the floor put there by others.

Until the child is able to identify with the ideal held up to him, and thereby turn against his own impulses, full toilet training cannot be achieved; and true *internal* conflict cannot be said to exist. In this respect, one of our Wartime Nursery children, Birgid, who had difficulty in acquiring control of her bladder, reached a turning point when she was able to announce, with feeling: 'No more wee-wee on the floor: Mummy doesn't like it; Nurse doesn't like it; *Birgid* doesn't like it.'

The crucial point that Birgid makes is that *she* does not like wee-wee on the floor; she takes an *affective*[5] attitude to unrestricted wetting and begins to find it repugnant, if not to hate it. Feelings play a considerable part in the defensive attitudes and inner controls that children build up and adults as a rule maintain.

Birgid has taken a step beyond that reached by Lisa in the story about the chocolates. Once Birgid had established true internal disapproval she would have been ashamed of herself had she relapsed into wetting. And if a child does something of which he is ashamed, he may not only hide his action from others, even the *thought* of his action may bring back the feeling of shame, and he may strive to hide the knowledge of it from himself. If Birgid's is an early step on the road to morality, it seems worth adding that not every adult has managed to take it. There are still many people for whom shame is experienced only when they are found out.

That is what Freud meant when he said that social anxiety is [historically] the essence of what is called conscience. The parents or their substitutes provide the social sanctions, and in some degree the sense of what is desirable, which form the foundations of internal authority. There is an internalisation of standards, as Birgid shows very well. The wish *to take pleasure* in wetting is no longer accessible to awareness. But it does not on that account cease to exist; it can sometimes surface again when a new baby is born and a child who, until that time had no competitors, reverts to an early mode of behaviour. It can re-appear, too, in less normal circumstances – in certain cases of mental illness for example, or be put to deliberate use when the social approval and endorsement of a peer group overrides any individual scruples, and house-breakers express their anger on finding nothing of value by urinating and leaving excrement around the room.

These early moves from outer to inner seem quite insufficient to anticipate the massive childhood amnesia that sets in so decisively around the age of five. Pride and shame may help to make certain inclinations unavailable to consciousness, as Nietzsche recognised, and so make some contribution to the effectiveness of repression, but they cannot in themselves account for the effectiveness of a *repression barrier* of such a fateful kind. Something more is required.

Shame is not guilt. The two may co-exist; they may complement each other; in both, external origins precede an internal presence. But they are not the same. Freud came to regard guilt as a specific form of fear – fear of what he called the *superego*, using that term to extend the everyday notion of conscience to include its unconscious sources – sources which continue to operate

---

5   i e emotionally charged. An affect is the general term for a state of feeling – happiness, sadness, anger, remorse or whatever else it may be. Some affects are complex, comprising mixed states of feeling: depression, for example, may contain, inter alia, a mixture of sadness and anger.

beyond the level of conscious awareness, beyond the level of the sense of guilt that *is* accessible to introspection. We now have to address the question of how this *superego* – this conscience, *a powerful part of which is unconscious* and therefore operates silently – comes into being.

We have in fact already made a start. What has been described up to this point are early moves from the use of an external policeman to the use of an internal one, but it does not follow that both constables exercise identical functions, even though they recognisably belong to the same (parental) force. At first we see, internally, an incomplete representation of the external policeman, a mere cadet, who is able to discharge only limited functions, and who repeatedly needs reinforcements, orders, and support from outside.

Oddly enough, there is a similarity here with something I touched on earlier, with the state of affairs in children who develop a premature sense of guilt, a *kind* of conscience that is so harsh it gives the child no peace. It is as if the internal police cadet has been rushed through his training, qualified long before he was ready, was unable to use the power entrusted to him with any sense of fairness, and threw his weight around with excessive zeal. In such an instance, the child may repeatedly appeal to the real policeman, to the parent, seeking assurance and reassurance that he is really 'good', in order to deal with the sense of "badness" that goes hand in hand with his failure to live up to the very high standards internally set for him and the severe and premature strictures of the internal cadet he has unwittingly imposed upon himself.

To pursue this matter further would take us too far into pathology, and we need to keep in mind a more normal state of affairs. More usually, in terms of our metaphor, the police cadet continues to rely for effective action upon external support. But harassed though he may be, he now draws strength from an unexpected quarter. *He draws it from the aggressive drive itself.* He turns to derivatives of that powerful force and uses them to re-enforce the internal prohibitions of the little person of whom he has taken charge. It is as if heavily armed ramparts bar the way to wishful impulses, thoughts, and fantasies that would otherwise get out of hand and threaten the small society in which the child is growing up and which he still needs for care and protection.

This remarkable advance in personal and social adaptation is presaged and reflected in certain changes to be observed in the fantasy play of children. Whereas, in the beginning, such play may tend to repeat, through imitation, the child's day-to-day experiences, he now begins to demonstrate a stand against powerful impulses to which, hitherto, he would have been tempted to give way. For example, one small boy who had always used dolls[6] to represent either himself or other children, and repeated with them the activities of his daily life around meal-times and bed-time, began to scold his dolls for their 'naughtiness' and 'dirtiness', for doing 'wee-wees' and 'poos', and for being smelly or stinking. The dolls were dealt with harshly: they were often smacked and even thrown about. It would seem that the anger and humiliation aroused in the child by external restraints and threats of punishment mobilised his aggression and the anxieties associated with it, so that they were defensively directed against the self.

It is impossible to understand the motivation behind these moves without giving due weight to *anxiety*. Indeed, it can be said that it is precisely the fear of loss of parental love which threatens the child with overwhelming anxiety, and which only appropriate internal measures can effectively keep at bay. Thus, on the one hand, the striving for pleasure makes it difficult for the young child to accept external prohibitions while, on the other hand, these selfsame prohibitions become an indispensable ally in the fight against his own pleasure-seeking demands.

How does it come about that the formation of the superego brings with it a sense of guilt? For its activities clearly go far beyond the exercise, conscious and unconscious, of simple checks and

---

6 Child therapists often provide miniature dolls representing girls and boys, men and women, people in occupations of all kind, for children to play with; often the child arranges the dolls in very informative ways that reflect their view of the state of the family, school-life as they see it, and so on.

controls. Freud came to his views about guilt and its *unconscious power* by the fact of infantile sexuality and the instinctual life of childhood. He had to account for the manner in which the 'child's first great love affair', with its jealousy of the parental relationship, is banished from the memory as early incestuous attachments come to grief. If, in this context, the word 'incestuous' calls for justification, two points can be made. Firstly, *we are talking about impulses and fantasies, and not deeds* (except in the rarest instances where action is initiated by the parents). Secondly, in the early years of life the child's instinctual impulses, and the love and hate derived from them and through which they find expression, can *only* be directed against the family *because there is nowhere else for them to go*. It is only in the context of the family or its substitute that relationships have any meaning. Although counter-measures against these impulses and the wishes that strive to express them are, of course, set up, eventually such wishes have to be abandoned. The reasons for this are many and various: the impossibility that childhood incestuous wishes could ever be gratified; the fears of fantastic punishment or revenge; and even perhaps the fact that these childhood strivings were ordained to come to an end for constitutional reasons – all these, and others, could play a part.

But, if these sexual and destructive wishes are forbidden by the objects of the child's fantasies; if the child is compelled, for whatever reason, to abandon his aims; and if, too, he has to give up such aims in respect of others – then internal interdictions have to be replaced, or rather re-enforced, by the kind of internal policeman of which I have spoken and, to be successful, a policeman of impressive power. And there is one further point of cardinal importance. Just as the younger child fears loss of love, and punishment from the external arbiter of his conduct, so the older child possessed of an *internal parent or parents*, fears loss of love from that fantasy parent, and a fear of punishment known to us all as guilt.

If, to the adult, all this talk of a childhood love affair and its resolution has an air of unreality, it is important to remember that it is not just a matter of *real* events, of *real* threats, of *real* determinations and intentions. It is very much a matter of psychological realities, of psychological forces, where anything can happen because it can be thought, where fantasy and reality do not always recognise each other for the different forces that logic knows them to be. The internal police are therefore not simply police: they are *thought police*. (The young child behaves as if he knows only too well the religious dictum that the evil thought cannot be distinguished from the evil deed, and may treat the one as if it were the other.)

It would not be true to say that the superego is simply an internal representative of the *real* parental precepts and prohibitions. Children of benign and understanding parents sometimes develop standards that are too harsh, too truly tyrannical, for their own good. Conversely, children who have been exposed to strict control and discipline sometimes achieve an unexpected degree of self-tolerance. There is no simple one-to-one correspondence: what is internalised is not an *objective* representation of the parents and their attitudes, but the parents as seen, consciously and unconsciously, through the child's eyes.

The child is not of course ruled internally simply by guilt or by shame and the fear of it. What is perceived by the child as loving and caring parental regard brings with it a wish for some degree of emulation. But it does more than that. It provides an *internal* source of love and self-esteem which helps to mitigate and modify the would-be tyrant within. The child is no longer exclusively dependent on the approval of others for self-regard. But early idealisation of the parents and the wish to be like them is one of the ingredients of those ideals that provide the child with aims, guidelines and models in the conduct of his everyday life. To these may be added the way in which the child perceives the parental behaviour in its sexual and aggressive manifestations and the degree to which, in this respect, he will identify with the *real* parents; the manner in which the parents convey their concept of *their* ideal child, that is, the child they would like him to be; and whether father and mother convey *different* ideals and whether there are discrepancies between what they consciously or unconsciously convey. All these elements will be compounded in the formation of the child's *own* self-ideal, which will include, in addition, the attainment of his pleasure-seeking wishes, suitably modified by later developments to take full account of reality.

To return to the matter of guilt. The upheavals of adolescence are yet to come. Puberty brings with it a biological intensification of sexuality and aggression which puts a severe strain on the personality. For all its importance, childhood sexuality is a pale thing compared with its adolescent successor; and childhood aggression still lacks the physical means to inflict the damage it may entertain in fantasy. Existing checks and controls can no longer contain these drives without reinforcement. On the other hand, total instinctual suppression runs counter to the psychological tasks of adolescence: psychic health demands that the extensive restrictions imposed during latency[7] are modified. Sexuality must be freed, but only *outside* the family, now that the physical means exist to translate wish into action. Conscience is at a crossroads.

Unconsciously, the tyranny within is denounced; consciously, the uprising takes the form of the 'adolescent rebellion'. The tyranny is perceived once more as if it came from without – from the parents and the social values they are thought to personify. Sexuality may be acclaimed and aggression and war attacked – as it was so forcefully in the sixties but still is today – in the most belligerent terms. The loving side of the superego may find expression in youthful idealism; but the incest taboo generally remains unscathed. Indeed, since the attack on the superego is, at bottom, an attack on the parents, it fosters, in turn, the shift of sexuality towards the outside world. This indispensable part of growing up is naturally painful to many parents when they feel the force of their child's hostility and are unable to understand the strength of the love behind it.

The adolescent process modifies the tyrant, but it does not do away with it. In any case, its loving aspects have to survive in maintaining self-esteem. And the fight is far from one sided; the struggle may be long and intense but it does not end in total defeat. What results, if all goes well, is an agency that gives guidance, sets standards and gives aims. It fortifies the ability to co-operate and fit in, but its standards will not lightly be set aside simply by social manipulation. *Behaviour* may change, but the way one feels about it may not. Shame and guilt may not disappear. Up to a point, perhaps that is just as well.

Social psychologists and sociologists need to recognise that while many radical changes in society are necessary or desirable, these changes will not in themselves provide a revolution in internal harmony or disharmony. It is true that those whose superego is weak will take extra comfort from social approval, and that social disapproval may add to the discomfort of those whose superego is stronger than perhaps it ought to be. The danger is that, in considering the relationship between the internal and external, the importance of the one may be emphasised at the expense of that other.

A great deal that is militantly written and said today about important social issues such as feminism and sexuality makes precisely this mistake. It treats 'traditional' attitudes to these questions solely as the result of the social forces. Essentially, they fail to see that, unlike Pavlov's dogs, people may be more than a product of their environment. Such a view is thoroughly insulting both to children and to adults, but it is not difficult to see how it may have arisen. On the one hand, understandably, it ignores the existence of the repression barrier. On the other hand, unconsciously, it takes sides with it and regards what cannot be remembered as of no account. But the fears, fantasies and improbabilities of childhood will not be dismissed so easily.

---

[7]   Latency is the period of relative sexual quiescence in childhood. It follows the ending of 'the first great love affair' when instinctual wishes are centred around the parent, when the superego is established, and when childhood amnesia sets in. The child's interests are generally turned outwards in this period, busily taking in the new and (generally) exciting new world outside the family. The period starts to come to an end in a time before adolescence proper, when sexuality returns with far greater force than it had before.

Unless we respect the child within, and the struggles he encounters, true social respect, and realistic attitudes based on it, may remain as elusive as ever. Perhaps the writers of fairy stories knew children better than we remember them through ourselves.

In children under five, access to the unconscious is not so impeded: the repression barrier is not yet fully formed and has not acquired the strength it has yet to achieve under the impact of the superego. The point may best be made through a true story. A little patient of mine, barely three years old, did not like some information about herself that I was trying to give her. Drawing herself up to her full height, she declared: 'Dr Yorke! I don't like you and I wish you were dead! Only you'd better not die just yet because next week I might have changed my mind.' No barrier, perhaps; and not yet conscience: but internal conflict, to be sure.

AFTERNOTE

This account is a generic one and does not address the complex issues of differences in superego formation in boys and girls, brought about by differences in sexual development. Nor have I examined the equally complex role of maternal and paternal contributions to superego formation – a difficult task in ay case and one in need of further elucidation.

Child Sexual Abuse Hearings in Family Courts: the Role of the Judge and the Value of the Expert Witness

*Lord Justice Wall**

The privilege of being invited to contribute to this publication is enhanced for me by the fact that in September 2005 the first of the interdisciplinary Dartington conferences took place, in which, as a relatively newly appointed Family Division judge, I participated. Its theme was *Psychoanalytic Perspectives on Child Protection, Assessment, Therapy and Treatment* and both the papers given at the conference, together with the fruits of the plenary discussions, were published by Jordans under the title *Rooted Sorrows*. It is a publication with which, I hope, a number of readers of this publication are familiar. The paper I presented at the conference was entitled *Issues arising from the involvement of and expert evidence given by psychiatrists and psychologists in proceedings involving children*. In it, I raised five issues for discussion. These were (1) the respective functions of expert and judge in the family justice system; (2) the tension between judicial and clinical findings and the methodology of the investigation of child sexual abuse; (3) the role of the expert in the assessment of the credibility of a child or patient; (4) the expert's role in advising the court on the therapeutic treatment of a child and on the manner in which the judge should dispose of the case; and (5) the expert's role in the concept of the 'assessment' of a child in the context of the investigation and treatment of sexual or emotional abuse. I shall re-visit that paper to see what changes there have been in the intervening years and what, if any progress, has been made.

Before addressing these particular topics, however, I think I need to set the context of what I have to say. I was at the bar for 24 years before becoming a judge in the Family Division. At the bar, I had a practice which included a large number of sexual abuse cases. I had the advantage of regular instruction by the Official Solicitor, who then often represented children in such cases. I also appeared for parents who had abused their children, and parents who had been wrongly accused of doing so. I appeared for local authorities seeking to establish abuse. On the bench I tried many sexual abuse cases: I have found abuse proved in some cases and dismissed others.

I mention this only in order to explain that my approach to the subject is very much that of the practical, evidenced based lawyer. That is not to say that I have no respect for research or for medical and academic hypotheses. What it does mean is that I have developed a considerable faith in what I can best describe as interdisciplinary good practice, and that in my court I expected the work of the medical and psychiatric expert to be examined rigorously and without unwarranted preconceptions. That process, conducted with courtesy, and combined with an equally rigorous forensic examination of the facts usually enabled me to reach a conclusion with which I could live and which, more importantly, was sufficient to protect the children who were

---

* This paper is adapted from a talk given on 10 October 2005, as the Glover Lecture.
  Lord Justice Wall is an Appeal Court Judge. He has worked within the Family Justice System all his professional life. He was a member of the President's Interdisciplinary Committee.

the subject of the proceedings. I will return to this point when I answer the last of the questions I raised at Dartington. I raise it now to explain that I was, on the whole, less concerned with the stable from which the expert came than with the objective quality of the advice I was given.

In answering the five questions I have posed, I am working on the assumption that many readers of this publication are not lawyers. For the family lawyer, what immediately follows is well-trodden territory. It will, however, serve to answer my first and abiding underlying question: why are cases of child sexual abuse so difficult for the family judge to resolve?

For the judge, an allegation of sexual abuse involves, first and foremost, a factual enquiry. The deceptively simple question posed to the judge is, usually: has this particular child been sexually abused or not? That, of course, is a question of fact. Thus, although one of the questions I raised at Dartington was the court's role in advising on therapy, the judge is primarily an investigator.

For the family judge, allegations of sexual abuse arise nearly always in one of two factual substrata. The first is what are known as private law proceedings: that is proceedings in which the state is not involved. The dispute is usually between separated parents. The contextual question for the court is usually with whom the child should reside or how much contact the non-resident parent should have with the child. Sexual abuse often arises as an issue in those proceedings, and the question has to be resolved before the court can reach a welfare-based decision as to residence or contact.

The second context in which issues of sexual abuse arise are care proceedings in which the state, in the form of the local authority, seeks a care order in relation to the child. To achieve a care order, the local authority has to establish what have become known as the 'threshold criteria' under s 31 of the Children Act 1989. It has to prove facts on the basis of which the court can properly hold that the child has suffered significant harm in the period leading up to the institution of the proceedings or is likely to suffer such harm in the future, that harm being attributable to the care (or lack of it) given to the child by his or her parents. A child who has been sexually abused has, self-evidently, suffered significant harm. The concept of 'likelihood' of significant harm in this context is more difficult, but usually arises where a parent or step-parent or cohabitee is accused of having abused a child who is not the subject of the proceedings, and the question is the risk to the subject child if that abuse is established.

Family courts nearly always deal with sexual abuse within the family: stranger abuse is rare in this context, except where, for example, inadequate parents prove incapable of protecting their children against abusive strangers, or, as in the example just cited, the mother of the subject child starts living with a Schedule 1 offender. In such cases, however, parental exposure of the child to abuse or the likelihood of abuse will usually provide a wider – and easier – route to the satisfaction of the threshold criteria.

Why are these cases so difficult for the judge? There are a number of reasons. The first is the context in which such disputes arise. In the private law sphere, allegations of sexual abuse usually arise in the aftermath of the breakdown of the relationship between the child's parents. As the growth in recent years of intractable disputes over contact demonstrates, this is a time of heightened emotions, irrational behaviour, anger, sometimes violence and the risk of mental illness. In my experience, there is a high level of false reporting in such cases, some of it malicious.

Secondly, from an evidential perspective, the allegations rarely emanate directly from the child him or herself. They are reported to a third party – often a child protection social worker – by one parent who has taken them from the child. The child may be very young. The parent may be unreliable: he or she may have misheard or deliberately misreported what the child has said. The parent is highly unlikely to have written down exactly what the child said. The parent may well have asked a series of inappropriate questions. An innocent remark by the child may be misrepresented or distorted. By the time the allegation gets to the judge, it will have been through several hands, and may well have become embellished.

Thirdly, one of the traditional methods by which a judge decides issues of fact is by an assessment of the credibility of individual adult witnesses under cross-examination. The judge in family proceedings never hears directly from the child him or herself, unless the case involves the alleged abuse of a child who is now an adult, where allegations by that adult of sexual abuse in childhood are relevant to the protection of younger children in the family. The classic example is the adult or teenage daughter who alleges sexual abuse against her father where the father has formed a relationship with another woman and has young children by her. These cases, in which abuse suffered many years ago is revived, bristle with their own self-evident difficulties.

Furthermore, the child may have been interviewed on video by a police officer or a social worker or the two in combination. This is known as the Memorandum interview, after the Memorandum of Good Practice published by the Home Office. The quality of such interviews is variable. The child may or may not have repeated the allegation. The interview is a crucial piece of evidence which has to be interpreted and fitted into the factual matrix, and it is in this area that the judge may become heavily dependent on expert advice in the assessment of the quality of the interview, the interpretation of what the child says in interview, and in an overall assessment of the child's credibility.

In the criminal law context, the jury not only sees the video, but also hears the child being cross-examined by way of a video link. Although I am not a criminal lawyer, I am very critical of this process. It means that a child is interviewed shortly after the complaint has arisen, and is then bought back to court many months, sometimes years later to relive the experience and to have his or her credibility impugned in cross-examination. During that interregnum, the criminal law discourages therapy for the child, since therapy (it is thought) may distort or contaminate the child's evidence. I have heard child psychiatrists describe this process as abusive of the child.

Irrespective of the question of the criminal process being abusive, however, it strikes me as not being the best method of getting to the truth. One of the major developments of the last ten years is the consensus which appears to have been reached in relation to the interviewing of children.

There is agreement that interviewing children who may have been abused is enormously difficult, and requires great skill. It is, I think, common ground that one of the critical tenets of an investigatory interview is that the interviewer should not ask leading questions, for the obvious reasons a suggestive or leading question contains or suggests an answer which is likely to be driven by the questioner's agenda.

In court, of course, leading questions are not only allowed in cross-examination: they are a standard technique for the advocate. The cross-examining lawyer in criminal proceedings has a duty to put his client's case to the witness: that case is unlikely to represent the truth, although it may do. So if a child is skilfully cross-examined on behalf of a defendant through leading questions, he or she may well give answers which are inconsistent with the memorandum interview. The result will then be the dismissal of the criminal charge.

That process does not, of course, prevent the family court reaching a different conclusion on the same facts, using a different standard of proof, a broader spectrum of evidence and admitting into hearing material not permitted by the criminal law. I have on a number of occasions found abuse established in family proceedings following an acquittal by a jury on the same facts, but the process is time-consuming, the delays are extensive, and the child is in limbo until the family proceeding are concluded.

A further difficulty, of course, is that perpetrators rarely – if ever – admit sexual abuse. I cannot think of a case in my time on the bench (or during my years as an advocate for that matter) when a person admitted sexually abusing a child. This applies both during the hearing and, perhaps more significantly, after a finding of abuse had been made when the admission is required for the purposes of therapy and outcome for the child. The reason for this is not far to seek. Apart from any social ostracism, an admission in family proceedings is likely to lead to disclosure by the court to the police, and whilst, under s 98 of the Children Act 1989 any such admission is not admissible in criminal proceedings, that fact has not, in my experience, provided much encouragement to any abuser to make an admission, particularly where the abuser is intellectually unsophisticated.

The judge thus has to attempt to distinguish between a genuine and a false denial. Given the seriousness of the subject matter, this is a critical point, and serves to demonstrate the importance of the subject, since, on the one hand, there few things more damaging to a child than the betrayal of trust involved in sexual abuse at the hands of a parent or carer: on the other, there are few things more destructive of family relationships and relationships between parents and children than a false allegation of sexual abuse.

Finally in this catalogue of difficulty is that fact that the court rarely has corroborative medical evidence. The cases in which there is evidence of a sexually transmitted disease, or unequivocal evidence of vaginal or anal damage caused by abuse are rare, and almost by definition they are the ones which are not contested. Far more common is an allegation of digital or penal interference, which has left no mark behind.

No doubt there are some readers who will be aware of further difficulties which I have not mentioned. These will, however, be enough to be getting on with.

I referred earlier to the criminal standard of proof. The judge has to decide on the truth or falsity of an allegation of sexual abuse by applying the civil burden of proof, known as the balance of probabilities. This means that if the judge can say that something is more likely than not to have happened, then, as a matter of law, it happened. There are grave intellectual difficulties in the proposition that that which a judge believes is more likely than not to have happened is in fact true, and in the criminal law, of course, the jury has to be sure. The standard there is 'beyond reasonable doubt'. Even that, as we know, is not foolproof.

Concern over the civil standard of proof being appropriate to enable findings of fact sufficient to trigger the threshold criteria under s 31 of the Children Act and thus provide the gateway into care, led a majority of the House of Lords, on 14 December 1995, in an important decision called *Re H and others (Minors) (Sexual Abuse: Standard of Proof)* (reported at [1996] AC 563) to conclude that the civil standard of proof on the balance of probabilities was the right test, but to add that the more serious the allegation, the more cogent must be the evidence required to enable the civil burden to be satisfied. As is customary, the case was heard by 5 Law Lords: the split was 3:2.

This case has its Dartington connections, because Lord Lloyd of Berwick, who was in the constitution which decided *Re H*, chaired the 1995 conference and wrote the foreword to *Rooted Sorrows*. I specifically recall that he was in the process of considering his judgment at the time of the conference. He was, in the event, in the minority when the decision in *Re H* came to be made: a fact which led some of us, at the time, to speculate what might have happened if those in the majority had also been at the conference.

It is worth spending a few moments on *Re H*, as it is a seminal, post Dartington decision, which has necessarily dominated the practice of the family courts since its publication. The issue in the case was a stark one. A mother had four children, all girls, the elder two by her husband, from whom she was separated, and the younger two by a man called R, with whom she was living. In

September 1993 the eldest girl, C, then aged 13, alleged that she had been sexually abused by R, since she was 7 or 8 years old. She was thereupon accommodated with foster parents and R was tried in the Crown Court on an indictment containing four counts of raping C. The jury acquitted him on all counts. The local authority proceeded with the applications for care orders in respect of the three younger children based solely on the alleged sexual abuse of C by her stepfather. It asked the judge to find that R had sexually abused C or that there was a substantial risk that he had done so, thereby satisfying the conditions prescribed by s 31(2) of the Children Act 1989 for the making of care orders. The judge rejected the evidence of the mother and R, but nevertheless held that he was not sure as to what he described as 'the requisite high standard of proof' that C's allegations were true. He decided, accordingly, that the statutory criteria for the making of a care order were not made out, even though he had his suspicions that there was a real possibility that C's statement and evidence were true. The local authority appealed unsuccessfully to the Court of Appeal and to the House of Lords. In both cases, the appeals were dismissed by majorities.

In *Re H*, the trial judge had gone so far as to say that he thought there was a 'real possibility' that C's allegations were true. The question for the House of Lords was thus whether or not such a finding was sufficient to satisfy the s 31(2) test as applied to 'likelihood of significant harm'. (There was no dispute that it was insufficient for a finding of actual significant harm.)

The minority said it was. Their position was that in contrast to an actual finding of significant harm, the assessment of the likelihood of significant harm was an assessment of risk which did not depend on specific facts being proved. The majority view was that whilst a conclusion that there was a likelihood of significant harm did not require a finding that such harm was more likely than not, it had, nonetheless, to be a finding based on facts, and since the judge had rejected the only evidence capable of giving rise to the threshold criteria (that is, he had found that the allegations of sexual abuse were not made out) the threshold criteria were not satisfied, and it was not open to him to proceed to the second stage and to consider the likelihood of further harm to the children.

I have spent some time on this decision in order to emphasise the fact-based nature of the judicial investigation. Suspicion is not enough. Where the threshold criteria are based on allegations of sexual abuse, the judge must be satisfied that abuse is more probable than not. The emphasis on this approach does, have some significance for the expert witness. If nothing else it means that the court will (or should) critically and rigorously examine an expert's methodology in order to ascertain whether it is capable of supporting a finding of fact.

Against this background, I return to the five issues I raised at Dartington.

THE RESPECTIVE FUNCTION OF EXPERT AND JUDGE IN THE FAMILY JUSTICE SYSTEM

In its essentials, the relationship between expert and judge has not changed. As I said at Dartington, where the question is in dispute, Parliament has given to judges the responsibility for making decisions both about what has happened to, and what should happen to children. In this context, the expert advises. The judge decides the case. But the judge does so, not simply on the advice of the expert but on all the multifarious aspect of the case, which include both the written and oral material, the assessment of witness credibility, and findings of fact outside the knowledge of the expert witness but which are contextually highly relevant to the ultimate finding of abuse, or its rejection.

The family court has the advantage, denied to criminal lawyers, that the rules of evidence are relaxed. Whilst the court exercises a fierce control over who is shown the court papers, and which experts are called to give evidence, hearsay evidence is admitted: the court looks at documents irrespective of their provenance and judges are entitled to garner evidence from all sources which they think will assist. The reasons for the different approaches are obvious. Criminal courts are concerned with the right of the state to punish individuals if an offence has been committed. It follows that the offence must be strictly proved. Family courts are concerned with child protection.

It is this wide-ranging, all-embracing judicial function which, in combination with a rigorous analysis of the medical and psychiatric evidence, have in my judgment, saved the family courts from the criticisms and the miscarriages of justice that have, of late, bedeviled the criminal courts. You will no doubt recall the announcement by the government that a number of criminal and family court decisions would be re-opened in the light of the decision of the Criminal Division of the Court of Appeal in the case of Angela Cannings. So far as I am aware, only two cases from the family jurisdiction have come to the Court of Appeal in this connection. Those two decisions are reported as *Re U* and *Re B (Department for Education and Skills Intervening)* [2005] Fam 134. The judgment of the court was given by the President, Dame Elizabeth Butler-Sloss, and is particularly authoritative because the other two members, who contributed to the judgment, were Mathew Thorpe and a highly respected criminal lawyer, Charles Mantell.

In dismissing the appeals, the court made it clear that the decision of a judge in a child abuse case was not solely dependent on medical evidence. He or she (in this case she, Bracewell J) was entitled to rely on the totality of the relevant and cogent evidence in the case, which included an assessment of witness credibility The court said:

> '26 It is for the purpose of satisfying that threshold that the local authority seeks to prove specific facts against the parent or parents. Only if it succeeds in that task can its application for a care or supervision order proceed. Thus the preliminary issue of fact constitutes the gateway to a judicial discretion as to what steps should be taken to protect the child and to promote his welfare. In those circumstances we must robustly reject Mr Cobb's submission that the local authority should refrain from proceedings or discontinue proceedings in any case where there is a substantial disagreement amongst the medical experts. For the judge invariably surveys a wide canvas, including a detailed history of the parents' lives, their relationship and their interaction with professionals. There will be many contributions to this context, family members, neighbours, health records, as well as the observation of professionals such as social workers, health visitors and children's guardians.

> 27 In the end the judge must make clear findings on the issues of fact before the court, resting on the evidence led by the parties and such additional evidence as the judge may have required in the exercise of his quasi-inquisitorial function. All this is the prelude to a further and fuller investigation of a range of choices in search of the protection and welfare of the children. A positive finding against a parent or both parents does not in itself preclude the possibility of rehabilitation. All depends on the facts and circumstances of the individual case. In that context the consequences of a false positive finding in care proceedings may not be as dire as the consequence of the conviction of an innocent in criminal proceedings.

> 28 So it by no means follows that an acquittal on a criminal charge or a successful appeal would lead to the absolution of the parent or carer in family or civil proceedings. It is also worth remembering that the decision of the Court of Appeal (Criminal Division) in *R v Cannings* [2004] 1 WLR 2607 turned on the very particular facts of that case.

> 29 In summary the decision of the court in *R v Cannings* has no doubt provided a useful warning to judges in care proceedings against ill-considered conclusions or conclusions resting on insufficient evidence. The extent of the retrospective effect remains to emerge. However practitioners should be slow to assume that past cases which have been carefully tried on a wide range of evidence will be readily re-opened.

> 30 In our judgment the responsibilities of local authorities have not been changed by the decision of the Court of Appeal (Criminal Division). Theirs is the task to protect the child; to assess the issues

within their competence and expertise; and to rely upon the legal team for the local authority to advise on the strength and credibility of the medical evidence. They will, with their legal advisers, continue to prepare applications for care orders in suitable cases based upon the civil standard of proof as explained by Lord Nicholls in *In re H (Minors) (Sexual Abuse: Standard of Proof)* [1996] AC 563. In our view the decision in *R v Cannings* [2004] 1 WLR 2607 does not affect their responsibilities under the Children Act 1989.

So in the family context, the respective functions of the expert witness and the judge remain what they were in 1995, albeit that – certainly in the field of paediatrics, the focus has shifted somewhat.

THE TENSION BETWEEN JUDICIAL AND CLINICAL FINDINGS AND THE METHODOLOGY ON THE INVESTIGATION OF CHILD SEXUAL ABUSE

Certainly, at Dartington in 1995 this was a major concern of mine. Prior to that date, I found it profoundly dispiriting both as advocate and judge to have participated in a number of cases in which the evidence of the psychiatrists, as clinicians, had been that the child has been sexually abused, whereas the finding of the court had been that abuse had not occurred. I made reference in my Dartington paper to the series of decisions reported in the Family Law Reports in 1987, in which in five out of six cases the courts had rejected evidence from child psychiatric sources that a child had been sexually abused.

I think it is fair to say that the issue in the pre-Dartington cases was, very largely, a dispute within the psychiatric profession as to how a child should be interviewed. The thinking was, as I understood it, that, historically, the adult response to a child's complaint of sexual abuse had been to believe the adult, not the child. This had resulted in considerable injustice as well as serious harm to children. Children had to be listened to, and taken seriously. Moreover, if they were reluctant to describe abuse, particularly if they were traumatised, or frightened of the consequence of disclosure, they could properly be encouraged to disclose abuse, and the resultant clinical findings of abuse were reliable.

It was, as I recall, the implementation of this approach which brought psychiatry into direct conflict in some cases with the courts, and no doubt led me, amongst others, to enquire at Dartington about the Holy Grail of a universally applicable psychiatric methodology.

When I raised these issues at Dartington 12 years ago, the distinguished group of psychiatrists attending the conference (including Dr Freedman) met to consider their response, which is also printed in *Rooted Sorrows*. I was extremely grateful for it. As it is in print, I will not repeat it *in extenso* here. However, in answer to my two questions: 'Is there a universally acceptable and uncontroversial methodology for the investigation of child sexual abuse? If not, is there any psychiatric guidance as to what is clinically acceptable and what it not?' the answer to the first question, unsurprisingly but nonetheless refreshingly, was 'no'. The group then set out child psychiatric guidance as to what was acceptable in the context of the four key questions which required clarification as far as possible. Those four questions were articulated as: (1) Has the child been abused? (2) If so, by whom? (3) Is the child safe from re-abuse? And (4) what are the child's and the family's therapeutic needs?

There followed a great deal of wise advice, which I fear I can only summarise in crude terms. However, it included the need for the investigation by the statutory authorities to be carried out appropriately and by individuals who had been properly trained. The process of assessment needed to pay particular attention to the early evolution of concerns. It was particularly important to ascertain the context in which the child had first described the abuse and the content of early descriptions. It was important to hear the response of the alleged abuser, whilst remembering that denial of abuse was common. Furthermore, there was no definitive clinical profile of a person who sexually abuses children. It was not clinically useful or desirable for the child to be seen and questioned repeatedly. However, this placed an onus on those who heard the early accounts from the child to record as fully and accurately as possible what the child had said, as well as their own statements and questions. This should be done at the time or immediately afterwards. Information obtained in an informal setting may be much more useful than what the child says or declines to say in a formal interview. There was much more, which I do not have space to paraphrase here, but which I commend to practitioners, both legal and psychiatric.

What I am about to say must, inevitably, be anecdotal, since it is based on my experience. I do not have statistics: it remains my impression. However, that impression is that the investigation of allegations of sexual abuse – particularly the techniques for interviewing children – have substantially improved in the last 12 years. Much of this, I think, is due to *Cleveland*. The Cleveland Inquiry was, I think, a true watershed. From it emerged the 12 points of agreement in relation to the interviewing of children, and from that emerged the Memorandum of Good Practice in 1992, subsequently, of course, revised and re-thought.

My experience since 1995, limited as it has been, has nonetheless been that the process of investigating child sexual abuse has settled down. The work of David Jones in this field has, in my view, been outstanding, and his extremely helpful and informative book *Communicating with vulnerable children, a guide for practitioners* should be on the shelves of all who work in the field. I have also found useful a framework document written by Dr Kirk Weir and published at [1996] 26 Family Law 673.

We have banished for ever a number of unacceptable practices. Indeed, even to remember them is to think of a different age – for example the 'dawn raid' in which the desire to avoid contamination of evidence or undue influence on a child by a suspected abuser led to the police and social services obtaining an emergency protection order and arriving at the family home in the early hours of the morning to remove children (often from their beds) into the care of strangers.

We no longer have untrained police officers using anatomically 'correct' dolls as a means of establishing abuse. We are still from time to time, bedeviled in the paediatric field by theories which have no foundation in medical science (I have in mind in particular the theory of temporary brittle bones). But these are exceptions. Over recent years, it seems to me, without I hope sounding remotely complacent, that the process of investigation of abuse has greatly improved. The problems the family justice system now faces in relation to experts has much more to do with supply and demand, and the reluctance of the expert witness to give evidence, than with any anxiety that the experts themselves will prove unreliable.

So it seems that the tensions I detected at Dartington in 1995 have been substantially reduced. This, in my view, is due to the development of good practice by the investigating authorities, as well as in psychiatry and the law.

THE ROLE OF THE EXPERT IN THE ASSESSMENT OF THE CREDIBILITY OF A CHILD OR PATIENT

This was the topic which, at Dartington, took up a great deal of my paper. The reason for this was that there were, at the time, two apparently conflicting decisions of the Court of Appeal on the subject, one of which said that the opinion of a child psychiatrist as to the credibility of a child's evidence was inadmissible. As I pointed out in *Rooted Sorrows*, however, the question as debated at Dartington had received a definitive answer by the time the book came to be published. In a second decision, the Court of Appeal was able to nullify the effect of the first decision by saying that it had been decided *per incuriam* (a phrase which AP Herbert said meant the court was asleep at the time it made its decision) but which in this context means that the court in the first case had not been referred to the terms of s 3 of the Civil Evidence Act 1972, which permitted such evidence to be given.

So not only is that particular controversy over, but I have certainly found, in a number of cases, that the evidence of a child psychiatrist or psychologist, who has expertise in child development, has proved of great value, either in an assessment of the child said to have been abused and/or in evaluating the weight to be given to the interview or interviews with the child. Assistance from an expert on the language used by the child, the spontaneity of the allegations, on their internal consistency, the amount of detail described, and the consistency of the child's description with his or her developmental stage, these are all aspects of the investigation of abuse on which I have found expert advice very helpful. And it becomes all the more helpful because we do have agreement on certain essential aspects of how children should be interviewed, and how such interviews should be evaluated.

THE EXPERT'S ROLE IN ADVISING THE COURT ON THE THERAPEUTIC TREATMENT OF A CHILD AND ON THE MANNER IN WHICH THE JUDGE SHOULD DISPOSE OF THE CASE

Ironically, although I raised this question at Dartington in the context of three of my own cases, it has since then not been a feature of many cases I have heard. The reasons for this are, I think, both practical and dispiriting. Therapy, to the lawyer, implies treatment on the basis of a firm diagnosis (or identification of a particular need) that the particular treatment is required. Thus, where there is an ongoing investigation as to whether or not a child has been sexually abused, therapy on the premise that the child has been sexually abused is not the issue.

However, when approving a care plan in care proceedings, the facts will have been established, and the likelihood is that there will be a recommendation for therapy as part of the care plan for the child. Unfortunately, however, in my experience, therapy is dependent on whatever is locally available. The expert who gives evidence in care proceedings relating to therapy has to make sure, before making a recommendation, that the particular form of therapy is locally available. Often it is not. Alternatively, if it is, the CAMHS waiting list for it extends well beyond the date of the implementation of the care order.

As I made clear in my Dartington paper, therapy is a primarily a matter for the clinicians, not for the judge. The judge is not often called upon to decide between rival proposals in this context. A reasoned psychiatric opinion as to what is required for a child is, however, extremely helpful.

THE EXPERT'S ROLE IN THE CONCEPT OF THE 'ASSESSMENT' OF A CHILD IN THE CONTEXT OF THE INVESTIGATION AND TREATMENT OF SEXUAL OR EMOTIONAL ABUSE. WHAT DOES A JUDGE REQUIRE OF A PSYCHIATRIC EXPERT?

At Dartington, this was a narrow issue based on the differing approaches required when making an assessment of a child as opposed to treating a child. For the purposes of this paper it would seem to me more appropriate to deflect the question to attempt to describe what a judge requires of an expert witness in the field of psychiatry when the judge is hearing a case involving allegations of sexual abuse.

The first criterion must be that the expert comes to the case without preconceptions, and has no professional bias either in favour of or against abuse. I do not think that this point can be over-stressed. The expert must investigate with an open mind, and should not reach a conclusion until he or she has considered all the material that is available.

Secondly, as I indicated at the outset of this paper, I have to say that the school from which the psychiatrist comes is less important than the wisdom, maturity and above all judgment of the individual expert. As Brian Jacobs put it at Dartington 12 years ago:

> When considering any framework of thinking about the human mind it is worth remembering that there are many conceptual frameworks that can be used. Psychodynamic models form some perspectives, but there are others which can be helpful. Different frames provide different slants on the same problem, but we should remember that whatever perspective is taken, it is the same human individual or relationship that is being described.

Those are, in my judgment, wise words.

The third factor by which I am influenced is the thoroughness with which the expert has carried out his or her task. This is not just a question of hours spent, but of the care and attention the expert has paid to the task. This includes such basic tasks as reading, note-taking, and recording of interviews and discussions.

This third factor nearly always carries over into the expert's report. I am always impressed by a report which is thoughtful and carefully written, and in which conclusions are moderately (albeit where appropriate firmly) expressed. A report should be a well-constructed process of investigation and analysis, written in as much plain and jargon free language as is possible, and covering all the ground set for the expert to cover.

In the same way that experts should never stray from the area of their expertise, they should never be afraid to say that they do not know the answer. Many think that because they are instructed to give an opinion, they must give an opinion one way or the other. But if the answer to the question: 'Has this child been sexually abused?' is from the psychiatric perspective: 'I don't know', the judge wants the expert to say just that. Equally, if the answer to the question is that it depends on findings made by the judge in relation to specific issues as to fact or credibility, the expert should tell the judge so. As I said at the outset, the judge has to make the decision. The expert does not decide the case.

Self-evidently, as with interviews, the psychiatric assessment of the behaviour of a child said to have been sexually abused in terms of age, development, relationships with peers, siblings and parents, as well as childhood norms is an aspect of the investigation in which the psychiatrist can play a critically important role.

Experts must, however, confine themselves to the area of their expertise. They also need to remember that they only see one part of the overall picture. It is only the judge who sees the whole. Thus experts who, for example, accept a parental explanation and found their opinion on it are providing a major hostage to fortune, since the judge may well find, as a fact, that the parent is not telling the truth, and that the explanation given to the expert is false. Similarly, where the issue before the court is which of several people is the perpetrator of abuse, that is usually an issue of fact for the judge, not for the expert.

Guidance for the expert witness in family proceedings is now legion. As I put it in my *Handbook for Expert Witnesses in Children Act cases*:

> What the court expects from you is an objective, independent, well-researched, thorough opinion, which takes account of all relevant information and which represents your genuine professional view on the issues submitted to you.

Give judges that, and there is nothing more they can ask of you.

Expert Evidence: Evident and Not Evident

Response to Lord Justice Wall's Glover Lecture

*Dr Judith Freedman**

Many readers will know that Lord Justice Wall has paid particular attention to the role of the expert witness. In his judgment, *Re M*, he outlined the manner in which the Courts would deal with expert witnesses: this included a provision for which I, and I am sure other expert witnesses are grateful.

> 'The court appreciates that experts are busy people and that travelling to court and giving evidence in court are time consuming. The court will always try to accommodate an expert by interposing him or her at a given time ...'

I shall respond to Lord Justice Wall from the perspective of an expert witness and I hope in so doing that I can address the interests of both legal and mental health colleagues. Lord Justice Wall has outlined the respective functions of the expert and the judge in the family justice system. He reminded us that 'Parliament has given the responsibility of making the decision to the judge. The expert advises.' I think that this point, which might seem self-evident, is an important one for us to consider. As a mental health professional, when I work in my consulting room, I am accustomed to making recommendations to other professionals and to my patients about the treatment that I think is necessary.

When I work in the court system, I have to shift my orientation in that I have to recognise that I am undertaking assessments for the court, which is to say, for the judge. I have to orient myself accordingly, no matter what theories of the mind I work by, no matter what might arise that interests me, no matter what questions I might otherwise be inclined to skip over, no matter what hypotheses I have, no matter what research says, no matter what I have been taught (such as that children rarely make false allegations); in the court system my task is to investigate, explore and then analyse and articulate what is true about a particular family.

If I develop hunches and hypotheses in the course of an investigation, I need to attempt to substantiate them and find corroborating evidence. As a psychoanalyst working as an expert witness, I can give weight to my counter-transference feelings in interviews and draw conclusions from those feelings, but because I do not have an ongoing therapy to test and evaluate such feelings over time, I need to look for additional evidence. If I find none, the counter-transference feelings are of little assistance. When conducting only one or two interviews, I remain aware that these feelings might amount to nothing more than feelings of aversion to the parent or near prejudice, whilst recognising that parents may present in an angry

* Judith Freedman is Consultant Psychiatrist in Psychotherapy at the Portman Clinic. She frequently prepares reports on parents and families for family courts. She is a Fellow of the Royal College of Psychiatrists and is a psychoanalyst.

or aggressive fashion because they are anxious about finding themselves in the midst of childcare proceedings. I cannot air unsubstantiated hypotheses in the family courts. I need to report to the court the facts I have learned, including substantiated opinions from others, and base my assessments and advice, in large part, on these facts and agreed views. In this sense, I am using applied psychoanalysis, which is not the same as treatment psychoanalysis. My experiences with other patients and my intuitions are important, but they must be used to guide me in my search for evidence. If I am surprised to find that evidence is missing, then I must say so.

As Lord Justice Wall said, it requires a shift in our position to recognise that as expert witnesses we form only one part of the evidence before the court. Other witnesses, including the parents, will give evidence. Although the statements and reports that are filed before the hearing are available, I have to recognise that I am limited by the fact that, unlike the parties to the proceedings, I do not hear all the witnesses give their evidence, as do the social workers, the children's guardian, the parents, and, of course, the judge. I come to give my evidence and leave immediately upon its completion. This should serve to remind expert witnesses that we provide one part, albeit often an important part, of the evidence that the judge considers in reaching a decision.

I have noticed that in the court papers containing reports from other professionals, sometimes certain ideas, fragments of statements or unproven allegations are repeated so often that they accrue some certitude. I find as an expert, that I need to 'turn down the volume' on these repeated ideas – and in some cases, turn them off completely. On the other hand, sometimes I need to 'turn up the volume' on information that has become underplayed and sanitised.

I also find that when working as an expert witness, it is increasingly important for me to read more widely than I did when I worked only as a psychotherapist and psychoanalyst. Now I read in general psychiatry so that I can be aware of how people fare on psychiatric medications; I read about the effects of drug abuse and the impact on the family; I routinely ask to see parents' GP notes, and I learn about the impact of physical illness on families.

How do I conduct my assessments and form the opinions that I provide for the court? As stated above, I must gather evidence and consider facts that provide evidence for my opinions. This will include what family members said to me, and I give the court a detailed account of what was said in their interviews. It also includes my psycho-analytically based understanding of how family members deal with difficulties in their lives, and how they manage their anxieties and their impulses.

As I begin to accumulate the evidence, including clinical facts from my interviews, it is beneficial if I am able to find corroboration. Let me give you a typical example, (the details have been altered, so as not to breach confidentiality). My team assessed a family at the Portman Clinic where the father of a young girl was accused of sexually abusing her older, adolescent half-sister; in other words this man's stepdaughter. The father had a conviction for sexual abuse of a young female relative, in his adolescence. The more recent allegation involving the stepdaughter had been tried in a criminal court, and the father was acquitted. Social Services then had to determine if it was safe for the father to stay at home with his young daughter. They asked for my view on the issue.

We interviewed the parents and felt uneasy, as we sensed that the parents were 'stonewalling' us and that the mother seemed particularly nervous. We asked for records from the father's first conviction, but these were no longer available. We also asked for reports from his recent criminal hearing, but Social Services were unable to locate these or to provide reports from their own files. We asked the father to give us the records from his recent hearing, and he agreed to do so.

I went to visit the family at home, where I found them with some of the father's relatives. There was also a pit bull terrier that was kept in the next room, barking and throwing itself against the door. I found the mother even more nervous and withdrawn than she had been in our interviews. Although the father was cordial, I felt uneasy. As I left, I asked the father about the records he had promised to give us. He said that he discovered that his papers had been destroyed. I then asked him – as a doorway comment, perhaps in a Detective Colombo moment – if he would give permission for his criminal solicitor to release the records. He said that he would. To his credit, he was as good as his word. We sent him a consent form, which he delayed in returning, but he did. His solicitor agreed to release the records, and a box of papers arrived at the Clinic.

The papers included multiple reports from Social Services, which the social worker had been unable to find in her archives. There were statements from the stepdaughter supported by her grandmother that revealed a concern about physical abuse, as well as sexual abuse. Reading the barrister's account of the criminal hearing, it was clear that although the jury had found the father not guilty, the stepdaughter said much that sounded convincing.

I felt that I had found evidence that corroborated our sense of unease about the family. When I reported this to the social workers, first by a written report and then in a meeting, they told me that this fitted with their worries that they had found difficult to substantiate. I think that this example usefully stresses the importance of starting with feelings and searching for corroborative evidence. Sometimes this might help to give a basis for the professionals' 'sense of concern'.

In his paper, Lord Justice Wall has focused particularly on the investigation of child sexual abuse, both in private law and in public law proceedings. In my team, we have learned that it is important for us to hear from as many members of a family as possible. We organise ourselves so that adult specialists interview parents, and child specialists interview children. We then provide an integrated report, in which we hope to address two questions: 'Is there a child who shows evidence of being sexually abused?' and, 'Is there a parent who shows evidence of being a sexual abuser?' Like Lord Justice Wall, I think that it is difficult to prove sexual abuse, particularly in the absence of physical evidence of damage to the child's genitals. Instead, I undertake to provide for the Court information about the personalities of the family members, an understanding of their past histories, and an exploration of their attitudes toward and experience of sexual matters.

A child care solicitor said to me recently, 'It's difficult having assessments based on what people tell you'. It is, but it is a difficulty with which the staff at the Portman Clinic are familiar. Early in my work for the courts, I learned a lesson that I was already learning with my other Portman patients, which was not to believe what people say about themselves until it is borne out in my experience of them, and even then, to try to hold onto a sense of possible doubt. In my work as an expert witness, I do not fully believe what anyone tells me until I have substantial reason to do so.

I would like to mention a case in which we thought that the father was a likely child sex abuser. We could not find evidence from the parents or the child, but in our interviews we noticed that the father believed that he could transgress boundaries. Whilst these were not of a sexual nature, they were of a sort that most people regarded as improper or impossible. We reported to the court that we could not prove that the father had sexually abused his son, but we were concerned about that possibility. Fortunately, our report coupled with other events, led to a holding situation that continued long enough for the local authority to gather more information. On the eve of the final hearing, the child made a clear allegation to his foster carer of sexual abuse by his father.

If I look at everyone in the family with an open mind, I sometimes find information other than what I was asked to provide. For example, in cases where we could not determine whether sexual abuse had occurred or not, we discovered that there had been physical abuse that had gone unnoticed; and in others that there was neglect or emotional abuse, which also had gone unnoticed. This should not be surprising, since there is often a correlation between sexual abuse of children and other forms of abuse. Nevertheless, once the alarming possibility is raised that there has been sexual abuse it becomes hard sometimes for professionals to take in the whole picture. In addition, it is important to recognise that emotional abuse may result in similar symptoms to sexual abuse, and that it is essential not to confuse one for the other.

Lord Justice Wall also spoke about treatment. At the Portman Clinic we have learned about and feel strongly about the importance of confidentiality for psychotherapy related to family court cases. I often give evidence, explaining the importance to patients of knowing that their therapy will remain confidential, so that they can feel free to explore whatever they wish to consider. I explain to the court that we also recognise the importance of the court knowing about the progress that a person does or does not make in therapy. For that reason, I suggest that there are assessments at the beginning and the end of the therapy with another professional, a process which is quite separate to the therapy. My aim, if I undertake such assessments, is to provide for the court an indication of the progress that parents have made, which, if it is meaningful they might be able to show in an interview.

I want to take this opportunity to say something about the limitations of the family court process. I think that it is unfortunate that there is often little opportunity in courts for open discussion. This affects us in a number of ways. When I read a judgment, sometimes I find that the judge has not understood something that I said – maybe the judge failed to understand; maybe I failed to be clear. Unfortunately, there is no opportunity to set this right. I also find that sometimes either the barristers or the judge do not ask me questions that I wish they would ask. When this happens I feel that I am not able to give as full an account as I would have liked.

Occasionally I hear criticism and disquiet about the 'adversarial' system permeating the family courts, as if it is not appropriate. In my view, this cannot be avoided. There are real conflicts and clashes of views that need to be exposed and argued in the service of discovering the truth of the evidence. In child care proceedings, where children's well-being is at stake, there needs to be a thorough investigation and thorough arguments. As an expert witness, I can find myself caught up in these conflicts when I am cross-examined but in my view, this is part of the work that is necessary.

I referred above to reading a judgment. It is more often the case that I do not see the written judgment, and even though I chase solicitors and guardians to find out what the outcome was, I frequently do not know. I rarely receive information from the judge about the ways in which my evidence was useful or not. I think that this 'feedback' would be helpful for expert witnesses.

And finally, I have been thinking recently about the limitations of my own practice and the absence of a dialogue about my reports with the families. They often complain about the report, but I do not have the opportunity to discuss it with them. Similarly, I do not find out what a family makes of my conclusions, apart from a final statement, which is often crafted by their solicitors in language that the family members would not comprehend, much less use themselves! Just as I learned in psychotherapy to make an interpretation and watch to see how the patient responds, I think it would be helpful for a later meeting between families and experts to take place. This would be especially helpful when I have recommended treatment, so that I am in a better position to advise the court about my view of the potential for family members to engage with treatment.

What is 'True Enough' to be Convincing Evidence? The Child Psychotherapist, the Family, the Team and the Court

Beverley Tydeman[*]

In this chapter I want to consider the role of the child psychotherapist as part of a multidisciplinary team whose task it is to undertake parenting assessments for the courts. Whilst this used to be a domain dominated by Child Psychiatrists, now Child Psychotherapists are increasingly going to court to act as expert witnesses in cases where they have been involved in assessing whether parents have the capacity to change. These parents might, in the past, have neglected, abused, or failed to protect their children. Through the process of our assessment work, which often involves seeing the children individually, we have to make up our minds and come to an opinion based on our observations; then be prepared to have our opinion carefully scrutinised through the process of cross-examination in court. In this situation we need to have a degree of *certainty* in what can often appear to be very uncertain territory. My interest is in how we make up our minds and come to an opinion to assist the judge with his/her decision-making. These decisions have serious consequences for many people's lives and judges need help from interdisciplinary viewpoints to reach their conclusions.

I will focus on the issue of truth and certainty and whether something can be 'true enough' to be convincing evidence. How much of a gap is there between that which I see as a 'clinical fact' and what can be accepted as a 'legal fact'? My notion is that making up one's mind about families and human relationships involves thinking and feeling, objective and subjective states, no matter what one's profession is. Whilst we all make use of various theoretical models to help us make sense of complicated phenomena, we come to a firm decision by getting in touch with what we know to be 'true' inside ourselves. We use our inner resources and emotional receptivity whilst we stare at the facts of the case. We need to use the reservoir of our own minds and selves, with theoretical concepts in the background and the experience of the emotional communication of the family members in the foreground.

The families we assess often have multiple problems at many levels, representing those aspects of society that are most damaged. They have not asked to be seen. Their deprivation, anger, despair, suspicion, resentment and guilt are aimed at us while we try to work with them. This can make things unpredictable and volatile. Often the families see themselves as defending their children against a hostile outside world. Our job is to challenge the family's view of themselves

---

[*]   Beverley Tydeman is a Consultant Child and Adolescent Psychotherapist working at the Marlborough Family Service, where the primary task is undertaking parenting assessments for court. She also runs the Infant Mental Health workshop. At the Tavistock she is involved with training mental health professionals, where she is the Organising Tutor of a course called Therapeutic Communication with Children. She has been on the Executive Committee of the Association of Child Psychotherapists for many years and is currently the Vice Chair.

or the care of their children. Frequently, we become seen as persecutors, the 'baddies' out to get them. Parents may *hate* the workers who are observing them; for example for getting them to face aspects of their lives where they may have been responsible for causing some damage to their children. These are realities that they would prefer to avoid and evade.

I will consider the emotional impact of these complex, high stress cases on the decision-making process using some examples to illustrate how both rational and intuitive processes, objective and subjective data are used to help form a professional opinion. As child psychotherapists we see things from multiple perspectives: (i) the child's inner world, the mind (ii) the outer world of real life events and (iii) how these relate to each other.

To function thoughtfully in court and in the consulting room is to say what you mean and mean what you say. In order to do this, mental space has to be created for the promotion of thought that can come close to the discovery of 'truth', in both internal and external reality.

There is a degree of overlap between the experience of being under cross-examination as an expert witness and being assessed in terms of your parenting capacities in a clinic. Your functioning is being put to the test. In both situations, because anxiety is high as are the stakes, there can be either a *'superego'* approach which is characterised by a dread or terror of being found out and harshly judged, or a more *'ego'*-driven approach which stems from curiosity and a wish to learn and perform better. These states of mind apply whether you are a parent willing to learn and change or an expert witness who wants to perform better. Questions of who is failing whom and who is fooling whom are dominant in both settings.

What equips a child psychotherapist for this work?

THE CHILD PSYCHOTHERAPIST – TRAINING AND PERSONAL ANALYSIS

Our training and experience of communicating therapeutically with children and families equips us well for this task. A central feature of our professional identity is to understand the individual in depth. We start from a lively interest in the particular child and his/her stage of development, paying detailed attention that extends to the family and the surrounding network. Our psychoanalytic training in observational skills and the capacity to be available on an emotional level to unconscious processes informs us about our experience of a child or parent, and how mental states can change from moment to moment in subtle ways. The training involves accumulating a knowledge base in ordinary child and adolescent development and current research in the area, as well as grasping an understanding of psychopathological behaviour and its aetiology. Part of this training involves a long personal analysis, which aims to put us in touch with the functioning of our own minds, separating our own issues from what belongs to other minds. Analysis provides a setting in which unknown areas of the self can be explored, discovered and integrated, so that one feels more in possession of one's whole self. This means struggling with areas of pain and fear in the self and coming to know about residual grievances or distortions of perception, which are usually 'traces' from our own history. Subjectivity and objectivity are scrutinised, so that the thinking process itself and the conclusions and beliefs one comes to are given the opportunity to be examined or reflected upon with an outside thinking and feeling person – the analyst.

Our cognitive and emotional responses in a work setting are not infallible, but they are the responses of a trained professional mind. Whilst child psychotherapists can be stretched to undertake a wide variety of tasks, our fundamental strength is our concentration on the individual child within the family context.

THE FAMILY CONTEXT

The children and parents we see often have problems that are largely determined by adverse external circumstances, which have had an effect on their inner worlds and their sense of what to expect from relationships with others. The cases that are assessed for court are full of issues relating to authority, control, power, impotence, trauma and emotional pain. The family members can seem utterly bewildered and can show us that they have learnt to trust no one. They often function in a particular way, which the psychoanalyst Melanie Klein called the *'paranoid-schizoid position'*. She explained the origin of this as follows:

> 'Unpleasant experiences and the lack of enjoyable ones, in the young child, especially the lack of happy and close contact with loved people, increase ambivalence, diminish trust and hope and confirm anxieties about inner annihilation and external persecution; moreover they slow down and perhaps permanently check the beneficial process through which in the long run inner security is achieved.' (Klein, 1940)

To elaborate this further, many of the families that come within the realm of the family court assessment arena are those that cannot communicate anxieties, thoughts and feelings, but enact dramas through the generations, which spill over into institutions like clinics, social services, police, and the courtroom. External reality is seen to be acting unjustly upon them and they are unable to view themselves as the agents of their own distressing situations. Such states of mind are described vividly in Selma Fraiberg's (1975) paper 'Ghosts in the nursery'. She states that the parents use their children in a re-enactment of their own past abuse and inflict similar treatment upon them. It is not just due to their lack of adequate models of nurturing that they cannot care for their children satisfactorily. They are *'identifying with the aggressor'* (Freud A, 1937), by inflicting on their own children similar emotional or physical pain that they experienced themselves. By doing this they protect themselves from suffering mental pain. They evade unbearable emotions that are *'projected'* into the children. They may terrorise, ignore, isolate or corrupt their children. Fraiberg's team worked on the principle that by offering home visits or 'kitchen therapy', the family's distress could be heard and understood, which would help the parents in turn to hear and comfort their children rather than abuse them, thus breaking the cycle. What they found was that this was more easily said than done. Families like this often cannot see 'help' as anything other than a further persecution. It is therefore not surprising that change is hard to achieve and that patterns of relating remain entrenched through the generations. Such patterns are recognisable to all who work with these families and are described by Britton as follows:

> 'The members of families whose relationships are experienced in the main in the paranoid-schizoid position, are likely to feel persecuted rather than guilty; ill rather than worried; enmity rather than conflict; desperation rather than sadness. They are liable to be triumphant or if not to feel squashed and to see others as either allies or opponents. Their tendency to take flight (e.g., by moving, changing partner, changing schools, etc.) is linked to their belief that psychic experience can be split off and left behind: by the same token there is a sense of being hunted and a fear of being cornered.' (Britton, 2005)

In such situations parents often find it difficult to face up to what has happened and may not always tell the truth, especially when a child has been injured and it is not clear who was responsible. The couple usually find it very difficult indeed to re-assess their relationship to one another in the light of possible injury to or neglect of a child, and conflicting stories as to their ongoing contact with one another are common. Couple relationships are put under strain when outside agencies are called upon to look at what has happened to the children in their care. We may hear a lot of 'lies' or accounts from different perspectives.

Most often the children we see do not volunteer to talk directly about what they have actually experienced, frequently because some of their experiences have been unbearable. They do not want to think about, let alone talk about what may have been too painful to register. We find that as a group they are often underachieving at school, they have developmental delay, they may be withdrawn and unresponsive, unsure of themselves, or they may be overly familiar and socially impaired. They use their bodies for action, rather than their minds for thinking. Their parents often have a history of unrewarding relationships, with intergenerational patterns of acting out. Domestic violence, sexual abuse, and substance misuse are common.

Children's symptoms can often be a clue as to what experiences they have been unable to take into their minds and to make sense of. Some symptoms are quite specific like aggressive outbursts against siblings or objects in the house, and may also include arson, promiscuity, stealing, bedwetting, smearing, not listening, and running away. In sessions, especially with younger children, much can be revealed through play. Typical sequences that we may see in doll's house play could include cars and people enacting disaster upon disaster. A specific sequence may be cars racing away from the house in fear of someone, the cars crash, children are hurt, the ambulance service arrives and runs over the victims, who are thus further abused; the police arrive but they run out of petrol and cannot get the children to hospital; or children lock each other in cupboards, run away to hide on the roof, try to balance there precariously and eventually, after clinging on to an edge by their fingernails, fall to the ground dying with any possible 'rescue' always failing. Such play often indicates that adult figures are not available, are not able to be effective or some that are actively physically and emotionally abusive. Sometimes there are no adult figures in their play at all, only other children, perhaps representing a gang left to their own devices, often in a very primitive world.

BEING IN A TOXIC REALM – WORKING TOGETHER TO KEEP THE CHILD IN MIND

Children who communicate in such ways through play evoke very powerful emotions within the professionals. These are difficult to manage precisely because on a personal level we have all had our own troubles in the area of parenting or being parented. When we consider parents who have been, or may be a possible risk to their children, or think about children who show signs of disturbance and damage, we are entering territory that is highly charged. I am going to refer to this as a *toxic realm* – the metaphor being one that refers to something poisonous – it causes harm or even death. In the psychological realm, children may suffer from a toxic impact that can be devastating. This can take various guises, from those who remain unnoticed by the network or, if noticed, claim they are 'not bothered', to those who 'act out' by bedwetting, not listening, lying and stealing and aggressive, disruptive behaviour that lets everyone know they are in trouble and need attention.

Children who live in a toxic realm have serious problems with their growth and personality development and capacity to form relationships. Their parents may have serious mental health problems, or they may be inadequate parents who are themselves victims of generational patterns of unconscious transmission. Cycles of neglect and abuse are notoriously difficult to alter. Kennedy (2005) has formulated five types of parenting patterns usually associated with parental mental illness: (i) the *psychically absent* parent, one who comes and goes, but is more absent during a period of acute depression; (ii) the *confused* parent – may be in and out of hospital and confusional states; (iii) the *unreliable* parent – usually associated with substance misuse and domestic violence; (iv) the *unempathic* parent – out of touch emotionally with their child's state; (v) the *enmeshed* parent – unable to be separate, merging identities with their child, so that it is difficult for the child to be independent. Such parenting styles may alternate within families, but whatever the pattern, the children's wellbeing is at stake as a result of the psychological difficulties of the parents.

If children receive too much toxicity it contaminates their inner world. They cannot take in a state of mind that reflects on experiences and deals with life's difficulties effectively and creatively. They may shut down and switch off in order to protect themselves. When such processes take place it is as though toxic experiences have remained un-metabolised and are handed on to the next generation like unprocessed nuclear waste.

As professionals we are exposed to this toxic realm at work, whereas the children have lived with it at home and it is often unbearable to think about their home life. Can the child psychotherapist strike up some communication and emotional contact in the wish to find out how this child's mind works and what this may reveal about what experiences s/he has had in the real world? The therapeutic task as a child psychotherapist is to try and make contact with this dangerous material in the hope that something may be available to be reflected upon, integrated into the mind and become part of the painful life experience of that person. It is through the capacity to tolerate these painful life experiences that the pattern of the family's defensive organisation will be broken, thereby safeguarding the next generation.

I will try and give you a flavour of the impact of such work. In order to preserve confidentiality details of the material have been changed.

This vignette describes a woman's outburst of anguish as she left the room at the initial network meeting, which is arranged with all the parties to establish the nature of the task to be undertaken during the Parenting Assessment work. She (I will call her Faith) had arrived 40 minutes late and began with a tirade of upset and distress as to how humiliating it was for her to be discussed by a room full of people, some of whom she had never met. Several people who knew her well tried to tell her that we had not had discussions about her and had been dealing with issues related to the children's father, whilst waiting for her to arrive. Faith could not take in the reality of the situation, which was unbearable for her and she obliterated all the voices of reason and concern for her as she swept out of the room. The meeting agreed that we should try and see if, after talking to someone alone, she might be able to return to the room. What she managed to communicate outside the meeting was the immense pain, which she described in words that went something like this: 'Do you know what it's like to have your children taken away from you? These are my babies. I grew them inside of me and now they've been ripped away from me. I can't believe how things like this can happen in a country that's meant to be civilised'. Her outrage was so strong that it was almost impossible for her to take in that, in order to begin the process of working to get her children back, she needed to prioritise them and try to contain her own feelings. She managed to work with us to some extent and she made it clear that her belief was that the statutory agencies were at fault, and that no neglect had taken place. She believed her children were fine and she was fine. There was nothing wrong with her, so why should she agree to see the adult psychiatrist? The team bent over backwards to find ways of reaching Faith and employed a cultural consultant to help us think about issues of immigration and loss in relation to her history. In the day-to-day work on the programme we witnessed her disciplining her sons in a harsh way, shouting and looming over them to the extent that one of them broke down in tears. When confronted with our view of this, she dismissed us as being in the pocket of Social Services, and so her denials and projection of guilt continued.

THE TEAM

Team members are often subjected to intense emotional pushes and pulls, being torn in opposite directions during the process of this work. For example, after some weeks of work, we might begin to think that certain children have sufficient 'good enough' care that they should stay with their parents who seem to be engaging well with what the professionals have to offer. A few weeks later, when pressure is applied, we may well question our previous view that the family should be given another chance. We might be wondering how we could ever have imagined that these parents could possibly prioritise their child's needs over their own, and wonder whether we can consider regular contact, let alone rehabilitation home. For those team members who have held the hope for this family, it is depressing to come to the conclusion that some people, because of their own early experiences, are either not capable of change or certainly not within the timeframe of their children's developmental needs. Conversely, it is heartening when work with a family concludes that the strengths outweigh the possible risk of further damage to the children and we can recommend that the family can remain together or be reunited.

When faced with such powerful emotional upheavals, it is natural that defensive processes are set in motion. Some team members might put on a thick protective suit, which results in cynicism, others get ill and burn out, some leave the job. Some lie awake at night worrying about coming to final decisions and meeting the deadlines for court reports. Before going to court many team members have sleepless nights. For others, the adrenalin of this work is exciting, leading to hyperactive states of taking on more and more work. Some write papers or attend conferences as a way of digesting experiences and focusing their minds.

We all have our limitations and we know that without our team meetings and supervision, burn out may result. Sufficient time and thought needs to be given to 'metabolise' our own responses to being in the firing line, both with these families and in court. The team acts as a check and balance for the individual practitioner, as it is here that multiple perspectives can be considered and there is the opportunity for an overview. These team discussions not only help us while doing the work, but are also a good preparation for court. Role-play can be done and possible questions put about the case from various points of view, which are helpful in anticipating the key elements of the case. However well you know your report, and the other reports in the bundle, there will often be an element of surprise in the witness stand, for which no amount of work will have prepared you. At such times it seems one simply speaks from the heart, gathering up all one's thoughts and feelings about the total situation under examination.

Sometimes there are disagreements among team members, or with other professionals in the network whose views can become polarised about particular cases. These conflicts usually concern the issue of whether care is good enough in the grey area of emotional abuse. Professionals get caught up in the underlying dynamics and may unwittingly reflect the relationships of the case they are working with, becoming intensely aroused, being uncharacteristically dogmatic, pressurising for urgent drastic action, or being complacent and rather unconcerned or insensitive. Quarrels and high-handed behaviour from colleagues, who have become incompatible in their views, may echo the disturbed behaviour of the family. Powerful feelings have been projected by family members who are looking for a receptacle for their unbearable states of mind. They need 'psychic containment' and different team members pick up various aspects of this. Mental space is required to reflect on such processes, so that frequent team meetings are vital for the healthy functioning of the organisation.

These forces are also likely to be present during the drama of the court process itself, with the various players at risk of being pushed and pulled into colluding with the underlying dynamic of the case. As individuals we need to work hard to stay in touch with, and reflect on, our own emotional inclinations and reactions in order to resist being drawn in to the family configuration unwittingly.

In the psychoanalytic framework such processes of 'acting out' or 'repetition compulsion' are explained as unbearable emotional experiences that are repeated and re-enacted as an alternative to being experienced as mental states that can be thought about and integrated within the mind. Instead they are externalised and others are enlisted to enact roles that fit in with the internal organisation of that family.

Working as part of a team gives one a sense of shared decision-making, so that one is not left entirely on one's own in this toxic realm.

THINKING AND FEELING – THE SEARCH FOR TRUTH

As expert witnesses we are required to report to the court the facts we have learned about the people in a particular family. A fact is something that can be substantiated. We have our opinion on the facts as we see them: a rational layer of facts as they are observed 'out there' and another layer which is beyond observable data, based on something from within. This layer includes our emotional responses, or subjective intuitions. Emotional states that can be felt, but not externally observed, are part of the mind set during the assessment. It is therefore right that the process of cross-examination would test how a professional opinion is formed to safeguard against *'wild'* subjectivity and views that may be prejudicial. The court process aims to arrive at a decision that is based on the 'truth', as far as it can be established on the balance of probability.

The word 'expert' means a person with special knowledge or skill, based on training and experience. An expert opinion of a child psychotherapist goes beyond external, observable facts, because the instrument of assessment is the clinician's own mind, in that an opinion is given about mental and emotional states that can be 'felt' but not always observed externally. Assessment sessions are not interviews with a set of pre-arranged questions and techniques. They are essentially an encounter with what may not yet be known about these children in this particular family, alongside what is already known as presented in the bundle of reports. It is not a question of gathering more information by asking more questions. It is a question of *how* this is done. We make ourselves available, with an open state of mind to what the child wants to communicate to us. Unstructured sessions may be used where we try to present ourselves in a relaxed and natural way, with some warmth, so that some beginnings of understanding may develop. We are not trying to coerce or influence, simply to be with them, listen and observe. Some clinicians use a semi-structured format, like the narrative story stems technique, where scenarios are presented to the child, who is then asked to say what happens next. This gives a picture of the figures that inhabit his/her internal world. We are often asked to assess whether the child seems to have suffered harm. We weigh up all the information received. We assemble all the data, using our theoretical framework to try and grasp the meaning of all that has been said, not said and done in the room with us. For example, within the field of child sexual abuse we have to make sense of the child's behaviour, demeanour, emotional responses, play, unusual or age-inappropriate knowledge of sexuality and the credibility of what has been reported to other parties. Searching for the 'truth' in cases of sexual abuse is very difficult, as allegations are often made in the context of the aftermath of breakdown in the relationship of parents. Perpetrators rarely, if ever, admit to sexual abuse. Our opinion is never a factual certainty. We have to decide, even though we can never know for certain. It is the expert's role to advise, having come to a professional opinion, while the judge has to decide by weighing up all the facts as presented in the reports and all the expert witness accounts.

THE COURT

The setting with which child psychotherapists are most familiar is the consulting room, whilst being an expert witness in court involves entering an alien setting. The court is a formal place with its own rules of conduct. Our aim is to inform the judge about what we have learned and to establish a good communication with him or her. Each barrister is there to put the best case for his or her client. Even though some lines of questioning may be less than courteous, it is important to avoid being provoked or getting caught up in the adversarial atmosphere. This is where skills for being a clinician and being a witness in court overlap. We must stick to clinical issues within our areas of competence. Occasionally we may be cross-examined by parents who have chosen not to be represented by a barrister, and who may be aggrieved by the reports and recommendations. Even if we are not being cross-examined by parents, when they are present restraint is clearly necessary. We need to keep thinking while fired at by questions. Being firm, clear, calm and refusing to be bullied is the best way of presenting ourselves as having authority and credibility. How we deal with cross-examination will be important in the impression we create and hence, how much the judge will rely on our evidence. Good evidence from a child psychotherapist involves having done a thorough report and communicating our findings in a clear and direct way, in language that makes sense and which is not jargon. Telling it as we see it requires confidence in our own ability to make decisions on professional matters.

What we discover about the child's inner world during our assessment sessions usually illuminates what is already known from more external sources that are present as 'facts' in the bundle. These 'facts' are brought to light through the child's communication with the therapist in the consulting room. As an expert witness this is then brought to life by the descriptions that the child psychotherapist gives to the court. We discover a lot about a particular child and his/her family during an assessment and it is what we *make* of the material that is cross-examined in court. How do patterns and meanings emerge from what we see 'out there' in the child? The court wants to know that our perceptions are based on clinical 'facts' and are not distorted by our own possible internal prejudices, weakness, blind spots or preferences.

Let us consider the following scenario to illustrate this: Two little girls, aged 4 and 2 come to the consulting room and immediately notice that there is no handle on the door to the room. (Some repair work was being undertaken in the clinic.) They are preoccupied with this and it reflects, quite by chance, something from their own experience. They had, in reality, been kept locked in a room by their mother who had removed the door handle on the inside so that they could not get out. This meant that they were stuck with each other and their own excrement that was smeared on the walls. In their play during this session there were scenes in the doll's house of a mother figure, alone, asleep, unable to be roused. There was an atmosphere of fear and sorrow in the consulting room. What the older child said was that they had been alone in an empty room and they couldn't get out, not even to go to the toilet. She said that the two of them played with the pet hamster, throwing it around and banging it against the walls until it died. The older child said it was the younger one who had killed it; the younger child did not speak.

According to the 'facts' from the external world, what had actually happened was that the children had been left in a room unable to get out and that faeces had been smeared on the walls. However, the hamster had died in very different circumstances from those communicated by the older child in the consulting room. The adults had been in the front room and the two children were scooting around in a plastic sit-in car, one inside and the other pushing. The hamster was not in its cage and it got run over. Why would the children tell such a different story?

This disparity of 'fact' is interesting. Children may distort the actual reality, but nevertheless they communicate some of the fear, guilt and sorrow about the hamster's death and perhaps their possible fear that a similar fate might have been theirs.

When I reflected on the difference between the two stories of the hamster's death, one the 'truth' of *external reality* and the other the 'lie' the children had told, I thought about it in terms of the children's actual experience: whilst they may have had adults present in the room with them when the hamster actually died, effectively they were alone and that is what was said. Perhaps the truth is worse than the 'lie' – the adults were present and were unable to take protective action to prevent a hamster dying. In their *internal reality* the children were alone in the room with the hamster when it died. They communicated their more *general experience* of being left on their own, which would be their internal working model of what to expect from the world of adults. The children might have had anxious thoughts and feelings about loss on many levels, including questions such as, 'was it my fault?' or 'what have I done to drive mummy away?' They could well have had the fear that things would never come right and be full of anxiety about what damage they may have done not only to the hamster, but also to their mother. Psychoanalytic thinkers, in particular Melanie Klein, recognised that the content of childhood play is significantly concerned with the impulse to repair damage or put things right. The tragedy of this kind of situation is that the adults, by dint of their own histories, need to obliterate their children's needs in order to continue to survive themselves. What is at stake in this situation is what happens when *appropriate* guilt is not acknowledged, but is somehow deflected on to others. Guilt is passed down the line and no one is capable of contemplating their own responsibility in a chain of events. In this case the child psychotherapist could give the court a vivid picture of neglect and harm suffered by the children, despite arguments in defence of the mother aiming to minimise her responsibility and blame the children for being 'naughty' and smearing the walls. If the parent is able to acknowledge the full horror of what has happened, the chances of reparation are greater than if guilt is denied, minimised or projected.

CONCLUSION

When parents and children find themselves in distressing situations where professionals are called in, they have usually been pushed beyond the limits of their capacities. Intolerable experiences have not been available for *'mentalisation'* and are kept so deeply buried that they are neither thought about, nor felt. Others suffer unless the split off guilt, pain or sadness can exist within the mind and be owned as a *subjective* experience that is part of the self. The personality can be enriched by this assimilation, but when this does not happen, such experiences become corrosive or toxic. Thus, 'facts' about ourselves can exist in different states – those which are taken on board as part of ourselves and our experience and those that are not.

The child psychotherapist tries to maintain a 'psychoanalytic attitude' so that details of the emotional impact on his/her self can be used as a guide to what meanings may be being communicated, either by the parents and children themselves, or from the facts of the case as presented in the reports. We need to beware of premature judgemental conclusions and let people reveal themselves over time, so that internal and external 'facts' are brought together through being held up to scrutiny. Thinking and feeling need to be integrated within the professional for an opinion to be reached that is based on inner conviction. But, are feelings not rather unreliable and imprecise? This is a valid question. A faculty for being receptive to emotional contact, whilst also bringing our cognitive skills to bear is at the heart of a psychoanalytic approach. Clinicians, through years of training and practice, develop a certain 'fitness' so that this skill can be a precise instrument for making decisions about what is 'true enough' to be convincing evidence.

ACKNOWLEDGMENTS

I would like to thank all the members of the team with whom a lot of this work has been done, as well as my clinical supervisor.

REFERENCES

Britton, R (2005) 'Re-enactment as an unwitting professional response to family dynamics' in M Bower (ed) *Psychoanalytic Theory for Social Work Practice: Thinking Under Fire* (London, Routledge, 2005)

Fraiberg, SH (1975) 'Ghosts in the nursery: a psychoanalytic approach to the problems of impaired infant-mother relationships' in Fraiberg (ed) *Clinical Studies in infant mental health. The first year of life* (London, Tavistock Publications, 1980)

Freud, A *The Ego and the Mechanisms of Defence* (London, Hogarth Press, 1937)

Kennedy, R Psychotherapists as Expert Witnesses (London, Karnac, 2005)

Klein, M (1940) 'Mourning and its relation to manic depressive states' in *Love Guilt and Reparation, The Writings of Melanie Klein Vol 1* (London, The Hogarth Press, 1975).

'Therapeutic Assessments': Assessing the Ability to Change

*Dr Eia Asen**

INTRODUCTION

Each year thousands of parenting assessments are carried out in the United Kingdom, by many different teams and individual clinicians. Various different models have been developed and the approach presented in this paper is one of these. It has been developed at the Marlborough Family Service, an NHS clinic which is a Child and Adolescent Mental Health Service (CAMHS) joined up with an Adult Psychiatry/Psychotherapy Unit. This setting allows for 'therapeutic assessments' to take place, with expertise available in not only assessing individuals of all ages, eg children, adolescents, parents and grandparents, but also providing specific interventions for individuals, couples and families (Asen et al 1989, Asen & Schuff 2004). Ample feedback over the course of the past 25 years suggests that this type of work is much valued by Social Services and the courts when making decisions about the long-term needs of children.

Independent 'Parenting Assessments', 'Family Assessments' or 'Risk Assessments', commissioned by Social Services and other agencies, are intended to assist the local authorities and courts in deciding public and private law cases which involve dependent children. A major aim of these assessments is to examine the past, present and likely future risks of emotional, physical and sexual harm to a child, and then to provide opinions and make recommendations as to how the child's best interests can be safeguarded in the short and long term. This implies above all that such assessments need to be child-focused, whilst they also need to take into consideration other significant persons and wider systems: the parents, the extended family, the social and cultural setting, the professional network and other dimensions. In other words, when planning assessments, we need to consider how to address the various different levels of the 'system': the individual (child, parent, carer), the parental couple, the family, the extended family, as well as the social and professional system.

An assessment is not delivered by merely taking a static 'snap-shot' of the risks, views and interactions of the family and its individual members. Instead it is a dynamic and interactive process, like a 'movie' made by the assessing professionals and the family together. The term 'movie' implies movement – and it is the ability to 'move', or change, that is so important when making recommendations about placement, residency and contact levels. As such changes need to address dysfunctional areas and risk factors, this may take time – weeks or months. Change rarely happens suddenly: it tends to be a rather slow process and needs to be viewed with

---

Dr Eia Asen is a Consultant Child and Adolescent Psychiatrist and also Consultant Adult Psychiatrist in Psychotherapy. He is the Clinical Director of the Marlborough Family Service, an innovative NHS resource in the centre of London. Previously, he worked as an Adult Psychiatrist in Psychotherapy at the Maudsley Hospital, as well as being a Senior Lecturer at the British Institute of Psychiatry. He trained as a family and couple therapist 25 years ago. He has written many book chapters and scientific papers, most of which relate to work with children and families and is involved in a number of research projects on depression, eating disorders, family violence and educational failure. He frequently appears as an expert witness in child care proceedings.

regard to the children's permanency planning or other timescale issues. Children can only be expected to wait if their parents can potentially make changes, and if this process is not too protracted. The focus on the parents' 'ability' to change helps to answer some of the important questions with regard to prognosis and likely outcome.

CREATING CONTEXTS FOR PARENTING AND RISK ASSESSMENTS

The independent assessor or team is usually sent a court bundle, detailing the work to date, including previous assessments, statements and opinions of professionals, as well as other information including the parents' respective views. Reading this prior to meeting the family can be problematic, as there is a risk that the clinician might be biased by the views and findings of other professionals. Furthermore, some documented 'evidence' is not infrequently disputed by the parents and can lead to them challenging the alleged 'independence' of the clinician. The same also applies to any verbal information a social worker, guardian ad litem or other professional, may wish to relay to the clinician(s) prior to the start of work. If such discussions take place thereby excluding the family, we have found that any subsequent work is often much more difficult, particularly if 'confidential information' has been shared. If the clinician gets caught up in a hidden alliance which excludes the parents and other family members, the result frequently is that the family regards the clinician as on the 'side' of the local authority, rather than being 'neutral'. This can have a paralysing effect. Total transparency is, in our experience, a pre-condition for 'therapeutic assessments'.

There are some disadvantages to not obtaining in-depth information about the family, its history and the various concerns prior to the first meeting. Going into a first joint meeting 'blind', armed only with the agreed Letter of Instruction, may make the clinician feel 'unprofessional'. Referring social workers, lawyers and guardians sometimes find it difficult to accept that their views are not heard, or read about, first. Why not be aware of all the information contained in the court bundle? Clearly it might help to focus the assessment and avoid having to go over old ground again. However, when weighing the 'pros' and 'cons', our team has found that this is a good way of engaging the family – and above all the parents – in the 'new' assessment work and to form a therapeutic alliance, which is best achieved by starting afresh in a transparent way. An initial network meeting is convened, which is attended jointly by the professionals and parents. Here each party can share information they regard as relevant in front of all the others. Such a meeting also provides a first 'live' observation of relationships between various professionals, as well as between the professionals and the parents.

UNDERTAKING THE ASSESSMENT

Once a request for a parenting assessment is received, hopefully in the form of a clear joint Letter of Instruction detailing the various areas of assessment required, we can begin the work. When there is no such letter, we compile and agree the areas of assessment during a network meeting with all the parties concerned. This includes the parents or carers, their own 'network' as well as the various professionals involved, which as a minimum requires the presence of the social worker(s) and the children's guardian. However, frequently other people attend the network meeting and the subsequent review meetings, depending on the intensity of their involvement: this may include members of the extended family, advocates and family friends, solicitors, health visitors, psychiatrists, teachers and so on. The purpose of this meeting is to:

- draw a 'map' of all professionals involved in the life of the family, including their specific concerns, tasks and positions;

- understand the relationships between the professionals and the family;

- share openly the concerns the different professionals have;

- ensure that the parents can respond and define what their own concerns and needs are;

- jointly agree on the areas of work, timescale issues and consequences of change – and what is to happen if there is no change.

For the network meeting to be successful for all, concerns need to be expressed in clear and comprehensible language. This may seem obvious but is frequently not the case. For example, the term 'attachment' to which many professionals feel quite 'attached', means very little to most parents and it requires an explanation in simple terms. Similarly, the term 'communication problem' can also mean all sorts of things: too little communication; too confusing; too aggressive or too emotionally abusive; some parents rarely say anything positive to or about their child; or they ask the child to be the referee in their verbal fights and then blame the child for siding with the other parent. Not listening to each other, or to their child(ren) can be another so-called 'communication problem'. The clearer and the more concretely any concerns are defined, or de-constructed into client-friendly language, the easier it is for the parents to understand what others are worried about and to know what changes they need to make. This then allows the assessing team to consider how to assist the family and its members to make the required changes.

It is important to remember that it may not only be the parents who need to make changes. One may encounter entrenched difficulties between professionals and the family. Occasionally one encounters very stuck systems, with professional paralysis and indecision making things worse. To enable parents to change, changes in the professional system or in the relationship between the family and professionals also need to take place. The assessing team may have to consider interventions that address these dynamics.

Therapeutic assessments can have very different time frames, depending on the nature of the task. Following the network meeting, it should be possible to make a detailed plan of how to structure the work: how many sessions, for how long, who should be present and where they should take place. The duration of work carried out by our team varies from short-term work, 5–8 sessions over a period of 6–8 weeks, to much more intensive long-term work lasting up to four months. We offer a variety of sessions: some with the parents/carers individually, others with the parental couple if there is one, and also sessional work with parent(s) and child(ren). In these sessions we not only ask a series of questions and listen to the accounts of the parents (and of significant others), but we also observe and question what goes on between family members. At times we will ask family members to carry out specific tasks, so that we can obtain 'live samples' of problematic and 'risky' family interactions. However, we not only make observations, but also feed these back to the parents, highlighting 'positives' – areas of competence – as well as 'negatives' – areas of concern, so that the parents can respond and consider making changes. This allows us to assess how the parents and other family members make use of feedback and whether they are able and willing to change. Since it is unrealistic to expect parents to change unaided, particularly if they are stuck in chronic patterns of poor parenting, one has to consider supportive and therapeutic intervention, such as straight advice, 'coaching', counselling or some form of family work. Risk can then be re-assessed, post-intervention, to determine whether it remains unaltered, or is increased or decreased. Another important concept that influences our parenting assessments is the basic idea that behaviour is also context dependent – people and families can behave quite differently in different settings. We therefore try and see parents in a variety of contexts: in the family home, when picking up their child from school, on hospital wards and other settings that are relevant to the family, be that their mosque, church, temple or synagogue. This 'wide angle' lens approach, if combined with the 'close up' look at the individual parent, permits us to assess the family and its support system.

OBSERVING AND INTERVENING

It is rare that spontaneous interactions occur during formal assessment sessions, particularly if these are based on a question and answer format, or if everyone is on their 'best behaviour'. Talking about problematic parenting in the absence of children is one thing, observing it 'in vivo' is another. In order to observe 'typical' communication and relationship patterns, we attempt to create scenarios that encourage 'live' interactions between the parents, as well as between parents and children. Eliciting 'live samples' of problematic family interactions and issues can be done in a variety of ways. The technique of 'enactment' (Minuchin 1974) can be adapted to therapeutic work with parenting issues. Here the therapist encourages all family members to 'show' some interactions that they themselves have identified as being problematic. Assuming that child and parent are not already displaying the very problems that have prompted the referral overtly, the clinician can say: 'Your child is behaving very well now. What is it that you would have to say or do now for your son to produce the type of behaviour that makes it so difficult for you to cope with him?' Almost all parents know how to trigger problematic responses in their offspring; they know, like their children, what button to push to get things going. Once in motion, entrenched interaction patterns unfold automatically, no matter whether a therapist is present or a camera is recording it. Studying 'in vivo' allows the therapist to get a clear idea of how problem behaviour evolves and escalates. If video-recorded it also allows subsequent joint reflections and analysis with the individuals concerned. There are 'tasks' families of all ages can be set to stimulate 'live' family interaction, many of which are described in the DoH's Family Assessment package (Bentovim and Bingley 2001). Asking a family to play a game together, or carry out some school-based homework activity, is likely to reveal serious underlying relationship issues. 'Show me how you all play … here is a board game (bricks, computer game) … why don't you all play for the next half an hour or so. I'll just sit back …'. As the temperature rises, the assessing professional may ask: 'I notice you are all getting quite heated … what normally happens next … what can each of you do now for it to be different, better?' It is then of interest to see what happens next: can the parents think about new possibilities? Do they blame the child or take responsibility for a different outcome themselves? This is an aspect of a 'therapeutic assessment' – promoting and assessing the ability to make changes and to sustain these.

INTENSIVE THERAPEUTIC ASSESSMENTS

Certain parental disturbances seriously affect the socialisation process of their offspring and an inability to change carries a poor prognosis for these children's ability to relate to others. Therefore it is important to assess and work therapeutically with children and their carers in 'familiar' situations, such as at home around mealtimes, when picked up from school, or during a shopping trip. Seeing people 'in vivo' helps to map the family's connections with their environment, or lack thereof: the space, state and location of the accommodation, and the immediate neighbourhood. Creating neighbourhood maps with existing or potential contacts helps to indicate possible changes. Getting parents to think about how to reach out, how to make use of their neighbours, helpers, local shops and the like can be a first step to questioning social isolation: "What would happen if you connected with that person? How could you do it? What would be the first step you would have to take?' These questions get parents to think about different ways of relating to their social environment, and they have both diagnostic as well as therapeutic value. Though home-based work is useful, in practice it is not necessarily the best or most realistic option. Firstly, it is very expensive for a team to assess parental functioning at home over weeks or months, with possibly two professionals travelling to the family home and observing just one family over the course of many hours. Secondly, the presence of outside observers, often in cramped conditions, tends to make feel parents like specimens who are being put under a microscope and, as a result, they may not behave 'naturally' at all. Thirdly, when children have been removed from the family home, possibly under rather traumatic circumstances, it is hardly a good idea to bring them back to their home merely for the purpose of an assessment. This may be upsetting and also raise false expectations.

In practice, time and resource issues seldom allow for such home and community-based work to be undertaken. For this reason multi-family day units or residential settings have become a useful context for therapeutic assessments. Sometimes assessments need to be intensive and prolonged because of the complexity and seriousness of the issues, and this is when day or residential units for families need to be considered. The Marlborough Family Service has a day unit for 6–8 families attending together at the same time. They attend for six hours a day, for a period of anything between a few days to four months, thereby making it is possible to assess the practical parenting ability of a mother and/or father, in a kind of 'home' away from home. In a multi-family setting, based in a family centre or a clinic, the family shares the 'stage' with a number of other families (Asen et al 2001). A typical day can be recreated in the centre so that naturalistic interactions can evolve. Although initially one-way screens and CCTV or video-links evoke 'Big Brother' associations, they are generally perceived as being much less intrusive than a pair of eyes trained to stare at their every action. With other families present the parents tend to feel less 'centre stage' or in the 'spotlight'. In other words, the observational procedures feel more diluted. Furthermore, multi-family settings also promote interactions between families. The parents' ability to make social contacts and form relationships can be observed, as well as assessing their capacity to supervise their children appropriately when meeting 'strangers'. Boundary issues are likely to emerge in a large group of families and can be quite a stressful experience, with a lot of noise and activity. Intense levels of stress are not unwelcome, as it requires parents to manage their volatile emotions in difficult circumstances. This is demanding for parents who are practiced in putting up a front, or presenting a 'normal' façade to impress the professionals. In this situation, amongst lively, challenging individual members, with sudden, unpredictable mini-crises arising frequently creating a distinct sense of impending chaos, it is not possible for even fairly well defended parents to maintain their studied composure. It is like being in a 'hot house' or in a 'pressure cooker' and parents have frequently used these metaphors to describe their experiences in our family day centre. However, it is also a context in which parents and families can support each other; where they bring their observations of other families and receive feedback about their own problematic or disturbed behaviour. Parents often see, mirrored in other families, precisely those issues that they find difficult to acknowledge themselves. Video-feedback sessions, using film footage from the day, are popular with families. They can see themselves from a different angle and reflect on how they could do things differently. Detailed study of conflict-ridden family interactions makes it possible to understand how sequences arise and how to avoid these. Multi-family settings offer an important assessment context, and yield data that cannot be obtained as quickly and in such detail elsewhere. This is also a cost effective form of assessment as 6–8 families can be assessed and treated simultaneously.

Feedback is an important feature. Most families attend on a semi-voluntary basis whilst awaiting the outcome of care proceedings, which will result in major decisions regarding their future. They are aware that their daily performance is being observed (if not judged) and are, not surprisingly, extremely keen to know what the staff's observations and recommendations are. Experience has shown that the best policy is to be as open as possible about all observations, positive and negative. This avoids disappointment later on. Moreover it curbs problematic collusions with clients who are addicted to keeping secrets. The fact that there are video cameras in every room, which may or may not be switched on, is a constant reminder to both patients and staff that everything is open to discussion. The staff share their observations with all families at the end of each day. Furthermore, at the end of each week there is a more formal meeting when the staff discuss in detail their weekly impressions of each family. This staff discussion is videotaped and then re-played to the families who can reflect on the staff's 'Reflections'. This feed-back process, chaired by a systemically trained psychiatrist or senior family therapist, is very popular and allows families to put themselves in an observer position – commenting on the staff's observations of themselves. Thus, it allows new perspectives to emerge, not only of themselves but also of the institution, the staff, other families and so on.

Any such intensive therapy does not need to be confined to the nuclear or extended family. Relevant others may include friends, a person from the religious community (priest, rabbi, imam), lawyers or other advocates whom the family experiences as helpful. It is the combination of interventions at a number of levels simultaneously, including the social level, which leads to change in these families.

WORKING WITH THE PARENTS TOGETHER

Domestic violence is a frequent occurrence in the lives of parents who present with borderline and emotionally unstable personality disorders. Exposure to domestic violence has highly adverse effects on children and their developing brains and minds (Schore 2003). Therefore assessing and changing a 'toxic' parental couple relationship is not only crucial when both carers live in the home, but also with single parents who have 'on and off' relationships with abusive partners. Exploring hypothetical scenarios is one of a number of effective ways of assessing risk: 'When you and your partner have these loud arguments, what do you think is the effect of this on your child?' Asking a parental couple to discuss a recent conflict 'in vivo' provides a good opportunity to study their difficulties. 'What are the issues that you tend to argue about – money, family, drink? When was the last time you argued ... what started it? What happened next ... so, you remember how it went .... keep going, try to sort it out now ... and what do you say when she says that? At what point do you think this argument is getting out of hand? What do you normally do – and what can you do now?' Encouraging such an 'enactment' under controlled conditions, can be helpful. It permits 'pausing' the interactions at any point for a short time to consider alternative actions and outcomes. Management of anger and exercising self control often become the focus of work. 'Keeping oneself and others safe' strategies may be developed by learning how to take 'time out' when a loss of control threatens. What can each partner do to de-escalate? How does one negotiate a 'break', and what actions and conversations need to take place before 're-entry' can be considered? This can be done by exploring hypothetical scenarios: 'Imagine you haven't slept all night, your partner has come back home early in the morning, drunk and he is fast asleep: your 5-year-old needs to be got ready to go to school, but your baby is teething and needs a lot of attention ... how do you manage all that?' 'You are in the middle of this argument, the temperature rises ... what can each of you do to maintain each other's and the children's safety?' This is followed by a detailed and concrete exploration of each partner's actions and reactions, with possible responses being explored in a mini-role play. It can be helpful to map the interactions in the form of a circle depicting each 'step' in a familiar escalation: how it starts, what happens next, how the other responds, and so on. Devising and studying this map from a more detached perspective helps carers to consider ways of breaking the cycle of violence and at each stage to think what alternative action could be taken. Such work is done without the child being present.

WORKING WITH THE INDIVIDUAL

Risk assessments may also need to involve assessment and therapeutic work with each individual parent. Their own past histories and how these impact on their present parenting requires exploration: 'Tell me about what sort of mother your mother was – and what sort of father your father was? What did your mother do really well? What not? What did you decide to do yourself as a mother? What did you want to do differently?' The repetition of 'scripts' from an individual's family of origin has to be explored, as well as identifying how such scripts have been or require rewriting. This necessitates the ability to reflect, and is another area that may benefit from therapeutic intervention. Reflection is the ability to have a measure of insight and understanding of any personal shortcomings, and also the ability to place oneself into the position of one's own child(ren). The ability, or inability, to develop empathy with the child's predicament, requires examination: 'Imagine that you are your 3-year-old daughter looking at you: what might she say is the one thing she'd worry about you most?'

The non-abusive parent's ability to act in a protective manner towards their child is another major assessment and intervention area. A mother can be asked to consider a number of hypothetical scenarios that pose potential risks to her child: 'Imagine that you notice that your daughter always leaves the room in a rush whenever your boyfriend turns up. What would you make of that?' By examining the mother's responses her ability to consider a variety of possibilities to explain her daughter's behaviour is assessed: for instance, that she might be threatened by the boyfriend. A parent who does not have an 'open mind', and who is unable or unwilling to consider a whole range of different explanations for specific unusual behaviour, may not be able to act protectively. The parent may also be asked to 'Put yourself in the head of your son ... pretend you are him ... imagine what he sees when he comes home and he notices that your partner has given you another black eye ... what do you think goes on in his head?' Audio-visual aids, such as a self-protection film, or books about risks of abuse, may help parents and children to get into a discussion about risks and how to avoid these.

FORMING OPINIONS ABOUT THE ABILITY TO CHANGE

A substantial number of families in private or public proceedings involve parents with mental health issues. There is now ample evidence that these can directly or indirectly impact on the welfare of dependent children (Goepfert et al 2004). In order to describe and quantify the type and degree of mental illness, together with treatment options, social workers and guardians tend to commission risk assessments from adult general psychiatrists. These reports are often disappointing as they tend to focus predominantly on the adult, and do not view the parent from the child's perspective. A child may be a 'young carer', one who has to 'parent' the parent, whilst also being exposed to the parent's mental state fluctuations. Psychiatrists are fond of making diagnoses, but a standard psychiatric diagnosis out of context is of rather limited value, as it says little about the risk this particular parent poses to his/her child. Merely to state that a parent has a 'personality disorder' is of little help; furthermore it is often assumed that this diagnosis means change is not possible, but this is untrue. Parents with the diagnosis of 'borderline personality disorder', notoriously the most difficult and perhaps potentially most dangerous or 'risky' condition as far as children's welfare is concerned, can be treated effectively, although these evidence-based treatments are not short (Bateman & Fonagy 2004). A mere psychiatric diagnosis says little about the prognosis with regard to the quality of current or future parenting, therefore it is important to undertake functional and not merely diagnosis based assessments. The prognosis with regard to the parent's future mental health and/or relapses is more useful if it is not merely based on general statistics, but takes into account the specific circumstances of that parent and his/her support system, be that family, friends or professionals.

CONCLUSION

A major aim of a parenting assessment is to predict future risks: what these are, how likely they are to occur, how they can be reduced, and which interventions – if any – might contribute to a risk reduction, over what timescale and whether any changes can be sustained. Therapeutic assessments with the ingredients described above challenge families and professionals alike. They imply that change is possible. Based on this assumption, a series of potentially therapeutic, change-provoking interventions are made at different levels: at the level of the individual, the parental couple, the family, and also the wider context. At times it is our task to help change aspects of the relationship between the family and one or more key professionals, who may also be stuck in unhelpful interactions with family members. Network and review meetings are a good context for such work though it can be tricky to challenge what some professionals do whilst not disqualifying them.

Therapeutic assessments allow us to form opinions as to whether families and their individual members are able to make even small changes and, equally important, whether they can sustain these over time. Given the relatively short time-frame of risk assessments, therapeutic work needs to start immediately and similar scenarios need to be revisited week by week, to see whether some progress is being made. We have found it possible, usually within three months, to come to informed opinions about the ability to change and to make some fairly reliable predictions about the ability to sustain these. Of course we need to make recommendations as to what continued support and interventions are necessary subsequently to sustain these changes, be that social work support and monitoring, home help input, individual therapeutic work for the child and/or parent, family work and other interventions.

Protective and good prognostic factors on the parent's part include the following:

- insight into own mental health issues and ability to identify warning signs of deteriorating mental state;

- ability to reflect about the child's predicament and to view things from the child's perspective;

- acknowledgment of and taking responsibility for past shortcomings, including neglect or abuse, and putting child(ren) at risk;

- demonstrating ability to take protective stance in hypothetical risk scenarios;

- making meaningful emotional connections with own past personal experiences;

- ability to change previously 'stuck' behaviours;

- demonstrating ability to be consistent and sustain changes;

- motivation for and compliance with treatments offered;

- good ability to co-operate with helping system, and/or family and friends;

- minimum of one year non-dependence on alcohol and substances (as verified by tests);

- ability to make feasible future plans for care of children.

REFERENCES

Asen, KE et al 'A Systems Approach to Child Abuse: Management and Treatment Issues' Child Abuse and Neglect, Vol.13, 45–57 (1989)

Asen, E, Dawson, N & McHugh, B Multiple Family Therapy — the Marlborough model and its wider applications (New York and London, Karnac, 2001)

Asen, E and Schuff, H 'Disturbed parents and disturbed families: assessment and treatment issues' in M Goepfert, J Webster & MV Seeman (eds) *Disturbed and Mentally Ill Parents and their Children* (Cambridge, Cambridge University Press, 2004)

Bateman, A & Fonagy, P *Psychotherapy for Borderline Personality Disorder* (Oxford, Oxford University Press, 2004)

Bentovim, A and Bingley Miller L The Family Assessment – The Assessment of Family Competence Strengths and Difficulties (London, Pavilion, 2000)

Goepfert, M, Webster, J & Seeman, MV (eds) *Disturbed and Mentally Ill Parents and their Children* (Cambridge, Cambridge University Press, 2004)

Minuchin, S *Families and Family Therapy* (Tavistock Publications, London, 1974)

Schore, A *Affect Regulation and the Repair of the Self* (WW Norton, New York & London, 2003)

Entangled Bonds: Psychodynamic Assessments of Sibling Relationships for the Family Courts

*Jenifer Wakelyn**

INTRODUCTION

When families break down and children can no longer live with their parents, it can seem unthinkable that they may also be separated from their brothers and sisters. However, although the hope is always that families will stay together, or be re-united when parents are more able to cope, sadly there are times for very troubled families when staying together would be at the cost of the children's physical safety or their emotional and mental stability. Both the Children Act 1989 and DoH guidance recommend that siblings be accommodated together if they are placed in local authority care, 'unless this is part of a well thought out plan based on each child's needs' (Lord and Borthwick, 2001). This chapter aims to describe how professionals in a multi-disciplinary assessment centre come to opinions about children's states of mind and their relationships in order to make recommendations about the placements of siblings for the family courts. It will also consider how children's overtly expressed wishes are taken into account to inform an understanding of underlying emotional states and attachments, rather than directly determining care planning.

When children have endured terrible experiences together, their mutual attachment may to some degree help them to manage the trauma of separation from their parents. Many writers have noted the protective and developmental features of sibling relationships. Research carried out by Dunn and Kendrick has shown that emotional experiences with brothers and sisters can contribute to a heightened awareness of self-identity and this in turn enhances the capacity to distinguish between self and other. Studies have also investigated the developmental aspects of sibling interactions: for example, Izard (1977) found that feelings such as anger or shame in sibling interaction motivate the growth of understanding of the self as a causal agent, which contributes to understanding of and interest in others. Research has also shown that in some types of adversity, such as maternal depression, sibling relationships often improve, as brothers and sisters turn to each other for attention and comfort that is not available from the parent (Dunn and Kendrick 1982). Fundamentally, as Silverstone suggests, 'siblings can hold the family narrative for each other, and become the containers for each other of a history of their own childhood' (Silverstone 2006, p 225). However, such research findings as there are on the benefits of keeping together brothers and sisters who have suffered highly traumatic early experiences, such as prolonged physical, sexual or emotional abuse, or chronic neglect and deprivation, are complex (Rushton, A, et al 2001). Separating siblings who have so far remained together is one of the hardest decisions that professionals are faced with, one that may be said to be of equal

---

* Jenifer Wakelyn trained as a Child and Adolescent Psychotherapist at the Tavistock after working in education. She has worked at Islington Child and Family Consultation Service, the Tavistock Centre and the Monroe Young Family Centre and currently works for the Tavistock/Haringey Service for Looked-After Children and Adolescents. She teaches at the Tavistock Centre and has written on psychoanalytic theory and art.

import to separating children from parents. But despite the current upsurge of clinical and academic interest in the nature of sibling relationships, there is still a dearth of research and follow-up studies of separated sibling groups.

Conflicts between the interests of different siblings may determine placement recommendations: a younger child may have a chance of being adopted, or the needs of one of the children may exceed the capacities even of devoted and experienced foster parents, requiring the specialist containment and support of a residential unit. Some children learn to protect themselves from the effects of trauma or gross neglect by means of defences that, in the absence of therapy or a highly specialised, supportive environment, would stunt their future development. Such children may split off their distress, presenting a calm, almost frozen exterior, keeping all emotional contact at bay, while others may find ways of losing themselves, and their painful feelings, in a gang, suppressing their own identity, thoughts and feelings. Attachment research has shown that these defences can become organised, leading to prolonged impairments in relationships which go on to be replicated in the next generation, as attachment disorders are predictive of parenting difficulties (Schofield and Beek 2006). For children in these circumstances, assessment involves meticulous observation of the defences each child has become most reliant on. Very careful consideration is given as to whether the continued presence of their siblings would be compatible with a slow and careful lessening of the grip of the defences that have hitherto been necessary for survival. If, on balance, it seems that ongoing interactions with brothers and sisters would be more likely to perpetuate and exacerbate these harmful ways of being, the assessment team may take the difficult step of recommending that the siblings are placed separately, in the interests of their long term development, while maintaining an appropriate level of contact in the form of visits, letters and telephone calls.

THE MONROE YOUNG FAMILY CENTRE

Drawing on clinical material which has been disguised to protect confidentiality, this chapter describes some of the thinking in the Monroe Young Family Centre (MYFC) about brothers and sisters for whom staying together seemed to be crucial to their emotional and social development, and goes on to explore situations in which separation of siblings is recommended. The centre, which was set up in 1989 by Professor Judith Trowell (Trowell; Huffington 1992) takes referrals from throughout Greater London to carry out assessments of families with young children where there are serious child protection concerns. The multidisciplinary team comprises professionals from a range of trainings and theoretical backgrounds, including child and adolescent psychiatrists, child and adolescent and adult psychotherapists, clinical psychologists and social workers. Each assessment is carried out on a case-by-case basis, informed by developmental and Social Services research. The expertise and experience of the whole multi-disciplinary team are essential in reaching recommendations that, as far as possible, reflect the interests of each child. Letters of joint instruction typically include questions about the placement of the children and about their therapeutic needs.

In the highly charged atmosphere of a court assessment, MYFC staff try to be empathetic, friendly and professional, with the aim that the intervention should have some therapeutic potential for the families who come to the centre. Time is given to thinking with the social worker and the parents or foster carers about how to prepare the children for their first visit to the centre, which follows a visit to the children's current home. The assessment begins with an introductory meeting when the purpose of the assessment is explained and, where possible, each family member's understanding of why they are coming to the centre is explored.

One aim of the assessment is to observe and gather evidence about the impact of traumatic experiences on children's states of mind and on their capacity to form relationships. Perhaps because of our need to remain hopeful, and the wish to be 'child-friendly', this impact can often be minimised. Contact supervisors, for example, often describe a calm, placid baby, or an excited, energetic toddler in positive terms, but these presentations may on further exploration mask high levels of distress or anxiety which cannot be expressed directly (Schofield and Beek 2006; Youell 2002). Observation and thoughts about the meanings that may underlie behaviour, play and talk, guided by the overall affect conveyed by interaction with a child or group of children, are at the core of psychoanalytical work in assessment as in treatment (Klauber 1997). Trying to be in touch with the painful and distressing feelings that children have as a result of traumatic or abusive experiences is the specialist task of psychoanalytically trained staff, who require the support of the multidisciplinary team and the understanding gained in personal psychoanalysis to carry out this work on a day-to-day basis. Without this framework and structure, cogently described by Anna Freud and her colleagues as providing a combination of 'hard-headedness and soft heartedness', the impulse to minimise the impact of children's experiences, perhaps under the catch-all 'they're too young to notice', can be irresistible (Freud 1980).

Sadly, experience and research show that young children, even babies, *are* profoundly affected by distress and trauma. The child who appears to be calmly contented, blithely oblivious, turning to self-comforting or self-stimulating practices, may, in effect, have carried out his or her own assessment of the parenting capacity of the adults around them. Faced with repeated rejection, assaults or neglect, many children set up powerful defensive barriers that, if untreated, would go on to impair their future development and personality. That children *are* affected in these ways, however, also suggests that they may be helped in the safe and reliable conditions of psychotherapy or of specialised therapeutic care, through sensitive, mindful, often long-term treatment.

The MYFC approach relies on observation and detailed description of interactions. In the course of each three to four week assessment, the children are usually seen on their own three times, as well as in sibling groups, and with their parent or parents. Detailed observational notes are written after each session. Children's overtly expressed wishes are thought about in the context of their play and interactions with each other, with their parents or carers, and with staff. Each child sees the same member of staff, where possible in the same room, with a box of toys and drawing materials, so that they are encouraged to make use of the experience of being with an attentive, friendly adult who is interested in them and their thoughts and feelings. Much of the time staff do not direct children's play or ask questions: the aim of the individual sessions is rather to follow the child's lead and to help them to name feelings that come to the surface, often in symbolic play with toys, or in drawings. When children have lived through traumatic experiences, or are still living in fear, the flow of their play may suddenly halt, or be diverted. The therapist notes these breaks in continuity, or avoidances of particular areas, and then by putting together their observations with colleagues in a team discussion, hypotheses will be formed about the defences that may have become habitual for this particular child. The therapist's observations also involve monitoring her own emotional state (or 'counter-transference') while she is with the child, as this may contribute valuably to the whole picture of a child's experience. With sibling groups, a more directive approach is sometimes taken: a task may be suggested, such as playing a game, or building a castle together. The therapist tries to support the siblings in carrying out the task, and notices how the group makes use of each other and how they respond to her help.

SIBLINGS IN PSYCHODYNAMIC THEORY

Many writers have commented on the enduring intensity of sibling relationships. Keats' description of his sister, as someone who 'walks about my imagination like a ghost', captures the way in which sibling relationships and shared histories intimately pervade the internal world (Keats, letter to Charles Brown, 1820, quoted in Dunn and Kenrick, p 221). The pressures of development into adolescence and adulthood often force conflicts in parent-child relationships to be addressed, bringing change and the possibility of some eventual resolution. Sibling relationships, on the other hand, with less drive to propel shifts in the predominant dynamics, can become more fixed. The position of 'big sister' or 'younger brother', persisting into adult life, may become entrenched in a personality. In psychodynamic theory, sibling relationships have tended to be seen as the backdrop to the Oedipal drama of parent-child relationships (Coles 2003; Colonna and Newman 1983; Mitchell 2006). However, Freud and later psychoanalytical thinkers did not overlook the contribution of family position to character development (Sherwin-White 2007). Freud himself grew up in a complex extended family, with much older half-brothers from his father's first marriage. He and his nephew were almost the same age, and he came to see this ambivalent relationship, alternating between closeness and enmity, as determining the future pattern of his friendships. Melanie Klein's intense relationship with her brother was reflected in the important role she attributed to sibling relationships in emotional development (Klein 1932, Rustin 2007).

In Kleinian thinking, it is the nature of unconscious responses and feelings – or phantasies – about the parents and parental relationships that determines whether sibling conflict and attachments are more or less benign or destructive. When the phantasies about the parents are dominated by sadistic hatred, the sibling relationships are more likely to be destructive, but Klein also thought that siblings could be 'possible facilitators of mental health', and that love between siblings can help to promote adult relationships, especially by mitigating relationships with parents that are dominated by hatred (Klein 1932, 1946; Coles 2003; Hindle 1995, 2000).

ASSESSMENTS OF SIBLING RELATIONSHIPS

In the following case examples, names and identifying details have been changed to protect confidentiality.

The children in the 'A' family came to the attention of Social Services after a call from a neighbour who had heard persistent crying from the house, night and day. The three children, aged 2, 4 and 5, were found in a horrifying condition. They had been locked up in a darkened room for much of their lives. Alex, the youngest, was emaciated, and badly bruised; it was his cries that had led the neighbour to call Social Services. The level of violence between the siblings seemed at first to suggest that separate placements might be indicated. However, observation of the children's play, in which toy police cars and ambulances repeatedly tried to reach a doll family, but were thwarted by a series of obstacles, suggested that the attacks on each other that had brought the children to the attention of Social Services also represented desperate attempts to arouse the attention and concern of their parents. It seemed that these children had been able to retain an idea, or an internal working model, of potentially concerned, helpful parents whom they wanted to reach. This suggested that there were benign and protective aspects to their attachment, despite the alarming nature of the injuries that had been inflicted on the youngest child.

Too much closeness can be as detrimental to development as too much conflict. In the case of the 'B' family, the two sisters, only 16 months apart, and with almost identical names, seemed unable to coexist together: their rivalry was such that any moment of adult attention, any idea of something to be enjoyed by one sister was immediately seized on by the other, suggesting an experience so rivalrous and crowded that each seemed to feel she could only live at the expense of the other. Here, the thinking about placement went hand in hand with therapeutic recommendations. The team recommended that the sisters stay together in long-term foster care in order to carry out the complex task of separating from each other in the context of intensive psychoanalytic psychotherapy for each child. Essential to this recommendation was the finding that each sister when on her own responded with alacrity and enthusiasm to the attention and interest of her therapist and was able to make use of the three individual sessions in a way that suggested she would benefit from long-term psychoanalytic psychotherapy. The team thought that the task of finding and maintaining the internal differences between them would be clearer if they were able at the same time to learn about ordinary ways of being two closely related, but separate, individuals in the external world.

In both the A and B families, the team recommended the siblings stay together, with the provision of professional support for the children and their carers. Their dysfunctional interactions, while likely to be demanding of future carers, were understood as communications about their experiences. Each child responded well when their interactions were received as communications and thought about. These were encouraging findings for their capacity to engage in psychotherapy and develop more positive relationships.

SEPARATING SIBLINGS

In *Together or Apart? Assessing brothers and sisters for permanent placement*, Lord and Borthwick (2001) summarise some key criteria for separating siblings. Recommending separate placements usually involves a combination of factors. In relationships where this eventuality is under consideration, there is likely to be extreme rivalry and jealousy; exploitation or scapegoating of one sibling by others; conflictual alliances between groups within the siblings; hierarchical positioning; highly sexualised behaviour between siblings; or extreme behaviours which amount to re-traumatising of each other. In some cases, especially where there are wide age differences, or a complex constellation of half-siblings, children have already been separated prior to assessment. One or more brothers or sisters may have been accommodated while others have remained in the family home, or they may have been accommodated at different times in different homes. Issues then to be addressed include the attachment each may have made to different foster families.

In the case of the 'C' family, the degree of Michael's chronic emotional neglect indicated a need to be placed on his own. In addition, his younger sister, Rosie, who had been referred at birth, had a good chance of being adopted. Michael, aged 13, had spent his life moving between his mother and her partners' homes. Listless and undernourished, he exuded a sense that he expected to be overlooked. His mother had been dependent on alcohol throughout his life, and her short-lived relationships with her drinking partners were marked by violent altercations. It seemed likely that Michael would have passed unnoticed by Social Services had it not been for the assessment of his baby sister. Like his mother, Michael was highly resistant to the idea of his going into foster care. The gut feeling that 'family is best', was entirely understandable as was the view, taken by previous Social Workers on this case, that the 'strength' of Michael's attachment to his mother was a protective factor for him. As Schofield and Beek emphasise, however, 'strength' of attachment is a misnomer (Schofield and Beek, 2006). Michael's intense clinging to his mother, whose attitude to him veered unpredictably from sentimental warmth to tempestuous violence to contemptuous indifference, was an aspect of an insecure attachment that left little scope for his own identity to emerge or for his needs to be met. It was 'strong', in that it was rigid and desperate, and therefore tenacious, but not in the sense of being nurturing or reliable.

Michael did show interest in his baby sister Rosie, and seemed to want to communicate with her, but he did not know how to do this, and their mother was unable to help him. In fact she seemed to turn to him for guidance as to how to handle and interact with the baby. As the assessment progressed Michael's interactions with Rosie were increasingly tinged with cruelty and jealousy. He chanted, 'Cry, cry cry!' as the baby cried and writhed in distress, watched impassively by their mother. Michael did not seem to have had good enough internal experiences in his own infancy to draw on, in his interactions with Rosie. In addition Michael would have had to manage his own feelings of deprivation and jealousy in order to allow Rosie to have a chance of a better experience, a demand that exceeded his fragile emotional capacities. It seemed particularly difficult for Michael to see Rosie being well cared for by her foster carer, in stark contrast to his own experiences of neglect and actual physical harm as a baby. In discussion the team came to the view that this would make it difficult for him to support Rosie's well-being as she grew up and this, together with the real possibility of Rosie being adopted, led to the recommendation that Michael be fostered separately. Six months later staff heard that Michael had thrived in his foster placement. In this situation, clinical experience and judgement overrode the expressed wishes of the child himself, who had not had sufficient experience of ordinary care and attention to be able to make an informed decision about his future.

Some sibling groups have the appearance of mutually supportive protective relationships, but on exploration there are gang-like dynamics in play that preclude the individual development of each child. This presentation is often associated with the entrenched scapegoating of one member of the family. In the 'D' family, a gang-like grouping of the siblings functioned as a way of protecting their mother, a waif-like young woman with a very troubled history of her own, but also as a way to avoid thinking about each individual in the sibling group. Ian, the oldest sibling, was identified as the problem child. He had been accommodated four years earlier following allegations that he had sexually assaulted his brother, Shane. Like a scapegoat, Ian seemed to carry all the sense of loss, damage and disturbance in the family, and this allowed the remaining family members to unite to expel him and the perceived threat that he posed.

While Ian was placed in an adolescent psychiatric unit, his two younger half brothers Kevin and Shane returned to live with their mother after a brief period in foster care. The assessment followed their return to the family home and came about as the result of continuing concerns about neglect and emotional abuse. Despite the appearance of warmth between mother and the boys, and mother's fluent use of psychological terminology, the experience of being with the family produced a sense of acute discomfort and anxiety among staff. There was an unreal quality to the rational-sounding discussions of relationships that contrasted starkly with the disturbing environment of the family home. Although the flat was in a well-appointed tower block, inside the rooms were dark and cluttered with broken toys and furniture. This proliferation of broken objects suggested that an unconscious communication was being made about a bleak internal world littered with damaged objects.

The assessment included sessions with all three children together, and with Kevin and Shane without Ian, as well as individual sessions. When the three were together there was a great deal of verbal cruelty between them, particularly when one of them was told off or upset. Any misfortune or sign of weakness was met with contempt followed by aggression, which their mother seemed to condone or not notice. It seemed that the presence of Ian, who had been ejected from the family with the idea that the problems would be got rid of with him, provoked further cruelty in the younger siblings (Waddell 1998). However, the assessment provided no evidence to support the contention that after Ian had been removed, the interactions between Kevin and Shane became more benign.

In fact, once it became clear that the MYFC staff were noticing and taking seriously the very disturbed interactions in the family, their cruelty and jealousy escalated. When Kevin came to the centre with a tummy infection, Shane jeered at him relentlessly, and bitterly resented any special attention his brother received. Less conflictual interactions were observed, but a disturbing, sexualised excitement emerged as the factor that allowed the brothers to join up. Playing a word game, for example, they vied with each other to suggest words for erections, laughing shrilly, and seeming to become fused in an excitement which shifted into cruelty as each boy began pretending to feed dolls and toy animals while at the same time assaulting them sexually. The collusion between the three children had a gang-like quality in which individual thinking was submerged (Canham 2002). It seemed that this gang state provided a kind of intimacy or togetherness, which may have offered some alternative to the desolation and disturbance that seemed to dominate their internal lives. For these children, separation seemed to be in their best interests, with contact meetings three times a year. A well-supported foster placement, together with therapeutic help, was recommended for Kevin, while Shane, whose disturbance was more entrenched, was placed in a residential therapeutic community.

CONCLUSION

Many difficulties and dilemmas face professionals when making decisions about the placement of brothers and sisters in highly troubled families where there are often transgenerational relationship difficulties and long-term mental health issues for one or both parents. In each family assessment, a complex interplay of factors determines what is likely to be the 'least bad' placement option for each child. Observation and psychoanalytically informed interpretation of children's play and interactions are key tools in developing an overall picture of a child's internal and external worlds so as to contribute to planning for their future care. Assessment on this model is complementary to and sometimes supersedes the overtly expressed wishes of the child or children. Judgments as to the benefits and drawbacks of different placements are among the most taxing decisions that have to be made by child care workers and placement panels, and as yet there is relatively little research on the quality of sibling relationships and the outcome of sibling placements. There is an urgent need for more research and follow-up studies in these areas.

ACKNOWLEDGMENT

I wish to thank Debnorah Steiner, my colleagues at the Monroe Young Family Centre and Anna Fitzgerald, Debbie Hindle and Margaret Rustin.

REFERENCES

Canham, H 'Group and gang states of mind' *Journal of Child Psychotherapy*, 28:2, 113–128 (2002)

Coles, P The importance of sibling relationships in psychoanalysis (London, Karnac, 2003)

Colonna, AB and Newman, LM 'The psychoanalytic literature on siblings' in *The psychoanalytic study of the child*, 38: 285-339 (1983)

Coles, P, (ed) *Sibling relationships* (London, Karnac, 2006)

DoH Framework for the assessment of children in need and their families (2000)

Dunn, J and Kendrick, C *Siblings. Love, envy and understanding* (London, Grant McIntyre, 1982)

Freud, A, et al *Beyond the best interests of the child* (London, Burnett Books, (1980)

Hindle, D 'Thinking about siblings who are seen together' *Adoption and Fostering*, 19:1, 14–19 (1995)

Hindle, D (2000) An intensive assessment of a small sample of siblings placed together in foster care (Unpublished D.Phil. Thesis, 2000)

Izard, CE 'On the ontogenesis of emotion and emotion-cognition relationships in infancy' in M Lewis and LA Rosenblum (eds) *The development of affect* (New York, Plenum Press, 1977) quoted in Dunn and Kenrick, 1982, p 212

Klein, M *The Psycho-Analysis of children* (London, Hogarth Press, 1932)

Klein, M 'Notes on some schizoid mechanisms' (1926), in *Envy and Gratitude* (London, Hogarth Press, 1946)

Lord, J & Borthwick, S 'Together or Apart? Assessing brothers and sisters for permanent placement' (London, BAAF, 2001)

Mitchell, J 'Sibling trauma: a theoretical consideration' in Coles, P (ed) *Sibling relationships* (London, Karnac, 2006)

Rushton, A et al *Siblings in late permanent placements* (London, BAAF, 2001)

Rustin, ME 'Taking account of siblings – a view from child psychotherapy' *Journal of Child Psychotherapy* 33:1, 21–35 (2007)

Schofield, G and Beek, M Attachment handbook for foster care and adoption (London, BAAF, 2006)

Sherwin-White, S (in press) 'Freud on brothers and sisters: A neglected topic' *Journal of Child Psychotherapy* 33:1, 4–20 (2007)

Silverstone (2006) 'Siblings' in Coles, P (ed) *Sibling relationships* (London, Karnac, 2006).

Timberlake, E and Hamlin, E 'The sibling group: a neglected dimensions of placement' *Child Welfare* LXI 8 (1982)

Trowell, J & Huffington, C 'Daring to take the Risks: setting up a Young Family Centre' *Bulletin ACPP 14(3)* May pp 114–118 (1992)

Waddell, M 'The Scapegoat' in R Anderson & A Dartington (eds) *Facing it out. Clinical perspectives on adolescent disturbance* (London, Duckworth, 1998)

Youell, B 'The relevance of infant and young child observation in multidisciplinary assessments for the family courts' in A Briggs (ed) *Surviving Space, Papers on infant observation* (London, Karnac, 2002)

A Child Psychotherapist's Assessment Tools

*Dr Janine Sternberg**

In my role as a child psychotherapist at the Portman Clinic (which specialises in forensic issues), I am often asked to be part of a larger team that has been instructed to comment on the future placement of a child. These requests frequently come from solicitors acting either for the Local Authority, or for the children. The team which includes child and adult psychotherapists, is led by a Consultant Psychiatrist who is responsible for liaising with the instructing solicitor, the Children's Guardian and the Social Worker, to clarify the questions they want answered. Our aim is to ensure that we gather the information that we need to present an informed opinion to the court. Concerns might include the extent of harm that the children have suffered, their developmental status, and needs for the future – including placement, contact, therapy and education – and also the capacity of their parents to understand and meet those needs. When many children are involved, I interview one or two whilst other colleagues in the service interview the others. This aims to ensure that each can have the opportunity to express their own feelings without undue influence from their siblings. Sometimes I see a number of children from the same family together if that seems appropriate, for either pragmatic or clinical reasons.

The clinic will have received instructions about the case, including background information often supplied by social workers and sometimes by previously involved professionals. Such instructions make clear the questions that they hope we will be able to answer. I know from discussions with child psychotherapy colleagues in other services that some practitioners defer reading the information until after seeing the child for the first time, but before subsequent interviews, so that their perceptions and thoughts about the child are not clouded by the information supplied. However I prefer to have all the information in mind, but at the back of my mind. I will use what I know of the child's history to guide me in the questions I ask. Since I usually only see a child once before furnishing a report on that contact, I think I need to have the concerns raised and questions asked in mind at the time.

I make it clear at the beginning of every interview, even with very young children, what I understand my role to be and also that I will be letting the other adults in the system know what has been said and done. There is no expectation that anything will remain within the normal bounds of confidentiality. Indeed as my colleague Dr Anne Zachary pointed out: 'assessment allows direct communication with the court. Therapy does not' (Rooted Sorrows, p 70).

---

*   Janine Sternberg is a Consultant Child Psychotherapist at the Portman Clinic, Tavistock and Portman NHS Trust, and worked for many years at the Tavistock Mulberry Bush Day Unit for children with complex difficulties. She is also an adult psychotherapist. She is an active member of the ACP, the professional body for child psychotherapists. She has published a book, (*Infant Observation at the Heart of Training* 2005). She is currently Joint Editor of the *Journal of Child Psychotherapy.*

THE PARTICULAR SKILLS OF A CHILD PSYCHOTHERAPIST

In *Rooted Sorrows*, Mr Justice Wall wrote of the propensity of some expert witnesses to claim the validity of their views without explaining sufficiently clearly on what evidence they based those opinions. Therefore I will endeavour to explain the concept of counter-transference, which in layman's terms could be called 'intuition', and to show it has a firm basis within our theoretical framework. I also make reference to 'the unconscious', child development norms, the internal world, and Attachment Theory.

When considering what the child psychotherapist may have to contribute to the information placed before a court, I was struck by the truism that what we see depends from where we look. I was made aware of this some years ago by my son and daughter after they saw their younger sister play in her 'end of term' concert. My elder daughter was interested in the other players and discussed with her sister what she had gleaned about their personalities from the way they had behaved on stage. My son, on the other hand, who plays the same instrument, had no curiosity about the other pupils but could name or sing the pieces and was keen to discuss their bowing technique. Each had responded to the event according to their interests.

Child psychotherapists and others working within a psychoanalytic frame work, have been trained over years to pay attention to what we call 'the internal world'; that is what the child thinks, feels or experiences rather than necessarily what may have actually happened or what 'is'.

I want to give a brief example from a case I was involved in to try to highlight how the specific skills of a child psychotherapist might be used. Haley, a 14 year old girl, was asked to see me because the Local Authority Social Services Department were trying to decide whether it was safe for her to remain in the care of her parents. They were a close-knit family, but the parents had a history of substance abuse and some involvement with the courts. Haley had recently called the police to her home following an incident in which she alleged that her father had attacked her, knocking her to the ground. She had subsequently withdrawn this allegation. She knew that she had been asked to see me in order that I might furnish information to aid the court in their decision about her future and whether she should stay at home. She was at pains to emphasise how much she wanted to do this. She behaved in a fairly typical teenage way: she wore a baseball hat that shaded her face and alternated her answers of shrugs and monosyllables with fast-rate emotionally charged 'rants' about the iniquities of social workers.

In order to protect confidentiality I cannot give details of her reactions when I expressed curiosity about her father's alleged attack, but I offer a number of possible scenarios to illustrate how I, as a child psychotherapist, would have used my professional skills to think about them.

Did she look distressed and then say she could not remember? Did she shift her position so that she had in effect turned her back on the therapist interviewing her? Did she suddenly become absorbed in disentangling her music system headphones? Did she make eye contact with the therapist brazenly, and declare that such an event never took place? And, importantly, what might be the significance of any of these reactions? The child psychotherapist conducting the interview cannot know the answer, but at this point she notices whatever the reactions are and tries to think about them later in context. So, we see that one of the very important skills of a child psychotherapist is the ability to notice and remember details.

PAYING CLOSE ATTENTION

We are trained to pay close attention to what is happening when we are with a child or with children and parents. The lengthy training (minimum 4 years post graduate) of closely supervised clinical work and theoretical seminars also involves the experience of infant observation, which teaches us to observe minute detail, (Sternberg, 2005). The skills used in on-going work with patients can be adapted for, and applied to, the assessments that child psychotherapists provide for the courts.

In the consulting room the therapist watches the patient carefully, taking note of all that s/he sees and experiences, before evaluating it. When writing of the technique used in psychotherapeutic work with adults Coltart (1993) and Langs (1973) wrote of careful auditory and visual observation of the patient, while Greenson (1974) suggests that noticing a patient's non-verbal bodily reactions can give clues as to what particular affect the patient is struggling with.

Nelson-Jones (1982) states that we are more likely to understand the client accurately if we respond to non-verbal bodily gestures, and he specifies head movements, posture, facial expressions, eye contact, proximity and spatial position. Schafer (1983) points out that all 'showing' is a form of communication whether intended or not. This ability to pay attention to minute, barely seen details is surely enhanced by the experience of paying very close attention to the minute hand or eye movements of a young baby when undertaking an infant observation as part of our training.

The therapist must also have a very particular way of listening. This again includes close attention to detail and listening at a more meta level. Rayner (1991) writes that the therapist must be sensitive to the intonations, syntaxes and linguistic habits of others, and to hear the meanings 'between and behind words', while Nelson-Jones (1982) is also concerned with procedures such as speech rate, timing, stress of utterances and silence. While manifest content is important, the therapist pays particular attention to what is being unconsciously expressed. Attention to when something is said may also be increased by the attention to sequence that the infant observation experience teaches.

Schafer's (1983) idea of narrative has profound implications for the way the therapist listens. Within the framework of 'narrative', which harbours no 'out there' reality, what the patient says is treated as 'narrative performance' and there is no final or definitive version: experience is always being constructed or reconstructed. The way of telling then becomes central; telling is not 'an indifferent medium or transparent medium for imparting information' (1983: 228), rather the therapist notes the how, when and why of telling, and pays close attention to gaps, evasions and non-sequences.

While all these authors cited are referring to the ongoing work with regular patients, much of what has just been described is of relevance when conducting interviews designed to give information to the courts. According to Goldstein et al, citing an Australian report on *The Emotional Needs of Infants and Young Children: Implications for Policy and Practice.*

> 'Children of all ages have a natural tendency to deceive themselves about their motivations … to shy back from full awareness of their feelings, especially where conflicts of loyalty come into question. To pierce these defences demands more than usual skill from the investigator. Verbal and nonverbal communications (attitudes, behaviour) have to be scrutinized, assessed, and translated into their underlying meaning; openings offered by the child, all unknowingly, have to be pursued and utilized'. (1986: 33)

We do not rely on the spoken word, the overt answer to the direct question. The psychoanalytic psychotherapist (or indeed any other acutely observant and thoughtful interviewer) is very aware that so much more needs to be taken into account. It is important to remember that we have not been asked to conduct interviews to uncover whether or not, for example, abuse took place. Memorandum interviews will already have taken place in cases of Child Sexual Abuse. Our role will be to try to understand what the experience might have meant to the child.

Sometimes I do hear information that had not been included in the papers sent and which might not be known to the professionals in the wider network, in which case I see it as my responsibility to alert them to this through the psychiatrist/team leader at the Clinic. I may have noticed that Haley's story of how she was knocked down by her father strains credulity as described, but that is not my specific contribution. Rather I notice small body movements or slight hesitation before saying a particular word, which alerts me to the fact that some emotions, which I may not yet – if ever – understand, accompany that part of the narrative.

AWARENESS OF THE SYMBOLIC MEANING OF PLAY

Child psychotherapy has a fundamental tenet. It is the belief that children's play (except, unusually, with some children on the autistic spectrum) has symbolic meaning and gives the psychoanalytically trained observer the opportunity to understand something of the child's internal world; that is their 'unconscious'. When a child is given the opportunity to play with toys, carefully chosen to give as much space as possible for them to be used in this symbolic way, he or she will usually show something of their internal preoccupations. If a child chooses to play at the doll's house, we are interested in what the detail of their actions might indicate. How do they organise the house: extremely neatly with all in its place, or with the furniture removed to create a rather bleak home? Are the children shut inside the wardrobe? If a child chooses to play with the toy cars, is the main emphasis on lining them up colour coded, or are they made to hover precariously at the edge of the table before falling off? Or is the predominant flavour of the game races or crashes? When offered a collection of figures including people, animals and dinosaurs, which are chosen for play? And what does the child make them do in relation to each other: are there vicious fights in which 'goodies' overcome 'baddies', or vice versa? Does the Mummy sheep notice that her lambs are being attacked by the tiger, or does it seem that she is too absorbed in conversation with the other adult animals?

It would be ridiculous and arrogant for any professional seeing a child do this on their first meeting to declare that they had understood the 'meaning' of such behaviour. What we can say with certainty is that these actions were not random and meaningless. With a child in ongoing treatment it would be possible over time to comment on what is seen, perhaps referring to how precarious and 'on the edge' life can seem for the falling cars, and possibly make links between the absent-minded sheep mother and the child's sense of not being sufficiently held in mind. Therapists and their patients together build up a shared understanding. Conversely, in these one-off interviews there is inadequate opportunity to find through gentle exploration and trial and error what the child is communicating, and the therapist must be careful not to be too assumptive. However it is possible to comment on what is seen, noting for example that the children are shut in the wardrobe and wondering in an interested way why that might be. Sometimes a child will explain this: perhaps they are hiding from a cross daddy, perhaps mummy has placed them there to save them from the monsters. Often the child will ignore the question and all the child psychotherapist can do is to note mentally the sequence of play and afterwards speculate on its possible meaning.

Noting the sequence is absolutely essential. *When* something is done is as important as *how* it is done. Child psychotherapists have been trained to remember in this way. In providing reports to inform others, it is vital that the interview is remembered and recorded in detail so that the readers can use their own thoughts and judgements. Reports that fail to give sufficient detail may seem to ask for the expert's view to be trusted 'because I say so', rather than giving the judge and others the opportunity to see how the therapist's views were formed, thus giving others a chance to agree so far but no further.

WHAT WE FEEL AT THE TIME

From these examples it will be clear that what *we feel* when observing a piece of play, or noticing how a young person responds to a question, is also significant. Nothing happens in an emotional vacuum. For instance with the car on the edge of the table, did I feel teased, hoping that maybe this time it would be safe, or was I in despair, already knowing that disaster was inevitable? When the fighting seemed endless did I shift uncomfortably in my chair, almost experiencing the blows being meted out or was I rather bored by it, experiencing it as rather routine? Why might I have felt teased? Is it possible that through his play the child was communicating his sense of being teased, kept hanging on? And if so, might this be related to the investigation and interview process or might it have reflected something of his early life at home? As psychoanalytic psychotherapists we are trained to be alert to our own feelings and question whence such feelings arise. Being with young people who have suffered abuse and deprivation, and may also have perpetrated abuse, can stir up all sorts of feelings within us. Trudy Klauber in 'Rooted Sorrows' offers a clear explanation of the process of transference and counter-transference.

Since Heimann's seminal paper (1950) on the subject, clinicians have realised that:

> 'the analyst's emotional response to his patient within the analytic situation represents one of the most important tools for his work. The analyst's counter-transference is an instrument of research into the patient's unconscious'. (1960: 74)

Therapists must allow themselves to experience whatever they are feeling in the presence of the patient; but simultaneously not be so overwhelmed as to be unable to think about why the experience is the way it is. Heimann specified that whilst the analyst must be receptive to counter-transference experiences he must not act on the feelings but use them to understand and help formulate interpretations. A*wareness* of counter-transference is an asset to analytic work, whilst any substantial expression of counter-transference in *action* is a liability that limits analytic work. Again we see the importance of a reflective space within which the therapist must hold on to feelings and think simultaneously.

Whilst a therapist will probably rely more on the use of counter-transference in ongoing therapy, what is felt in these brief one-off meetings offers an important tool that the psychoanalytic psychotherapist is uniquely well placed to use. It is therefore also a subjective experience that the therapist is trying to report on, and it is understandable that it may be received with misunderstanding or considerable scepticism by those unused to the idea that our emotional lives exert a powerful influence on conscious thoughts and ideas.

For example, as a supervisor of a trainee child psychotherapist I listened to a student describe her terror when, at the child's instigation, she and the child were pretending that it was night and the monster was approaching the bedroom door. Her description of how *her* heart was beating and *her* palms were sweaty gave us both considerable concern. It seemed likely that she experienced this terror as the result of unconscious communications from her child patient: terror which made us concerned as to whether someone was currently approaching the child's bedroom door in order to abuse him. Such concerns, together with many others gathered from his behaviour at his special school, were shared with Social Services.

Fortunately when I report to the courts, other necessary investigations have already taken place. Nevertheless the child's behaviour may make me *feel* things in a way that I understand as being caused by his, rather than my, experience. It may be difficult for those outside the therapeutic world to appreciate the significance of this.

WHAT WE THINK ABOUT WHAT WE NOTICE

Goldstein et al in urging professionals not stray into decision-making territory that rightly belongs to the judges, warn professionals against being swayed by their personal views as to what is 'right' for the child: 'we have to separate our personal commitment to children from our professional knowledge about child development and the status of children in law' (1986: 11).

What we think about is strongly influenced by the theoretical framework that lies behind our work, and child psychotherapists are trained in a psychoanalytic tradition, having regard for ideas about unconscious mechanisms and intergenerational transmission of trauma.

However, I think it is reasonable for child psychotherapists to claim, along with others such as nursery workers and health visitors, a certain level of expertise in child development such that we can state whether the behaviour that we are witnessing falls within certain developmental norms. It ought to be possible for us to gauge whether the behaviour of the child in the room is that which we might expect of a child of the same age who had not suffered the similar abuse or deprivation. Obviously developmental norms need to be thought of in quite a wide way, but it is useful to be able to have an internal yardstick against which to measure observed behaviour.

Theoretical ideas about transference and counter-transference, as described very briefly above, are at the core of how we understand what we see. The way the child or young person behaves may give us a clue as to what they expect from other adults and their anticipation of adults' behaviour towards them. Of course we must make allowances for the strangeness of the particular setting, but something of the way a child interacts with us is likely to offer useful information about their general, as well as their specific, expectations. The picture of the 'other' that the infant builds up based on repeated experiences is termed 'the evoked companion' by Brian Jacobs (Rooted Sorrows, p 14). If, in our initial meeting with a young person, we find ourselves being treated as if we are interested and basically compassionate people, we might hypothesise that their experiences so far have led them to expect such an approach from the world. Conversely, and sadly far more frequently, when we see the child behave in a wary and suspicious manner we would wonder what experiences have predisposed the child to this. Given that I might interview a child to inform a decision as to whether he can return to live with his mother (a result he may both consciously want and unconsciously dread) it is not surprising that wariness and hostility abound. If, however, I watch closely and use the feelings evoked in me sensitively, I may notice that he treats me as if he expects me to sneer at his failure to manipulate the toy in the way that he wants or may be startled when I repeat a phrase he has used earlier, possibly indicating that he is not familiar with being intimately attended to.

Together with the traditional psychoanalytic ideas that child psychotherapists have learnt, we are also familiar with and influenced by Bowlby's work on Attachment (1969, 1973). Therefore, with younger children the child psychotherapist may choose to interview the child in the presence of a trusted adult. It would not be appropriate to expect a young child to go easily with a stranger: although many do, and this in itself may be an indicator of their indiscriminate attachment patterns. The child to be interviewed may at that point be with its parents, other family members, or in a foster family or under the care of other professionals. Although the child may not be able to express any negativity towards their current living arrangements in the presence of an adult, or say what particular arrangements they wish for, it is less likely that their play will be seriously inhibited by being in their presence: in fact this gives the child psychotherapist an opportunity to see how the child is in the presence of that adult. Again the same careful observation and attention to detail will reveal a wealth of useful information. When a young child discovers a toy he finds appealing, does he turn to his mother with a gesture that says 'look!' or does he act as if she would not understand his excitement? When a little girl removes her shoes to use the dressing up clothes, does she turn to her foster carer for help or struggle silently for some time, indicating that she has no expectation of a helpful and involved adult? And what does the adult do? Is father too busy trying to impress the professional about his involvement to notice the little boy gouging the wall with the end of a pencil? If he notices does he shout at him to stop or take the pencil away silently? It is important not to assume that the way *we* would have dealt with the situation with our own children is the 'right' way. We must remain aware that the situation itself may misrepresent the usual interaction because of its artificial nature. Nevertheless we are in a favourable position to comment on what we noticed about the interaction between that child and the adult. On occasions when we are asked specifically to assess the relationship between children and parents at the Portman, we will organise a meeting in which both adult and child psychotherapists are observers in order to create a more rounded picture.

Reports on the individual meetings need to be written independently. However, the opportunity to discuss our thoughts with other members of the multidisciplinary team who are contributing to a family report is always useful and informative. Sharing impressions about what was seen can be illuminating. A child's rather odd way of phrasing something might have been echoed in the parents' meeting, suggesting that this was simply this family's way of talking. A boy's swagger and toughness might mirror that of his father. Observations of the whole family at home, or in a contact visit, might highlight undesirable alliances between family members that had shown up in symbolic play, but not been previously understood by the child psychotherapist when alone with the child. It is vital that the child psychotherapist holds on to her awareness that what was seen and noticed is a 'snapshot', a one-off impression.

We can state with absolute clarity what we have seen, what we think about what we have seen, and why we think it: but we must also acknowledge that our view is inevitably partial. In ongoing psychotherapeutic work it is possible to say something that links conscious behaviour with what we suspect to be its unconscious roots by making an interpretation, and the child's response then gives us further information as to whether that idea was correct, or not. In the interviews for court we are not in a position to make any links for the children between what they do with us and what we believe may be bothering them. The interviews are not therapeutic in and of themselves. Indeed, although we try to work in a very gentle and affirmative way (far more so than would be my style in ongoing psychotherapy where negative feelings about the therapist are an integral part of the work), they can provoke anxiety in the children. On her way back from a meeting with me, a 3-year-old girl put a small stone up her nostril that had to be removed in hospital. While those outside the psychotherapeutic world might see this simply as coincidental, I could not help feeling that she had enacted her sense of being intruded on; having been hurt by someone being rather 'nosey'!

Mr Justice Wall also said 'the medical profession owed it to the judiciary in particular, as well as to the litigating parties, to explain the philosophy/methodology behind their work in order to justify their conclusions', (p 34). This chapter has been my attempt to do that.

REFERENCES

Bowlby, J *Attachment and Loss: Volume 1 Attachment* (London, The Hogarth Press & The Institute of Psychoanalysis, London, 1969)

Bowlby, J *Attachment and Loss: Volume 2 Separation* (London, The Hogarth Press & The Institute of Psychoanalysis, 1973)

Coltart, N *How to survive as a Psychotherapist* (London, Sheldon Press, 1993)

Goldstein *The Emotional Needs of Infants and Young Children: Implications for Policy and Practice* (1986)

Greenson, R *The Technique & Practice of Psychoanalysis.* Vol 1 (London, The Hogarth Press & The Institute of Psychoanalysis, 1974)

Heimann, P 'On Counter-transference' [1950] Int J of Psycho-Anal 31. Also in Tonnesmann M (ed) (1989) 'About children & children-no-longer' in *Collected Papers of Paula Heimann* (London, NY, Tavistock/Routledge, 1989)

Jacobs, B *Rooted Sorrows* (Bristol, Family Law, 1997)

Klauber, T *Rooted Sorrows* (Bristol, Family Law, 1997)

Langs, R *The Technique of Psychoanalytic Psychotherapy* Vol 1 (New York, Jason Aronson, 1973)

Nelson-Jones, R *The Theory and Practice Of Counselling Psychology* (London, Cassell, 1982).

Rayner, E *The Independent Mind in British Psychoanalysis* (London, Free Association Books, 1991)

Schafer, R *The Analytic Attitude* (London, The Hogarth Press, 1983)

Wall, N *Rooted Sorrows* (Bristol, Family Law, 1997)

Zachary, A *Rooted Sorrows* (Bristol, Family Law, 1997)

Examining the Evidence Base in Child Protection: a Paediatrician's View

*Professor Jo Sibert**

There can be little doubt that one of the most important parts of the multi-disciplinary process in child protection is the diagnosis of abuse. Without a sound diagnosis it is very difficult to be certain of the right course to be taken in the best interests of the child. The certainty of diagnosis reflects clearly on the Social Services analysis of a child's case but also throughout the whole legal process. In many cases, and certainly in most cases of physical abuse, the diagnosis is made by the paediatrician. The child protection process therefore depends very much on the paediatrician and how good the evidence is that s/he is able to give to that process in cases of physical abuse and neglect, and some cases of sexual abuse.

I was fortunate to work with Dr Christine Cooper in Newcastle during my training. She was a well-respected paediatrician: when she gave evidence either to a Case Conference or to the Court it was generally accepted. She believed that she was in the lead in the child protection process. She taught many paediatricians and child and adolescent psychiatrists. As we look today at the state of expert evidence we see a very different picture. Paediatricians feel much less confident about giving evidence and there is little doubt that the attitude of most paediatricians to child protection has changed since the travails of Roy Meadow and David Southall. Why is this?

WHY HAVE PAEDIATRICIANS LOST CONFIDENCE IN CHILD PROTECTION CASES?

Twenty years ago, child abuse was seen and managed on the general paediatric ward, which was often used as a 'place of safety', whilst complex clinical and social issues were addressed. Paediatricians and the Children Act recognised that hospitalisation was inappropriate for the majority of child protection cases and as paediatrics changed, so child protection became the domain of Community Paediatricians. This has to some extent lead to a de-skilling of general paediatricians who have lost confidence in the field.

The legal system evolved so that, in any but the most straightforward child protection cases, the examining paediatrician gave little more than basic professional evidence. An expert from away was appointed to assess the case, make a report and give 'expert opinion' in court. The court appearance was often intimidating and many paediatricians felt exposed and humiliated by the

---

* Emeritus Professor J R (Jo) Sibert recently retired as Professor of Child Health at Cardiff University and as a Consultant Paediatrician working for the Cardiff and Vale NHS Trust. Until April 2005 he was Officer for Wales for the Royal College of Paediatrics and Child Health and President of the Welsh Paediatric Society. He is an Honorary Member of the NSPCC and was a member of the National Commission on the Prevention of Child Abuse. He has a wide research portfolio including work on child protection, childhood injury prevention and disability. He has over 130 scientific publications. He was awarded the Sir James Spence Medal in April 2006 by the Royal College of Paediatrics and Child Health for his contribution to extending paediatric knowledge.

aggression of defending barrister. The national media throughout this period had become heavily polarised against the profession. Fewer and fewer paediatricians were inclined to give evidence in court or felt capable of the assessments needed to protect children.

This meant that an increasingly small number of people were available to be the experts in complex child protection cases. These doctors were faced with increasing demands on their time for legal work and became increasing targets for criticism particularly in the court situation. Few paediatricians involved in expert witness work have not been subject to problems (1), and in many cases the problems have threatened both their careers and mental health. This further added to the vicious circle of concern regarding any involvement with child protection. Paediatricians previously prepared to advocate for the victims of child abuse are dwindling.

EVIDENCE-BASED MEDICINE

If all this was not enough, there have been concerns on the science available to paediatricians in child protection cases and through them to the courts. Twenty years ago it was sufficient to look at textbooks before giving evidence in court. However, it has become clear that this was insufficient for many legal cases. Many of us were increasingly worried about the standard of the science available to us in child protection and the separation from the mainstream assessment of evidence in medicine.

Colleagues in disciplines outside medicine may be unaware of the revolution that has occurred in the assessment of diagnosis, treatment and investigation in clinical matters. This has been with the introduction of randomised control trials and the systematic review of the evidence. In many ways this was started by Professor Archie Cochrane. I was also fortunate to have met him when I was younger. He was born in Kirklands, Galashiels, Scotland in 1909. He qualified in 1938 at University College Hospital, London and joined the Medical Research Council's Pneumoconiosis Unit at Llandough Hospital in 1948. Here he began a series of studies on the health of the population of Rhondda Fach – studies that pioneered the use of randomised controlled trials (RCTs). In 1979 he stated: 'It is surely a great criticism of our profession that we have not organised a critical summary, by specialty or subspecialty, adapted periodically, of all relevant randomised controlled trials.'

Archie Cochrane and those following him developed the technique of the Systematic Review, which is now the standard way of evaluating evidence in clinical medicine. The key feature is that all the evidence is put together: papers are searched for systematically and not just in English. The papers are reviewed critically by a team of people using standardised forms. Results are combined often using a technique of meta-analysis. A Systematic Review studies scientific papers giving real results: not papers giving personal opinion. In the case of a Systematic Review involving a child subject, the results in children must be able to be separated from those in adults.

The result of this technique means that all the evidence on a particular topic can be considered together. The quality of the evidence can also be assessed. The statistical analysis of the results means that individual papers do not bias the overall results. All this means that nowadays the effectiveness of all clinical interventions is assessed in a systematic way.

WHAT ABOUT CHILD PROTECTION?

Despite all the changes that this evidence based approach has made to medicine generally, it seemed to us to have passed child protection by. We felt there was a clear need to evaluate the basis for diagnostic decision-making for all of us in child protection. This view is not universally held however and in the British Medical Journal on the 22 July 2006, the front page stated that the evidence for child protection was 'well established'. The distinguished American paediatrician David Chadwick further amplified this theme (2). He describes the evidence behind child abuse as 'robust' based on the 16,000 citations for child abuse in the world literature. We believe that it is important that the quality of the literature is assessed as well as the quantity and when a standard systematic approach to the critical appraisal of this literature is adopted, the findings are very different and there are significant scientific limitations to many of the published studies.

OUR SYSTEMATIC REVIEW

Because of this background, three years ago my colleague Alison Kemp and I believed there was a need to review the evidence for key areas in physical abuse in a systematic way. We have developed a team in Wales to do this: **the Welsh Child Protection Systematic Review Group**. Sabine Maguire was appointed as Coordinator.

As one of the few systematic review teams in this field we have interrogated the scientific literature on several key questions around the diagnosis of physical child abuse: www.core-info.cf.ac.uk. We have been fortunate to have the benefit of a first class library service: an absolute essential for this work. Also essential are a dedicated and efficient organiser, statistical advice and a team of reviewers with child protection experience. We have been very grateful to funding from the NSPCC and the RCPCH.

We have had 27 reviewers, all with child protection expertise.

Each paper is reviewed by two independent reviewers, with a third reviewer used to resolve any disagreements. Reviewers used standardised forms to critically appraise and extract data if included based on NHS Centre for Reviews and Dissemination, 2001.

We reviewed papers in all languages from 1952 to the present. We search 10 Databases: ASSIA, Caredata, Child Data, CINAHL, Embase, HealthSTAR, Medline, Social Science Citation Index, TRIP and SIGLE. We also make a hand search of textbooks and references.

We study the literature on children and young people under 18 years. This is important as in some papers it is impossible to distinguish between adult and child cases. We exclude papers on review and personal practice, those with a mixed adult and child population and those on complications or management.

So far we have completed reviews on bruising in children, fractures, oral injury and bites, and thermal injury. A review on non-accidental head injury is ongoing at present.

OVERALL MESSAGES FROM OUR REVIEW

Important as assessing the literature scientifically is, we believe that an injury must never be interpreted in isolation and must always be assessed in the context of medical and social history, developmental stage, explanation given, full clinical examination and relevant investigations.

We have been disappointed in general by the paucity of literature on key questions in the diagnosis of physical abuse. Most studies are performed in the United States and while these studies are invaluable, the difference in health systems, demographics, definitions and types of abuse and legal systems mean that the study findings are not necessarily directly transferable to

UK. Another problem is that many studies are compromised by the differences in definition of abuse used in different countries over the 50-year time period of this research and the variation in diagnostic techniques.

The numbers of cases included in many studies are small and highly selective. Most observational studies are of a case series design, inherently compromised by selection bias and lacking any comparative data.

Our first review was on ageing of bruises: 50 years of international literature identified three studies that give good evidence that the age of bruises cannot be accurately judged on a visual interpretation of bruise colour (3). This refutes the dogma that a way of telling abusive bruises is that they are of different ages. On the other hand there was quite good evidence on bruising in non-abused children (Maguire, Mann, Sibert, Kemp, 2005(b)). Bruising is strongly related to mobility. Bruising in a baby who is not yet crawling and therefore has no independent mobility is very uncommon (seen in <1%). This is really important in the assessment of injuries in infants where the risks of serious injuries and deaths are at their highest. On the other hand approximately 17% of infants who are cruising have bruises (range 1–5 bruises) 52% of children who are walking have bruises.

Bruising in abused children (4): the head is by far the commonest site of bruising in child abuse. Other sites that are commonly bruised in abuse include the ear, face, neck, trunk, buttocks and arms. Although bruising is the commonest injury in physical abuse, fatal non-accidental head injury and non-accidental fractures can occur without bruising.

Our work on fractures again revealed an area that refutes widely established dogma. When we evaluated the evidence surrounding the dating of fractures we came to the overriding conclusion from the only three studies in the world literature that addressed the topic (5) was that fractures can only be dated in the broad time frames. Again on the other hand **rib fractures in young children that have a high specificity for abuse.**

Our work on rib fractures and cardio-pulmonary resuscitation (CPR) (6) could be of relevance in a number of court cases where this is given as an explanation for rib fractures in babies. Our review showed rib fractures are a rare complication of CPR in children (only 3 out of 923 children). The fractures caused by CPR were all multiple and anterior. Two were bilateral and one unilateral. There were no posterior rib fractures due to CPR.

When we reviewed the investigations need to exclude fractures in potentially abused children, we found that both skeletal survey and bone scan missed fractures. We concluded that both should be performed in optimal investigation (7). This again may well result in more abused children being recognised and demonstrates the value of combining information from a number of studies.

CONCLUSIONS

So there are areas where the quality of evidence is good: another example is the profile of non-accidental scalds where the literature defines clear differences between intentional and non-intentional scalds. However, there is a profound lack of published evidence around the recognition of adult bites, cigarette burns and the specificity of a torn frenulum for physical abuse.

Systematic reviews have begun to provide a sounder basis for evidence in physical abuse. The Royal College of Paediatrics and Child Health is undertaking a similar process in sexual abuse. However in many areas of child protection, clinical experience and clinical judgement are the tools we have and are likely to rely on for some time. There is no reason why this systematic review process should not be extended to emotional abuse and neglect.

In emotional abuse and neglect, including the components of emotional abuse that accompany physical and sexual abuse, we have indicators such as hyper-vigilance, panic attacks and separation anxiety, but no definite signs. There are no systematic reviews to guide clinicians or experts, only their clinical experience and expertise as to the presence of emotional abuse or neglect, despite its fundamental importance when considering the psychological health and emotional well-being of the child.

This field of research is challenging in several areas. It is difficult to perform standard diagnostic studies in the absence of a gold standard test for abuse that is independent of the presenting injuries or symptoms of neglect. Consent issues for the inclusion of abused children and the relative rarity of abuse make it difficult to undertake cohort studies: not to mention the challenges of defining ideal control cases.

We believe this work is of relevance not just for paediatricians and other doctors. It should be of great importance for all those involved in child protection: in particular social workers and lawyers. The information is available on the website www.core-info.cf.ac.uk and with two leaflets (on bruising and fractures) published by the NSPCC. We hope as well that the lawyers will become familiar with the principles of reviewing the literature in a systematic way. If this is done the role of individual experts with individual views will be reduced.

Despite the value of the review process we have been disappointed with the limitations: particularly the lack of decent studies in important fields. All those who have tried to undertake child protection research have been appalled by the difficulties in finding adequate funding. There has been much media concern about the quality of evidence that is available in the courts in important cases. We hope that at least some of this concern can be focused on encouraging research.

The overriding priority must be to encourage optimal research in this field. There are many paediatricians and allied professionals who have worked in the child protection field for many years and continue to do so. Many have experience that could be translated into scientific published evidence if they were able to publish their data from often meticulously kept retrospective case series. Better still they could use their experience to set a hypothesis and under take well-designed multi-centred prospective comparative studies. This work urgently needs the support of research funding bodies.

Expert witnesses appearing in court require a thorough understanding of the quality of the available scientific evidence and must be able to convey this to the court in an understandable manner. Courts and clinicians need to appreciate that child abuse evidence base is a long way from being robust or complete and that 'absence of evidence is not necessarily evidence of no effect or no association'. Where opinion is drawn from personal practice, this must be explicit. As Baroness Kennedy stated 'A doctor can be convinced, based on his or her experience, that a defendant is guilty – but unless there is compelling evidence supported scientifically, he or she should not express that view in criminal proceedings' (8), which sets the standard for an expert opinion in the British courts. We would like to see the paediatrician in clinical charge of the case being the lead figure in the presentation of the medical issues to the court.

Although the clinical field of child protection has gone through a difficult period in the UK, the current situation has the capacity to stimulate good quality scientific research and redress the imbalance. A collaborative approach across the UK, with high quality multi-centre trials addressing the key questions is essential, and requires appropriate support and funding. By so doing the profession will regain scientific credibility and support those clinicians who are carrying out this crucial work.

ACKNOWLEDGMENTS AND THANKS

None of this work would have been possible without Alison Kemp, Sabine Maguire and the other members of the Welsh Systemic Review Group. Alison now leads the Group following my retirement.

REFERENCES

(1)   Kmietowicz Z 'Complaints against doctors in child protection work have increased fivefold' (BMJ, 2004; 328: 601)

(2)   Chadwick DL 'The evidence base in child protection litigation' (BMJ 2006; 333: 160–161)

(3)   Maguire S, Mann MK, Sibert JR, Kemp AM 'Can you age bruises accurately in children? A systematic review' (Archives of Disease in Childhood 2005; 90: 182–186, 186–189)

(4)   Maguire S, Mann MK, Sibert JR, Kemp AM (2005(b)) 'Are there patterns of bruising in childhood, which are diagnostic or suggestive of abuse? A Systematic Review' (Archives of Disease in Childhood 2005; 90: 186–189)

(5)   Prosser I, Maguire S, Harrison SK, Mann M, Sibert JR, Kemp AM Welsh Child Protection Systematic Review Group 'How old is this fracture? Radiologic dating of fractures in children: a systematic review' (Am J Roentgenol, Apr 2005; 184: 1282–1286)

(6)   Maguire S, Mann M, John N, Ellaway B, Sibert J R, Kemp AM 'Does cardiopulmonary resuscitation cause rib fractures in children? A systematic review' (Child Abuse and Neglect 2006; 30: 739–751)

(7)   Kemp AM, Butler A, Morris A, Mann M, Kemp KW, Rolfe K, Sibert JR, Maguire S 'Which radiological investigations should be performed to identify fractures in suspected child abuse?' (Clinical Radiology 2006; 61: 723–736)

(8)   Kennedy H *Sudden Unexpected Death in Infancy* (The Royal College of Pathologists and The Royal College of Paediatrics and Child Health, 2004)

SECTION 2

With one exception the contributions in this section are by lawyers.

Mr Justice Hedley demystifies 'the judge' with a paper showing warmth and humanity alongside his legal acumen.

Stephen Cobb, QC, a barrister, demonstrates the reasoning involved in his work, focusing particularly on the confidentiality versus openness debate and considers the question of children appearing in person.

We include a paper by **Dr Anne Zachary** because in it she looks back and considers what she learnt from court proceedings in which she appeared, and the events that surrounded the case.

Khatun Sapnara, a barrister originally from Bangladesh, writes about the particular cultural issues that accompany cases from the Asian continent that are at variance with our legal system.

Katherine Gieve, a leading solicitor working in Public Law, moves away from familiar legal issues to consider the inter-dependency of parents and their children that can be lost in the legal territory.

Isn't the Judge Human Too?

Mr Justice Hedley[*]

Pivotal to the family justice system is the role of the judge, a role that is both indispensable and determinative for so long as societies adhere to the need to have courts as the means by which public and private disputes are subjected to binding resolution. Traditionally no human awfulness or tragedy can disturb the serene tranquillity in which his/her office is exercised. This, of course, has never been true but it is only in comparatively recent times that this fallacy has been recognised and then principally in the field of family law. Many now recognise that decision making in family law may leave its mark on the decision maker, though many judges will still insist that their capacity to 'switch off' at the end of a day, or the end of a case, is protection enough. I know myself to be one of the marked men.

My experience stretches over 35 years as advocate, circuit judge and judge of the Family Division of the High Court. That means I try at first instance many of the most difficult cases involving the future of children and of adults who lack capacity to make their own decisions. I sit mainly in London, or as the Family Division Liaison Judge, in Wales and Cheshire. By way of variety I also sit as a judge of the Court of Appeal, Criminal Division, where all the work is appellate (so we rarely see a live witness), and responsibility for decision making is shared with other members of the Court.

The greatest stress on the family judge is the fear of making a wrong decision, coupled with the recognition that being a fallible human, some error is inevitable. No one wishes wrongly to find that a parent has killed his/her child, (or indeed not done so) and I always dread not believing an honest witness. The stress is heightened by the fact that the one thing a judge really has to do is to make a decision. If there is no decision this means there is no resolution, with the parties remaining captive in their dispute, in reality the worst of all possible worlds. The imperative to decide heightens both the chance of error and the potential consequences of error.

Beyond that, different judges experience differently the strains of particular types of cases. For me three classes of case impose the most conscious strain. First are those that involve the permanent separation of children from parents who are not 'bad' people. They may have been hopelessly inadequate parents, or sometimes the unlucky victims of circumstance or even official bungling. I still remember the extraordinary generosity of a natural father deprived of his child by some very poor official adoption practice, whose first comment outside the court was: 'I'm glad I did not have to decide that case'. The second group is where a serious risk as to the future of a child has to be taken: for example a placement with a fragile member of the family that might succeed or might go horribly wrong, or with a family member who has caused the death of a much younger child, or in a family redolent with suspicion of sexual malpractice but lacking real proof of it. The third and perhaps the most obviously difficult cases are the life and death decisions involving sick children or adults who are unable to make their own decisions.

---

[*] Mr Justice Hedley is a judge of the Family Division of the High Court. He was a member of the Children Act Advisory Committee 1993–97 and Judicial Studies Board Course Director in Family Law 1997–2002. Until recently he was the Liaison Judge for Wales and Chester Circuit.

We are faced by questions such as 'do we remove from the ventilator?', or 'should artificial nutrition and hydration be withdrawn from an adult in persistent vegetative state?'.

One may recognise the stress of a specific case, but be much less aware of the toll of emotional wear and tear over a period of time. Moreover, it is not just the enormity of the subject matter that breeds stress. It may come from the sheer emotional investment of the parties themselves in the case. And it certainly emanates from the fact that the work is done in public and is open both to appellate scrutiny and sometimes to much wider public scrutiny. From wherever it comes, stress remains a real consequence of this work. The importance of recognising this lies in its impact on the individual judge and on the capacity of each judge to give their best possible effort to each and every case, almost all of which will represent a critical point in the life of the individual parties to the case.

There are perhaps two distinct approaches available to the family judge. On the one hand one can put the maximum possible emotional distance between oneself and those involved in the case. That approach certainly offers protection and some find it congenial, but that way lies the road to cynicism; and a cynic has no place in the proper despatch of family law. On the other hand one can enter into the emotional life of the case. Perhaps empathy lies that way, but it is likely to be personally costly and also may impair mature and balanced judgement, which is above all what the difficult case requires and the judge is required to give. We all know lawyers who have succumbed to one extreme or the other. Of course what is needed is a balance between these extremes: distance to permit sound judgment and empathy so as to understand the human personalities and issues which have given rise to the need for an exercise of judgement. Wisely all family judges are volunteers and no one is required to do this work, so those that do are a self-selected group.

In my view it is essential that a judge recognises that this work does exact a personal cost and that it is necessary to address it. For me there are three essential safeguards. First, that I do not do an unremitting diet of family work but have some variety blended into my itineraries. Not all agree with this and maybe not all need it, but most do and the experience of other work (especially if intellectually rather than emotionally challenging) is likely to refresh and prevent that world-weariness that all too easily leads to cynicism. Secondly, a family judge needs a sound philosophical framework within which to see and understand the cases that have to be resolved, a framework that avoids both cynicism and sentimentality or mindless optimism. Cases are much easier to grapple with if one can see why things might be as they are, as well as seeing how things should be. Thirdly, a family judge needs sound and effective support systems through which others can understand the issues and the implications for the judge personally, and can offer that critical solidarity that can only be based in trust and love or friendship. A recluse or deeply unhappy person will struggle to be effective as a family lawyer. These ideas require a little further elucidation.

1   Variety is increasingly difficult to achieve as specialisation becomes increasingly necessary, with specific areas of the law growing in complexity. It may be easy for the new district judge to acquire a varied diet of work, but it is very difficult for the Family Division Judge. The Family Division faces an ever-increasing workload and that creates a pressure shared by many an experienced circuit judge. Yet variety for most of us is an essential ingredient in the making of an experienced and effective family judge. It is essential that this is understood by those who administer the judiciary's itineraries.

2   In a pluralist and secular society, each may choose their own philosophical framework and the breadth of choice is likely to reflect the breadth found in society as a whole. Yet I want to advance a series of principles, which substantially address the issues that confront family law, and to which most could and probably would subscribe.

(a) Each person is unique and of infinite worth as a person. This will hold good, however inadequate the personality or however bad their conduct. It is conditional only on the fact of humanity.

(b) Evil is a real and potent force in human life. Evil needs to be recognised as such and not disguised in language that may explain why someone has perpetrated it, so that the deed (rather than the doer) appears to be defended.

(c) Human beings find nasty easier than nice. That is not to deny either the existence of goodness or the pleasure in doing good, but is to recognise that all too often first instincts point elsewhere, especially once the emotions are heavily engaged.

(d) Human beings have within themselves a reservoir of altruism. That is not inconsistent with the above. It is to recognise that we have both the resources to overcome first instincts and an innate capacity to do good.

(e) Small things may have great consequences. That is classically illustrated by the catastrophic consequences that can flow from a casual punch or a frustrated shake of a baby. Its significance in family law lies in keeping a proper sense of proportion and not judging principally by consequence but by intent. The resulting conclusion will not only be more merciful but also more just.

(f) Human beings retain their capacity for choice and self-autonomy. This is vital to maintaining personal value by ascribing personal responsibility to the consequence of choice and thereby acknowledging personal freedom, which inevitably entails the making of bad choices as well as good and taking responsibility for them.

(g) The same human being can both delight and appal us by the choices made in life. Just as one must never invest infallibility in anyone (especially the judge), so one must never despair of good in anyone. Human beings are an ever-varying manifestation of good and ill.

Now all of that can be expressed in religious language, as the basic God-given tenets of the created order as discerned in the opening three chapters of the Book of Genesis. However, there is no need for it to be expressed in the language of any identifiable religion or philosophical genre. It can equally be expressed as principles derived from human experience, reflection and culturally conditioned intuition. We may disagree on why things are as they are, but that does not preclude agreement that they are as they seem. What is necessary is a coherent framework that describes things as they are and identifies how they may develop. The question of 'why', however fascinating and important, is of less significance to the family lawyer.

Each judge requires effective support systems but once again there will be wide variety in their provision. For many, family or friends will be critical in enabling us to locate our experiences as a judge within our philosophical framework. They will comprise those few whose love or friendship inspires that confidence that can embrace encouragement and criticism, without engendering false confidence on the one hand or being undermined destructively on the other: in other words enabling the judge to confront Kipling's 'Twin Imposters'. I should no more exult in the House of Lords preferring my approach to that of a critical Court of Appeal, than I should be crushed by being buried 8–0 by those two august bodies unanimously declaring me wrong: both have occurred to me. The purpose of such a system is to help steer a course between the Scylla of cynicism and the Charybdis of sentimentality and mindless optimism; it is to enable an acceptance of the way the world is whilst being able to delight in goodness where it is found.

A conspicuous absentee from my thoughts so far, is the question of professional support in the form of psychotherapeutic input or an equivalent professional contribution. This is, I suspect, a highly controversial topic. It is not so much that it would be opposed by a strong 'macho' culture of judicial self-efficiency, (though I suspect that many of us would continue in some measure to hold to that), but that the informal systems I have described are sufficient for the purpose. In my experience they normally suffice. But where they are absent, fresh questions may need to be asked and we may need to take stock of where we are and what we need. In my view, what is not needed is the provision of professional support as a matter of course.

This chapter is offered as an individual (and perhaps idiosyncratic) insight into the impact of this work on those who try it. There is an increasing awareness that the impact is real and that this may in due course be reflected in the way we do our work. This should be a concern not only for judges but also for those who manage us, our workloads and our itineraries. I hope that at the very least this may be a small contribution to initiating discussions about those issues.

'This Even-Handed Justice'

Stephen Cobb, QC[*]

In all cases concerning the upbringing of children, the family court seeks to identify and bring about outcomes which are in the best interests of those children. This basic and essential standard has stood firm in legislation and in practice since at least 1925.[1] The principle, over the last century or more, has withstood challenges presented by continual and fundamental social changes, within and beyond the family. Those societal changes have required that principle to be applied with considerable flexibility.

It is the structure and *practice* of the family courts, and the *process* by which the courts seek to attain the outcome which best promotes the best interests of the child, which is presently the subject of unprecedented scrutiny and challenge. In this respect we are, in my view, in an unusually dynamic era in the development of the administration of family justice. Over the last 12 months or so, reviews and consultations have been initiated to examine a unified court's administration,[2] judicial resources,[3] procurement of public funding for legal representation,[4] child care proceedings,[5] the system of family justice,[6] case management and the Protocol ([2003] 2 FLR 719);[7] recently, media access and transparency,[8] and separate representation of children.[9]

This paper does not endeavour to review the reviews, the consultations, or the challenges to the system, nor does it purport to anticipate what I believe will be a number of changes which will follow the reviews and consultations. This paper is an entirely personal perspective of some of the current issues thrown up by the reviews and the challenges, which in my view are highly relevant to the promotion of even-handed justice in the family courts, in cases concerning children.

---

[*] Stephen Cobb, QC specialises in family law; the majority of his work concerns children, in 'public law' and 'private law' proceedings, and occasionally by way of judicial review. He was appointed to the Family Justice Council in 2004 and has been re-appointed in 2006 (three year term). He is a member of the Expert's Sub-Committee, and the 'Safeguarding Children' Sub-Committee. As a member of the Family Justice Council, he has also directly participated in consultations on the use of experts in family cases, and on transparency in the family courts. He is a general editor of Clarke Hall & Morrison on Children, having previously edited Essential Family Practice (Butterworths).

[1] Section 1 of Guardianship of Infants Act 1925 amending the Guardianship of Infants Act 1886, bringing the test more in line with the courts in the courts exercising the *parens patriae* jurisdiction (the courts of Chancery, or their predecessor the Court of Wards and Liveries or their present successors the courts of the Family Division of the High Court).

[2] HMCS *Management Proposals to Develop a Unified Family Service* (2005) 17 February, Position Paper, Sheridan Greenland, Area Director (Family) HMCS; *Moving Towards a Single Family Court.*

[3] (2005) July 2005, Judicial Resources Review.

[4] *A Fairer Deal for Legal Aid* (2005) July, Cm 6591, TSO, and the Carter report (July 2006).

[5] *Review of the Child Care Proceedings System in England & Wales* (2006) May.

[6] The Constitutional Affairs Select Committee (2005) 1 March, HC 116-1, TSO.

[7] The Judicial Review Team (JRT) review of the Protocol and its associated Practice Direction.

[8] DCA Consultation *Confidence and Confidentiality: Improving transparency and privacy in family courts* Cm6886 (2006) July.

[9] DCA Consultation: *Separate Representation of Children* CP/20/06 (September 2006).

The title of the Dartington Conference in 1995 was borrowed from *Macbeth*, Act V, Scene III, line 37 ('Pluck from the memory a *rooted sorrow*'). In the context of this new compilation (Re-Rooted Lives), I borrow the theme of my paper from one of the famous soliloquies in the same play (Act I, Scene VII, line 10):[10] '... *this even handed justice*'.

PROMOTION OF INTER-DISCIPLINARITY

Lord Justice Thorpe observed in Family Law in August 2004:[11] 'Whatever be the problems and shortcomings of the family justice system they will never be solved or resolved unless family justice is truly recognised to be an inter-disciplinary system with a need to find and to adopt only those remedial measures that have gained inter-disciplinary support'. It is true that although we share one language and enjoy 'a common speech', there has been in the past, and to some extent there still is, often much lack of understanding – both as to the language spoken and as to the roles and functions – among the family justice community.[12] Elizabeth Walsh in her publication 'Working in the Family Justice System' [2006] commented (para.5.1) that 'the key skill requirement in multi-agency inter-disciplinary working is not to be able to think like a professional from a different discipline, but to understand how other professions think and to know the legal and knowledge boundaries within which they work ... inter-agency work is essential within the family justice system'.

The need for inter-disciplinarity has been most boldly addressed in recent times by the creation in 2004 of the Family Justice Council, whose primary purpose is to promote an inter–disciplinary approach to family justice. Specifically, its terms of reference includes the promotion of 'improved interdisciplinary working across the family justice system through inclusive discussion, communication and co-ordination between all agencies', and also the promotion of a 'commitment to legislative principles and the objectives of the family justice system by disseminating advice and promoting inter-agency discussion, including by way of seminars and conferences as appropriate.'

Through consultation and research, the Family Justice Council has been charged with monitoring how effectively the system both as a whole and through its component parts delivers the service the Government and the public need, and advising on reforms necessary for continuous improvement. One of the key strengths of the Family Justice Council is its inter-disciplinary composition; issues central to the delivery of 'even handed justice' in the family justice system can be debated by representatives of the many members of the family justice constituency.

An important objective of the Council – materially assisted by the work of the local councils in liaison with the national Council – is the provision of guidance and direction to achieve consistency of practice throughout the family justice system. In this way, the best examples of even-handed justice will be disseminated around the country in order to promote the best interests of the children, the subjects of the proceedings.

---

[10]   'But in these cases / we still have judgment here; that we but teach / Bloody instructions, which, being taught, return / To plague the inventor: *this even-handed justice* / Commends th'ingredience of our poison'd chalice / To our own lips' (Macbeth).

[11]   [2004] Fam Law 558.

[12]   Somewhat reminiscent of Genesis, Chapter 11, vv 1–9.

JUDGES AND THE COURT PROCESS

In order to determine the outcome in the best interests of children – and, where relevant, the determination of facts to support such outcome – the family courts have developed (in my view justifiably) a more relaxed code for the collation and admissibility of evidence than other jurisdictions. To that end the process feels, certainly to the practitioner, largely inquisitorial. The courts have emphasised and re-emphasised that there is a wide discretion vested in the court to consider the 'wide canvas' of material when reaching relevant factual conclusions: indeed it has been said that 'the range of facts which may properly be taken into account is infinite'.[13]

In public law cases, even the first stage of the proceedings, the 'fact-finding', 'threshold' or 'causation' stage has been held to be 'quasi-inquisitorial'. Butler-Sloss P so characterised the first stage in *Re U; Re B* at p 273, paras 26–27, as follows '[27] In the end the judge must make clear findings on the issues of fact before the court, resting on the evidence led by the parties and such additional evidence as the judge may have required in the exercise of his *quasi-inquisitorial function*'. But public law proceedings have a strong adversarial element, particularly at the 'first (fact-finding) stage'. I find it easy to recognise Charles J's comment[14] that: '… some tension exists between the statements that such proceedings are essentially non-adversarial and the points made as to establishing the threshold criteria and the establishment of facts the purposes of ss 31 and 1 of the Children Act 1989'. He commented (rightly in my view) that the requirement of proof of threshold facts to the civil standard 'both at the threshold stage and, then, at the disposal stage in, for example, assessing risk', to his mind 'reflect an adversarial procedure'. He referred to the 'causation' or 'threshold' stage as 'largely an adversarial process', and added: 'Human nature and the respective roles of the parties at that stage of public law proceedings have the result that those proceedings are treated at that stage as being adversarial or as having a substantial adversarial element.'

The adversarial element[15] is highlighted by the fact that the outcome could involve what for many of us would be the unimaginable prospect of permanent separation from one's own child; as has been said on occasion before, since the abolition of the death penalty, there is no more draconian order for a judge to make than to order the permanent removal of a child from their natural family.[16]

There is no doubt that the 'threshold' part of the case *feels* adversarial for the lawyers, and I am quite sure for the clients; indeed, the might of the professional bodies – medical or social work – must often seem overwhelming, particularly those who come to the courts vulnerable through their life experiences, whether through drug and alcohol dependence, mental health problems, and learning difficulties, which epitomise many of the respondents to these types of application.

It is often a consequence of this process – which on any view has an adversarial component – that parents feel disempowered and unable to engage with the professionals who they see as oppositional. It is clear, following the decision of the House of Lords in *Kent County Council v G*

---

[13] *Re H & R* [1996] at page 101, and see also *Re T (Abuse: Standard of Proof)* [2004] 2 FLR 838 at para 33, p 848, Butler-Sloss P. This has been recently re-stated in *A County Council v A mother, a father and X, Y, Z by their Children's Guardian* [2005] 2 FLR 129 (Ryder J): findings of fact must be based on all of the available materials, not just on scientific or medical materials, no matter how cogent they seem to be in isolation. Investigation of fact should have regard to the wider context of social, emotional, ethical and moral factors.

[14] In *Re R (Care: Disclosure: Nature of Proceedings)* [2002] 1 FLR 755 specifically 771–772.

[15] Reinforced by the (proper) requirement on local authorities to articulate their case with clarity (see for example *CL v East Riding Yorkshire* [2006] EWCA Civ 49) rather as in an indictment, and the onus falls on the authority to prove it (per *Re H & R*).

[16] Munby J in *Re B* (supra) also Coleridge J 'Another Big Bang' [2003] Fam Law 799. See also McFarlane J in *Re X (Emergency Protection Orders)* [2006] EWHC (Fam) 510 'there can be few more Draconian or important orders that justices are called upon to consider than making an EPO; particularly one made without notice to the child's parents' (para [91]).

& others [2005] UKHL 68, that it is no part of the Children Act 1989 (most notably s 38(6)) to facilitate any sort of treatment programmes to effect change in parents. As Baroness Hale indicated 'It is still the *present* capacity [of the parent to meet the needs of the child] with which the court is concerned. It cannot be a proper use of the court's powers under section 38(6) to seek to bring about change' (para [67]). Without change, or signs of change, many parents will fail in their endeavours to persuade the court to consider reconstitution of the family. It is therefore remarkable and impressive to see a change in attitude by parents towards authority figures in public law proceedings in the absence of treatment. I am clear in my own role to endeavour to effect the re-engagement of such families and re-direct proceedings to achieve positive outcomes. However, the difference between a good outcome for a family (and rehabilitation) and a poor outcome is often the ability of the social worker and the family to engage constructively one with the other.

The general state of public ignorance (or, more fairly, innocence) of the family court process coupled with the range of complex and intense emotions (commonly high levels of stress, distress, regret, anger, sadness, despair) with which clients present, does little to prepare or equip parties (or witnesses for that matter) for active participation in the crucial determination of their family's future lives. Many find even the process of giving of instructions painful and slow; many are resistant to receiving advice – some because they do not want to hear it, others because they cannot. Often parties are unable to focus on the *real* issue and are distracted by other pressing issues or agenda. Many clients are mistrustful of the litigation process and its outcomes because of their cultural or societal background. Many enter into litigation as the victims of domestic (physical and emotional) abuse, and are for that reason disempowered and unable to engage fully in the process. Clients (particularly in private law proceedings) are advised of the potential benefits of settlement and agreement, and need to contemplate conciliation, yet simultaneously have to be prepared literally to confront the issues, and the personalities, from the witness box.

We have an impressive body of specially trained judges at all tiers of court available to determine family cases; they are appropriately vested with wide discretion to determine issues on a wide 'spectrum' of procedure.[17] Oral testimony is often vital to the judicial assessment of a case (witnesses '… may have in their demeanour, in their manner, in their hesitation, in the nuance of their expressions, in even the turns of the eyelid, left an impression upon the man who saw and heard them which can never be reproduced on the printed page.'[18]). A case 'on paper' can take on a very different character when it is spoken to, and tested in cross-examination. Appellate decisions have reinforced the value to the trial judge of receiving oral evidence – emphasising the broad and subtle advantage of the judge in seeing and hearing the witnesses. All practitioners in the field have seen cases fall apart, or conversely rally, when subjected to 'live' testing and review. I recall once in conference referring to this 'forensic fate' (raising an eyebrow of a senior matrimonial solicitor who was in attendance); I was simply trying to convey the element of unpredictability of the courtroom process.

In private law proceedings in particular, many litigants come to the family courts without representation at all; many may well feel that 'even-handed justice' may not in the circumstances be achieved. I am unfailingly impressed by judicial accommodation of a perceived (or real) disadvantage which lack of representation may produce. The inevitably daunting prospect of litigating in person is, in my view, mitigated in many instances by the assistance of a '*McKenzie* friend'; whose role has been the subject of recent guidance.[19] The presumption in favour of allowing a litigant in person the assistance of a *McKenzie* friend is very strong. A request for such

---

17   See Butler Sloss LJ in *Re B (Minors)(Contact)* [1994] 2 FLR 1.

18   Per *Powell v Streatham Manor Nursing Home* [1935] AC 243 at 250. In a passage which Viscount Sankey cites from *Clarke v Edinburgh Tramways Co* (1919).

19   *Guidance from the President's Office* [2005] Fam Law Vol 35, p 405 and the Court of Appeal in *In the matter of the children of Mr O'Connell, Mr Whelan, and Mr Watson* [2005] EWCA Civ 759, [2005] 2 FLR 967, in which the Court of Appeal

assistance should only be refused for compelling reasons, which, if found, must be carefully and fully explained to the litigant in person and the would-be *McKenzie* friend.

In many cases concerning children there is not really a right solution.[20] This makes the delivery of the decision an extremely important part of the legal process. A judge at first instance is expected to deliver a judgment after the oral evidence and arguments which appropriately records the key components of the evidence which have informed his/her opinion, his/her assessment of that evidence, the relevant law, and (where relevant) the arguments advanced. It is of course a critical feature of the case, delivering for the parties – particularly parents – the objective judicial evaluation of the material laid before the court. Judges adopt different styles: some prefer delivering the decision (ie outcome) at the outset of the narrative judgment, followed by the lengthier discussion of the evidence. Others (the majority) prefer to engage in the discussion and review of the case (requiring the parents to listen to the evaluation of their circumstances) before revealing how the evidence has been assessed, and the conclusions reached. In a judgment, the material should not be ritualistically trawled, nor formulaically reproduced; the arguments do not need to be minutely examined. It is sufficient if what the judge says shows the parties, and if need be the Court of Appeal, the basis on which he/she acted.[21] Inevitably, (as Lord Hoffman observed in *Piglowska v Piglowski* [1999] 2 FLR 763) the exigencies of daily court room life are such that reasons for judgment will always be capable of having been better expressed. This is particularly true of an unreserved judgment, but is also true of a reserved judgment based upon notes.

A balance needs to be struck in each case between ensuring that the evidence has been adequately considered and rehearsed, while not making the judgment excessively long. As Thorpe LJ observed in *Re B (Appeal: Lack of Reasons)* [2003] 2 FLR 1035 (at para [11]), 'there is a huge virtue in brevity of judgment …the more experienced the judge the more likely it is that he may display the virtue of brevity'. The essential requirement is that the terms of the judgment should enable the parties and any appellate tribunal readily to analyse the reasoning that was essential to the judge's decision.

It is very much to be hoped that judgments – and transcripts – will more routinely be available for the experts who have given expert evidence in family proceedings. There is provision in the Public Law Protocol[22] for the solicitor instructing the expert – within 10 days of the final hearing – to 'provide feedback to the expert by way of a letter informing the expert of the outcome of the case and the use made by the Court of the expert's opinion. Where the court directs that a copy of the transcript (of the judgment) can be sent to the expert' then this should be requested within 10 days of the final hearing. Regrettably, this provision in the Protocol is often ignored, and all too commonly the expert is left ignorant of the outcome of the proceedings, and of the value of the contribution he or she has made. The legal profession, and the courts, need to be much more assiduously attentive to this.

It is also to be hoped that judgments – and transcripts – will more routinely be available for parents/children, so that they can have the opportunity to digest the review of their case, and the outcome, in the quiet reflection of their own time.

---

re-affirmed that the purpose of allowing a litigant in person the assistance of a *McKenzie* friend was to further the interests of justice by achieving a level playing field and ensuring a fair hearing.

20   As Cumming-Bruce LJ observed in *Clarke-Hunt v Newcombe* (1982) 4 FLR 482 at 488 in many cases: '… there were two alternative wrong solutions. The problem of the judge was to appreciate the factors pointing in each direction and to decide which of the two bad solutions was the least dangerous, having regard to the long-term interests of the children, and so he decided the matter'.

21   *Eagil Trust Co Ltd v Piggott-Brown* [1985] 3 All ER 119.

22   *Protocol for Judicial Case Management in Public Law Children Act cases* (2003) (Appendix C, para.7.1).

We must never forget that the conclusion of the family court process is not the judgment; that is often the beginning of the process. For after the court proceedings are over, the delicate, difficult and often painful work of implementing the court's decision begins.

A contemporary consideration on whether the courts deliver 'even-handed' justice would be incomplete without reference to the serious impact of delay upon the process. Delay is a significant fault-line which underlies both public and private law proceedings in the family courts. Although there is plainly a duty to exercise exceptional diligence in family proceedings in view of the risk that the passage of time may result in a *de facto* determination of the matter,[23] it is, regrettably, probably singly the most serious failing in the delivery of effective justice to families. Regrettably, delay can often influence an outcome in proceedings – often adversely. Much attention is being rightly given by the Government, the Judiciary, the Family Justice Council (among others) to tackle the endemic delays in the system, and the consequences. Proposals for reducing delay are far-reaching and imaginative. Time will tell whether they are practical and effective.

CHILDREN AT THE HEART OF THE PROCESS

In both public and private law proceedings, it is the often expressed wish of the parent(s) to place before the court the voice of their child, or children. In public law proceedings, of course, the child is an 'automatic' respondent, and his/her voice is received through representation by a Children's Guardian. The older child may be represented independently.

Section 122 of the Adoption and Children Act 2002 amended the Children Act 1989 to allow court rules to be made to provide for children to be separately represented in all section 8 private law cases by making such cases 'specified proceedings' in line with public law proceedings. However, the Government has always been clear that such provision is only relevant for a small proportion of children who are involved in private law proceedings arising from parental conflict.

There is undoubtedly great value in an agreed outcome for children in which they themselves have contributed. There is also value in permitting children of maturity to voice their views directly – most recently and clearly illustrated by the Court of Appeal's decision in the case of *Mabon v Mabon* [2005] EWCA Civ 634, [2005] 2 FLR 1011, in which Thorpe LJ referred to the fact that 'Unless we in this jurisdiction are to fall out of step with similar societies as they safeguard Article 12 rights, we must, in the case of articulate teenagers, accept that the right to freedom of expression and participation outweighs the paternalistic judgment of welfare' (para [28]).

The case of *Mabon* provided 'a timely opportunity to recognise the growing acknowledgement of the autonomy and consequential rights of children, both nationally and internationally. The Rules are sufficiently robustly drawn to accommodate that shift. In individual cases trial judges must equally acknowledge the shift when they make in individual cases a proportionate judgment of the sufficiency of the child's understanding' (para [32]).

On the other hand the potential for either or both parents to seek to influence the child is high; overt manipulation of the child is abusive. Almost as unattractive is the willingness of the parents to subordinate the exercise of their own parental responsibility to the child.

For my part, I value greatly the independent representation of children in complex private law proceedings (in accordance with *President's Practice Direction (Representation of children in Family Proceedings pursuant to rule 9.5)* [2004] 1 FLR 1188), through representation by a Children's

---

[23]   See *Haase v Germany* [2004] 2 FLR 39 at [54].

Guardian. All too often, in my experience, the interests of the child are lost in the adult conflict. I also welcome the court's increasing recognition of the need to give mature children a clear voice in proceedings of this kind. This is reflected in the recent consultation paper which drew on the Cardiff University research showing that giving the child party status and separate representation was most beneficial in intractable cases because it enabled the parents to refocus attention on the child, putting the child centre stage. A well-trained and experienced guardian was often able to unblock these cases and provide a 'balanced and reasoned report' verifying the wishes and feelings of the children.

But relevant checks do need to be observed relevant both (a) to the level of maturity of the child, and (b) with regard to the nature of proceedings. I have despaired of parents' endeavour to manipulate the legal process by facilitating the introduction of their children (sometimes younger than teenage) to solicitors, the child carrying with him/her the cant of the 'facilitating' parent. Solicitors may well take a view that the child has the relevant degree of maturity (applying the test in rule 9.2A) but perhaps too glibly regard the important words of Sir Thomas Bingham MR, in *Re S (A Minor) (Independent Representation)* [1993] Fam 263, 276G, [1993] 2 FLR 437 at 445: '... any solicitor accepting instructions from a child in this situation must exercise a scrupulous, conscientious and responsible judgment'.

Research at Cardiff University (which has informed the DCA Consultation) produced findings which showed that bringing the child into the proceedings could be stressful and put too much responsibility on the child, 'particularly if they believe that the judge will make a decision based entirely on their view'. The research revealed that children can feel confused and manipulated by their parents, 'repeating unfounded allegations or simply reciting the parent's view to the guardian'. In the circumstances, the court has to (and generally does) exercise relevant discretion not to permit engagement of the child unless it is right to do so.

IMPROVING AWARENESS OF THE WORK OF THE FAMILY JUSTICE SYSTEM

If my own experience of meeting and discussing family law issues with clients (and others outside the profession) provides a reliable measure of the state of general public knowledge about the family justice system, then it would appear that there is still a relatively low level of awareness about the work of the family courts, and the principles with which we work. Regrettably, still commonplace is the belief that 'custody' is awarded in private law proceedings; the concept of parental responsibility (which is highly relevant to much private and public law work) is little appreciated or understood. I fear that equally endemic is the misconception, widely propagated periodically through the popular media, that the threshold for state intervention in family life is low, and that local authority applications are widely rubber-stamped by the courts without full or proper investigation.

Family law, and its processes, are ill-served by such a low level of understanding in the public domain.

This lack of awareness of the family court's processes, and its principles, is likely to be addressed – at least to some extent – by reforms which are likely to flow from the proposals set out in the recent DCA consultation paper *Confidence and Confidentiality: Improving transparency and privacy in family courts* Cm6886. The 'transparency' debate was stimulated (not for the first time) in 2004 by a number of causes within and outwith the courts: two particular cases provoked this re-evaluation, namely *Pelling v Bruce-Williams* (Fam Div and C/A) [2004] 1 FLR 171 and [2004] 2 FLR 823 and *Re B (A child) (Disclosure)* [2004] 2 FLR 142 (Fam Div).[24]

The challenge to the legitimacy of holding proceedings in private was rejected in *Pelling* (supra); the Court of Appeal's ruling that it remained justifiable to hold children's proceedings in private, and to limit the extent to which judgments were made available to the general public, was tempered by a recognition of the validity of much of Dr Pelling's argument, and by a clear statement of the need to scrutinise in its own courts the need to impose a blanket of confidentiality on the reporting of proceedings (which are of course in public). This chink of light into the otherwise private corners of the family court was significant. In *Re B*, Munby J highlighted the need for re-appraisal of the current convention of privacy by adverting to the fact that 'It is all too easy to attack the system when the system itself prevents anyone correcting the misrepresentations being fed to the media: see Harris at para [386].' Munby J commented that 'too relentless an enforcement of the privacy of family court proceedings may be counter-productive' adding that 'the courts should perhaps in future be more willing than they have been in the past to exercise the disclosure jurisdiction so as to permit matters such as these to be put into the public domain.' (see paras [133], [134]).

I value the essential private nature of family proceedings. I am of the view that children (often the involuntary and innocent subjects of the process) are entitled to the protection of privacy from the public gaze. Plainly, judges do need to receive the best evidence available in order to inform these vital decisions, and I have no difficulty in accepting Bennett J's comment[25] (at para [48]) 'In order for me to gain as full and accurate picture as possible of this case, of the facts, and of the options available to me, it is, in my judgment, essential that the parents, the child and family reporter and other witnesses should feel able to express themselves candidly on personal issues without fear of public curiosity or comment.' Although the Family Proceedings Rules 1991 confer on a judge in any case the discretion to lift the veil of privacy, 'there is such a strong inherited convention of privacy that the judicial mind is almost never directed to the discretion, and, in rare cases where an application is made, a fair exercise may be prejudiced by the tradition or an unconscious preference for the atmosphere created by a hearing in chambers. Judges need to be aware of this and to be prepared to consider another course where appropriate.'

I have no doubt that greater openness is essential to promote greater understanding of the work of the family courts, and to restore confidence with the public in the even-handed manner in which critical decisions are made for families.

Greater transparency will permit greater freedom to show off the accomplishments of the family justice system; it should, in my view, promote confidence in the system. The family justice system is, I believe, essentially a very good one. We have a well-refined statutory code, buttressed by case law which is scholarly, humane and practical. We have a strong body of dedicated, specially trained, judges at all tiers of court. There is a thriving specialist bar, and a

---

[24]   Other cases contributed to the debate at the time, notably Munby J in *Re D: F v M* [2004] EWHC 727 at [4]: 'There is much wrong with our system and the time has come for us to recognise that fact and to face up to it honestly. If we do not, we risk forfeiting public confidence. The newspapers – and I mean newspapers generally, for this is a theme taken up with increasing emphasis by all sectors of the press – make uncomfortable reading for us. ... We delude ourselves if we dismiss the views of journalists as unrepresentative of public opinion or as representative only of sectors of public opinion we think we can ignore. Responsible voices are raised in condemnation of our system. We need to take note. We need to act. And we need to act now.'; Ryder J in *Blunkett v Quinn* [2005] 1 FLR 648, and in public law proceedings the 'miracle babies' case *Haringey London Borough Council v C E and another intervening* [2004] EWHC 2580 [2005] 2 FLR 47. Most recently the Court of Appeal's decision in *Clayton v Clayton* has further added to the sum of judicial commentary.

[25]   *P v BW* [2003] EWHC 1541, [2004] Fam 22 (first instance decision).

specialist solicitors' profession. The law and its application has been proven, in my view, to be flexible and versatile to the changing face of society. This all needs to be showcased more confidently.

Inter-disciplinary cooperation is key to many successful outcomes in the delivery of family justice. This is most readily defined by the recent creation of the Family Justice Council and increasingly nurtured by its activities. Greater transparency should promote better inter-disciplinary practices, by allowing perhaps wider access of the public, and particularly of the medical profession, to the judgments given in the complex medical cases. Greater transparency will promote greater accountability and investigation into the processes by which decisions have been taken.

Greater transparency will undoubtedly (and properly) more widely expose the flaws of the system. There is unacceptable delay in the resolution of family disputes. There is insufficient consideration to pre-proceedings intervention, and to alternative dispute resolution. The achievement of family justice comes at a very substantial cost to the public purse and to the private purse; those costs are often driven up by lax case management and lack of judicial continuity. As Mr Justice Munby said in *Re B* we have to have the humility to recognise that there have undoubtedly been miscarriages of justice in the system. Transparency may assist in exposing the shortcomings, highlighting the deficiencies; motivating better practice.

These arguments point inexorably to greater openness. Greater openness will, I hope, lead to greater understanding of our work by the public at large. I am currently unconvinced that the media is the appropriate agency (or only appropriate agency) to be the 'watchdog' of the family courts, though plainly media access to the courts is an inevitable component in the achieving of wider transparency. The DCA together with the Family Justice Council should urgently channel its respective (and joint) efforts to making more generally available information about the work of the family justice system; this would in my view materially assist in de-mythologising the system and its practices.

We have to be careful to ensure that in the quest to answer the critics of the current private nature of proceedings, greater public access may have the effect of neutralising some of the strengths of the family justice system; I am concerned that publicity – far from correcting its flaws – may indeed multiply or deepen them. Specifically, we have to ensure that judges are able to continue to make decisions in the best interests of children. We must be careful to ensure that by seeking to promote accountability, we do not compromise the willingness of parties to litigate, and/or the ability of witnesses (expert and lay) to come to court and assist the judges by giving evidence in a manner and context which yields the most reliable information. As the DCA consultation paper on transparency rightly points out, we plainly do not want to add to the delays in prosecuting family cases with cumbersome disputes about media and/or public access, and/or reporting. We do not want to add to the costs or the uncertainties of litigation.

Perhaps ten years on from now, when the third edition of the 'Rooted'[26] papers is published, we should take a moment to reflect on the debate which is engaged now, and reflect on whether we got the balance right.

---

[26] *Rooted Sorrows* (1997), *Re-Rooted Lives* (2007).

Standing Firm Beside 'Fact'

*Dr Anne Zachary**

Soon after the implementation of the Children Act 1989, now more than 15 years ago, I gave a talk entitled 'Vulnerability exposed: children, parents and professionals'. I set out to make two points and I used Family Court cases in which I had been involved as an expert to illustrate them. A recent case reminds me that, although change is slow, there have been significant improvements in our practice over the past 10 years. I will describe one of the early cases here.

The points in the talk were:

(1) how much the different professionals' perceptions of a situation can vary, depending on whom they are representing,

(2) that we are all easily fallible in court, even under oath, and that having heard all the evidence the decision is up to the judge.

The Children Act sought to reinforce the autonomy of the family through the exercise of parental responsibility. A central change in the law and a principle of the Act was the concept of parental responsibility that replaced parental rights. Another principle was that children should be able to be parties separate from their parents in legal proceedings.

Therefore the Children Act involves not only children, but also parents. At the time of its inception I heard it referred to as 'the Parent Act'. Richard Williams (1992) in 'A concise guide to the Children Act 1989' commented that, 'The major changes in law relating to children that result from this Act will have their most significant effect upon parents, others having responsibilities for children and local authorities ... It will have substantial implications for the NHS and all health care workers who come into contact with children.' One of the main themes of the Act is the encouragement of greater cooperation between those with responsibilities for children and the statutory and voluntary agencies. Clearly, it involves professionals as well.

The family I describe here, to whom I was linked as an expert, illustrates this. I will concentrate on the perspective of a single mother by describing how she related to the professionals and indirectly to her child within the framework of the then new Act. With this case in mind, I will try to understand distortions and complications that can arise in terms of 'projective processes', which is an expression used by psychoanalysts to describe certain interactions. In object relation terms, this can be understood to include a repetition of the relationship with the primary object (first significant relationship which sets the template for what is expected from consequent relationships), with the subsequent counter-transference responses felt by those professionals involved.

---

* Dr Anne Zachary is a Consultant Psychiatrist in Psychotherapy and has been employed by the Tavistock and Portman NHS Trust for 17 years. She works at the Portman Clinic, which assesses and treats patients with problems of violence, sexual perversion and delinquency. Currently she spends two days a week seconded to the High Security Hospital, Broadmoor, and is an approved doctor under s 12(2) of the Mental Health Act 1983. Formerly a member of the President's Interdisciplinary Committee.

The term 'projective processes' also refers to what may occur between an individual or a group that finds managing their own emotions difficult or even intolerable.

People who are highly emotionally aroused can evoke very powerful feelings and responses in those they are in contact with: it is this that gives rise to the expression 's/he gets under my skin'. When this happens to a professional who is involved with a distressed client or patient, the professional may speak or act upon these 'projected' feelings unaware of their source. On the other hand, if the professional manages to recognise that the patient has 'got under his/her skin' yet simultaneously manages to retain a distance and continues to think and feel from their own perspective, it may be possible to help the disturbed person understand the situation and their part in it, in a different way. Psychoanalysts use the phrase, 'to process the projected feelings psychologically' to refer to this ability. The psychoanalytic concept of projective identification is explained well by Segal (1973) and Ogden (1982) amongst others.

I am going to use the concept of projective identification to describe how powerful interactive forces between individuals (eg parent and child) can be transposed on to institutions (eg court and clinic) and become located in the individuals representing those institutions, causing the professionals to re-enact the feelings and wishes of the parent and child unconsciously. This in turn causes the parents and children to become passive observers, whilst their painful feelings are contained by the system attempting to provide them with a service. Work by Isabel Menzies-Lyth (1985), and Richard Davies (1992) shows us that this is a useful way to conceptualise what can happen intra-psychically and interpersonally in an institutional setting.

Whilst describing this mother and child, I have s 1(3)(a) of the Introductory Part 1 of the Children Act in mind: '... a court shall have regard in particular to – the ascertainable wishes and feelings of the child concerned (considered in the light of his age and understanding); ...' In my view, the child in this case was over-exposed to court proceedings which became rigidly polarised despite a genuine wish on the part of the professionals to collaborate.

The situation centred around the *absence* of a telephone call by the mother during an assessment process and its effect on the related court proceedings. There was, as so often in such cases, a proliferation of paperwork with regular correspondence and telephone calls from the range of professionals involved. This included solicitors, previous assessors in the medical field, borough council social workers, and a guardian ad litem.

In a psychoanalytic treatment undertaken in a consulting room setting, there may be great significance in a telephone call, or its absence. Telephoning is not part of the recognised treatment model; on the contrary, the aim is to contain as much of the contact between psychoanalyst/psychotherapist and patient within the treatment setting. In an ideal situation, the only transaction that would take place outside of this is a brief initial telephone call, made by the patient to set a date for a preliminary interview. This is a solid baseline, and any deviation from it becomes part of the work to be taken up in the transference. When the psychoanalytic model is adapted to an institutional setting, and being applied to an assessment interview such aspects still hold true, but the therapist is unlikely to find an appropriate way to make use of the transference. In this setting, the patient will relate to the receptionist by telephone, as do the relatives if necessary. Much work on the telephone might be done subsequently by social workers, or others in the multi-disciplinary team, particularly by following up enquiries and consulting other professionals.

THE CASE

The case I want to focus on in detail involved the mother of an adolescent boy who, after her son's assessment received an appointment to see a social worker. Routine though this sounds, it was arranged because of the strong messages that pervaded both the correspondence and the boy's account of his situation, indicating that his mother was very angry at having been left out. Initially the boy was considered separately because at the time he was in care and due to go back to court for consideration of an extension of his care order. A worker from his residential school setting brought him to his assessment with me. I learned that both the boy and his single mother would like his care order to be terminated, so that he could spend more time at home rather than having to abide by the very strict holiday arrangements under the care order. They were in agreement that his education away from home should continue, though during the assessment it was not clear that this was what the boy wanted. He was happy at school and doing relatively well; nevertheless his index offence had recently come back into focus, not in a repetition as such but in some anxiety over his beginning to have age appropriate contact with girls. It was a cause for concern that the exposing behaviour itself had only occurred when the boy was in the home situation, and not at school. (The behaviour occurred whilst in the presence of a gang of mainly younger boys, but included his elder brother). There was certainly a case to put forward that the work was not finished in an emotional sense, and that to disrupt the restrictions put on his movements could be detrimental. As his mother seemed keen to have him at home and to have the parental responsibility returned to her, we wondered whether the impetus for the change might possibly be coming more from her than from him. It was decided to offer her an appointment to examine her view of things.

The institutional 'mental set', somewhat naively, expected the mother to be full of enthusiasm for anything that would facilitate changing the arrangements concerning her son. So there was surprise and then a need for reflection when the day of her appointment came and went without her making any contact. A second invitation was sent to no avail and the court report had to be prepared without contact; it recorded a lack of communication despite having heard that an appointment was what she wanted and that it had been offered.

Here is the telephone call that was not made. Was her lack of response an attempt to communicate that, in her view, the clinic was letting her down? On a more practical level, if she had telephoned to cancel there would have been a great difference in the situation. It might have been that she had a previous commitment that day and she requested another date. Or she might have been short of money and needed help with her fares. But we were in the dark as to her position and her feelings. However, her anger was conveyed through the silence that had a rather sinister feel to it, and by using the institutional adaptation of the truly valuable concept of 'counter-transference', we were able to perceive it.

Looking back over my assessment of the boy, there was a definite sense of hostility and achievement underlying the flat adolescent indifference that tended to mask his real feelings. What came into focus was his description of his relationship with his mother whilst he was at school. He said that she liked him to telephone her on Saturday nights. Usually he did not mind doing this, but sometimes he was too busy with his own plans, or short of money, or there was a queue for the pay-phone. He explained that his mother did not have a phone in her flat and that she would go round to a neighbour and wait for his call at an appointed time. It seemed that he could have quite a powerful effect on his mother by not making telephone calls, just as she had had on us. Nevertheless, the boy had certainly given the impression that his mother was feeling left out of our clinic assessment, and that she was putting pressure on him by expressing anger about this when they did manage to speak on the telephone. Perhaps this represented a projection of a failure of the object, as although she had been invited she needed more, which may have been to be 'sought out' and instead she made do with nothing.

The court case was scheduled for two to three days, and in accordance with the terms of the Children Act, the boy was entitled to attend the whole of the proceedings. His mother was also in court on the day I was called. The guardian ad litem had acted as a coordinator of the preparations for court, and in my mind filled the gap left by both the elective absence of the mother and the formal absence of the father, (the parents were divorced). Witnesses were called with due attention to their own commitments and I was called immediately before a lunch break. I did not anticipate that my discussion with the barrister representing the mother would centre on the telephone call. A question arose about her non-attendance at the clinic and its relevance. Whilst not wanting to sound punitive or judgemental, I had to declare that we had been surprised at her lack of contact when we knew how keen she was to have the care order rescinded. 'Just a telephone call would have sufficed.' Then an example followed of how quickly expectations are reduced to fit in with reality. There was no discussion about the fact that it had been felt to be important that she actually attend and relevant reasons why she did not. Instead there was a distortion of the proceedings whilst the barrister gave an impassioned account of the home circumstances where 'there was not even a telephone', and which included details of the mother's difficult personal financial situation. It seemed unconstructive to go very far into an argument about the cost of a simple call from a pay phone, whilst under what felt like an attack on the perceived loss of reality of those 'in ivory towers' like myself. I felt that the barrister was viewing me as a community psychiatrist who might have gone to visit the mother rather than expecting a telephone call. Instead of the mother's projection of failure being taken up, it was enacted.

I was aware of the boy sitting watching the professionals in dispute, his characteristic flat adolescent indifference now clearly coloured by an omnipotent look of achievement and control. Here was a chance to get back at his mother indirectly, by using this gathering of professionals to act their (that is his own and his mother's) parts. He might have preferred a less rigid plan, and been able to phone her or the neighbour when he wanted to, then perhaps the neighbour could call her … Yet any direct confrontation of his feelings about the control his mother tried to exert over him in terms of his brightening up her Saturday evenings, was completely bypassed.

There was another level to this re-enactment. This mother's divorce had occurred long ago when the boy was young. There had been stormy periods between the couple even before his birth, although there had been a reconciliation when he was born. The father finally left when he was 14 months old and the divorce took place about three years later. The reconciliation had occurred around a post-natal depression when she had not been able to look after the baby, and for a time the father and grandmother shared his care. There was a bone of contention between the boy and his elder brother, because the brother had memories of father living at home, whilst he did not. He knew from his mother's affidavit, which he had read, that his father favoured the elder brother and he felt that his mother did too. He was especially close to his grandmother who was also in court. The boy had recently discovered that his brother had been meeting father secretly.

The court adjourned for lunch and on return there was a distraction. The mother had lost her coat and was convinced that she had had it in court during the morning, and that she had probably left it there by mistake. She did not remember having it at lunch. Unfortunately, several foreign professional observers who had been present in the morning had not returned. Immediately an air of suspicion and intrigue arose from the family whilst the professionals shifted uncomfortably. With great dignity the court clerk issued instructions for certain enquiries to be made and the court resumed eventually about 20 minutes late. There was a very brief exchange between the barrister for the local authority and me before I was dismissed.

DISCUSSION

I had never met the mother and was advised not to look at her in court, but her powerful presence was central. Whilst knowing little of her own personal background and nothing of her early experience, it can be said that this was a needy mother whose vulnerability made her demanding and attention-seeking. She had an adolescent son whose affect was flat. Both exerted powerful, passive forces on to each other and on to the professionals involved with them, who were thus given roles to enact. The mountain of paperwork contained the expression of mother and son's hostility towards each other and their wish to control the other. It is typical of situations like this that there should be a cumbersome file and an anti-climax when it comes to actual contact. In this example the interview with the boy was flat and affect-less and the interview with the mother non-existent.

In court only practical reasons were put forward as to why the mother did not make the telephone call. The barrister and I became locked in a confrontation that mother and son could use to feel reassured that their vulnerabilities were recognised, because they could observe us playing them out. I felt that we had missed a valuable opportunity to process the projection, and grasp an understanding of the emotional rather than the practical needs of the family.

The loss of the coat was expertly handled by the clerk of the court, demonstrating just how valuable and important the formal structure of an institution can be, especially when under attack or suspicion. The suspicion which rested on the foreign professionals who had not returned, again illustrated projective identification at play, representing an opportunity to project neediness into another; in this case, the fantasy of a poor relation of the court who needed a coat and relinquished her integrity to acquire it. The projection was controlled at that point, in that the assembly felt uncomfortable and the court proceedings were delayed. Eventually, through the clerk's instructions, the projection is returned, reprocessed, in a form now acceptable to the mother and she could feel rightfully needy without her coat and reassured that her neediness had been recognised.

CONCLUSION

By using certain psychoanalytic concepts and their adaptation to institutional work, I have tried to illustrate how human nature persists and undermines defensively. In order to negotiate this as constructively as possible, the interactions, conscious and unconscious, intra-psychic and interpersonal, need to be recognised then understood and addressed. In the workings of the mind and in the interaction of individuals there is always the possibility that distortions will occur and that re-enactments will be performed. In fact these are to be hoped for as long as they are recognised, for they offer a therapeutic tool; they are doorways into the individuals' inner worlds. I hope that the circumstances of the boy and his mother will serve to stimulate thought especially in the area of their vulnerability and also our own vulnerabilities as professionals. I have purposefully referred rather anonymously to the boy and his mother to illustrate that whilst I had only fleeting contact with them, one interview with the boy and a glimpse of his mother in court, there were extremely strong feelings generated not only in me, but also in everyone concerned in the case. This was further illustrated by the size of the file. In the adversarial climate of the court system these feelings became rigidly polarised as an expression of how the mother tried to exercise control and how her son rebelled against her.

In my recent case, there has been the modern exchange of papers and the opportunity for discussion between experts before the polarising experience of the court. This 'best practice' of communication, preferably in an experts' meeting and in joint instructions, arises not from the Children Act itself but from the growing cooperation between the professions that has resulted. This has been an evolutionary process to which the first Dartington Interdisciplinary Conference made an important contribution.

REFERENCES

Davies, R (1992) Psychodynamic aspects of the professional network with forensic patients. (Unpublished) 1st International conference on forensic psychotherapy

Menzies-Lyth, I The development of the self in children in institutions in *Containing anxiety in institutions* (Free Association Books, 1985)

Ogden, T *Projective identification: psychoanalytic technique* (Aronson, New York, 1982)

Sandler, J, Dare C, Holder A *The patient and the analyst* (Karnac Books, 1982)

Segal, H *Introduction to the work of Melanie Klein* (Hogarth Press, 1973)

Searles, H *Collected papers on schizophrenia and related subjects* (Int Univ Press, New York, 1963)

Searles, H *Tactics and techniques in psychoanalytic psychotherapy* (Aronson, New York, 1975)

Williams, R (1992) *A concise guide to the Children Act 1989* (The Royal College of Psychiatrists, Gaskell, 1992)

Representing Asian Families in the Family Courts

*Khatun Sapnara**

INTRODUCTION

In order to understand the specific issues frequently raised in proceedings involving families from the Asian sub-continent, it is essential to have an appreciation of the cultural context within which such families live. Culture provides a context for behaviour, expression and development, as well as for problem formation and resolution. There are significant differences from the dominant culture in the UK. Culture is, of course, not monolithic and is subject to variation: individual differences from cultural norms can always be found. However, if no effort is made to understand culture generally, the family justice system is ill-equipped to evaluate where a family/individual fits in with regard to adherence to a given culture or where they transcend boundaries. My view is that this is appreciated best through a multi-disciplinary approach.

Over the last 15 years I have represented a large number of adults and children in the family courts who are from South Asian backgrounds, with roots in Bangladesh, India or Pakistan. Proceedings have included domestic violence injunctions, private and public law Children Act proceedings, as well as wardship, international child abduction and forced marriages.

THE ROLE OF THE FAMILY

The role of the family is central to South Asian communities where importance is attached to collectivistic rather than individualistic values.

This can be traced back to the class, caste, and social backgrounds in the country of origin. In the past, the migrants came here because there was 'pressure to emigrate'. The values they brought with them remain powerful influences today and can be observed in the structure and dynamics of families who come to court, irrespective of whether they are first, second or third generation immigrants. These values are often more pronounced within the communities settled here than can be seen in comparable families in the country of origin. There is a degree of inevitability about this, given a diaspora which commonly faces socio-economic disadvantage, compounded by experiences of racism. Consequently, the community seeks to harness its culture and faith for fear of dilution within the dominant culture, leading to a loss of identity.

The first generation of communities that settled here were frequently from poor socio-economic backgrounds that were largely rural with high rates of illiteracy, and therefore litigants from this background are usually publicly funded.

---

*   Khatun Sapnara is a committee member of the Family Law Bar Association and a member of the Family Justice Council. She was born in Bangladesh and speaks Sylheti and Bengali, and regularly undertakes diversity training of Judges on behalf of the Judicial Studies Board. She will be appointed as a Recorder this year.

Traditionally, land would be jointly owned by brothers or owned by the male head of household, and would be the main asset of the family in the country of origin. This gives rise to joint economic endeavour and interdependence that also establishes both an age and gender hierarchy. The father owns the land and power descends through the line of sons in age priority. The wives enjoy similar status according to whom they are married. Subservience to the point of exaggerated acts of deference may be expected of women and children. This could range from women covering their heads in the presence of the parents-in-law and elder brothers-in-law, to the touching of the feet of elders as a sign of respect.

Marriage (the emphasis being on arranged or, at the very least, marriages assisted and approved by the family) is central to family life in Asian communities. Traditionally, an Asian woman, whatever her faith, is literally and symbolically passed from her own family to that of her husband's family during the marriage process itself.

Paradoxically, within the confines of the home, matriarchy frequently reigns supreme and the female head of the household exercises significant power. Very often allegations of physical, verbal and psychological abuse by a wife against a husband involve members of the paternal family – often the paternal grandmother or aunt – as a perpetrator. If one accepts the notion that domestic violence represents abuse of power, then the power structures within Asian families provide fertile ground for such abuses.

It is very rare that a case involving Asian families is uncontested, or that a litigant fails to attend court or engage with the legal process, or indeed that he/she attends court alone. It is not just the issues between the parties that are at stake but also the honour of the respective families. A frequent problem for the practitioner is how to obtain direct instructions from the lay client. The risk is that instructions are refracted through the prism of the family and decisions are often made for the universal good of the family unit as a whole. Inevitably, with the increased numbers of witnesses and the need for interpreters, litigation is necessarily lengthy and therefore expensive. For example, it may be the case that a younger brother feels unable to make decisions in respect of his application for contact with his own children without recourse to discussion with his parents and elder brothers. The children's mother may feel similarly constrained by the fact that she is utterly dependent on family members for financial and practical assistance in facilitating any contact. She may have never travelled alone before and may not speak English, but is then expected by the court to travel considerable distances with young children on public transport to attend a contact centre. Frequently family members would have accessed legal services for such mothers, and they therefore actively participate in the process.

One of the most difficult aspects of representing women such as these is to obtain any instructions at all. They are often used to playing very passive roles in life and I have lost count of the number of occasions a lay client will simply say, 'Please do whatever you consider to be for the best'.

'IZZAT' AND 'SHARAM'

Key to understanding the dynamics of Asian families and communities are the concepts of '*izzat*' (honour) and '*sharam*' (shame).

Izzat is a patriarchal notion meaning reputation, respectability and status and any deviation from this has very serious consequences and implications, as an individual can be deemed to have broken ranks with the whole family and to have brought the family/caste group and even the entire community into disrepute.

Izzat extends to children honouring their parents and older siblings. There is, for example, an expectation that sons will marry and bring the wife to live in what would have been the family compound back in Bangladesh, Pakistan or India. Here that translates into living in the family home at worst, or next door, or otherwise within close geographical proximity. Even with second and third generations, it is not unusual to find that a frequent source of dispute upon family breakdown is the struggle to try and 'move out', with the young men caught between two very powerful and competing forces and causing a complete conflict of loyalties. Such pressure on the men is known to manifest itself in depression and substance abuse, together with allegations that the husband spends unacceptably long periods out of the home. Most families do not have the means to live in expansive accommodation and this inevitably leads to overcrowding and yet more pressure on relationships. These living arrangements are not always a result of economic necessity although there appears to be an increasing trend towards economically independent younger couples living in nuclear households, not without some cost to the relationship with the paternal family.

Sharam (shame) can mean modesty and is a highly prized virtue that many Asian women are encouraged to adopt. It can also refer to a state of disgrace. The inter-relationship between *izzat* and *sharam* can be understood thus: if honour serves to control behaviour then shame serves as a reminder of the consequences of dishonour.

Izzat is often maintained through control. Asian communities are closely-knit and hence concepts of shame and honour take on extra significance when it is within this context that issues such as domestic violence, forced marriage and so–called 'honour killings' are viewed. Such actions – however misguided, wrong or reprehensible – are seen as a method of mitigating or redeeming shame. Upholding family honour may be borne of practical imperatives eg to avoid social ostracism. These communities are often self-regulating, with employment and financial arrangements dependent on being an integral part of the community. Consider the impact on younger, unmarried daughters whose prospects will be severely diminished by association with actions of an older sister that are considered disreputable. There have been numerous instances where this has resulted in the expeditious divorce of another sister (often where siblings have married within the same families, sometimes other cousins) simply as punishment for the sins of the errant sibling.

I have had experience of interpreters (male and female) at court applying pressure on women who have initiated proceedings, to settle matters and reconcile with the husband rather than air the family's dirty laundry in public and thereby bring shame and dishonour on their community in general. Formal accreditation of interpreters may go someway towards addressing such difficulties and in reducing costs that are incurred as a result of proceedings being lengthened by the quality of interpreters available, in what is a specialised area of law.

In many cases before the courts, attempts are made to bring the credibility of an individual into question by reference to the lack of support they have from their own family members who choose to give evidence in favour of the other party. There is need to exercise caution in such situations, as often the only way of redeeming the perceived shame – for example a woman leaving the family home and initiating divorce/injunction/private law proceedings – is for the family to demonstrably distance itself from the individual in order to attempt to mitigate/redeem the shame. To condone would be to compound the shame.

Bearing in mind the consequences of shame, it is very rare to obtain admissions of wrongdoing from any party to litigation. Issues of denial present a particular problem for courts dealing with South Asian families, as I will discuss later.

In a case that I appeared in, the only way in which the Muslim Bangladeshi mother could be rehabilitated into her family and community after marrying a Sikh man (whom I was representing), was by ensuring that the name of her child – which readily identified him as Sikh

– was changed to a Muslim one. During her evidence she claimed that she had not known the father was Sikh at the time that she married him and that he had actively deceived her. This was not a matter requiring adjudication but my feeling was that she had had to present the facts in this way in order to minimise her culpability in the eyes of her family. It is not an uncommon device used by women who have entered what are considered to be 'inappropriate' relationships, to say that they were in some way forced to do so.

FAMILY BREAKDOWN

Given the consequences for individuals and the number of other people immediately affected, issues of family breakdown are extremely significant and divorce proceedings are not entered into lightly. It is almost never the case that marriages end amicably or by mutual consent.

Experience suggests that there is often a precipitating factor, which will frequently be domestic violence, involving the woman (and sometimes children) as the direct victims of physical harm. Whilst the emotional and psychological harm to children that arises out of witnessing or hearing domestic violence is widely recognised in the family justice system, these are concepts that have not yet been fully appreciated within Asian communities, (although this could also be said of society at large, albeit to a lesser extent). Similarly the well-documented reasons why women stay in violent marriages/relationships, such as children and economic necessity, apply equally across race and class divides. However, the problems are magnified in the case of Asian women, who may face social isolation as a result of rejection by families and communities subsequent to their decisions and actions.

The Asian women I represent are often expected to remain within the home and serve the needs of all three generations living there. Control frequently extends to limiting their interaction with the outside world, and often the only time a woman may be free to be outside the home un-chaperoned, is on a visit to the doctor or to collect the children from school. When such women flee an abusive household or relationship, it is often with direct and active assistance from outsiders such as family GPs and schoolteachers.

The other possibility is where the woman's own family makes a rare visit with the specific intention of taking her back. In such dramatic and urgent situations, women are frequently forced to leave children behind. Courts can be slow to order the return of the children to the mother's care, citing the continuity of familiar surroundings (especially if the mother is living in temporary accommodation) and care by family members who have assisted in rearing the children, as adequate reasons for maintaining the status quo of living arrangements. Insufficient regard seems to be given to the primary care hitherto provided by the mother, and the effect on a child's emotional welfare arising out of relentless, vociferous denigration of the mother in the child's presence. Whist this may be common enough in other cases, the number of people reinforcing these derogatory views, in the child's own home, compounds the problem of alienation.

The work of voluntary women's organisations, and in particular those created to assist Asian and other minority women in this field, is invaluable. They provide safe accommodation for women and children, help in accessing appropriate legal services, provide childcare and interpreters and generally support, assist and empower women towards an independent life.

CASE EXAMPLE

I recall appearing on an emergency injunction application whilst still in pupillage. The lay client was a Pakistani woman in her mid-twenties with three children under four years old. She appeared very tired and much older than her years and she and the children were poorly and inadequately dressed, dirty and dishevelled.

Her parents had arranged her marriage to her cousin. She had recently arrived from Pakistan with the children, to live with him in a privately owned flat. She was made to remain in one small room with her children all day, whilst he regularly brought home a number of different women with whom he had sexual relations in the next room. She was expected to cook and clean for him and his 'guests' and to attend to their every need. He was frequently absent from the home, leaving her locked in with little or no provisions. When he was at home she would be abused and beaten on a regular basis. She arrived at court having managed to escape the home during a particularly savage beating when she sustained a serious injury. She had run screaming out onto the street. The police were called and put her in touch with a women's organisation. She had no family or friends she could turn to and spoke virtually no English.

I battled with the judge to obtain an order ousting him from the home, in addition to the protective orders he readily granted. The clerk from the solicitor's office disappeared after the hearing, leaving the woman stranded and unable to get back to the refuge. I finished my other hearing and travelled with her, back to surroundings in which she was familiar and confident. I went home and wept tears of frustration, certain in my belief that despite having obtained a bit of paper with an injunction she could not even read, she would still be powerless to change much about the wretched circumstances of her life.

I was unable to represent her further owing to other commitments. About six months later I was in Chambers one evening when my clerk informed me that someone wanted to see me urgently. I was met by a very attractive woman, smiling at me. I did not recognise her but it was the same woman I had represented. She had just finished a conference with a colleague with regard to divorce proceedings. The transformation was incredible. She had moved to her own property, learned to speak English and to drive.

To me that case represents an object lesson in the power of the legal system to change people's lives profoundly. Obtaining that injunction represented a significant first step on the road to her empowerment and emancipation. It provided a very valuable lesson, which I am grateful to have received at the very outset of my practice.

ISSUES ARISING IN PRACTICE

I have encountered a number of cases where the paternal family worked actively to disable a mother from caring for her own children. The paternal grandmother would insist on feeding the children (food prepared by the mother) and play with them while the mother undertook household chores. Food plays a profound role in notions of motherhood for Asians from a background where, historically, it may have been a scarce commodity. Food and the feeding of a child by its mother, holds a particular symbolic and emotional significance. Sometimes it is the only way a mother is able to physically demonstrate love and affection. It is not unusual to see allegations of maltreatment that include the withholding or rationing of food to a woman by the paternal family.

This may go some way towards explaining why so many issues, relating to the provision and consumption of food during contact visits, arise in care proceedings. The parents wish to prepare traditional food and to feed this to their children. Social workers, when supervising or observing contact will frequently criticise the quantity of food brought and the over-emphasis on feeding the children. Sometimes it is said that the children have come to prefer western food as a result of being in a culturally inappropriate placement for a lengthy period. The danger is that attempts to feed are often viewed as bad parenting, without an understanding of why such problems arose in the first place.

The lack of Asian foster carers and adopters means that children are frequently left in culturally inappropriate placements. In such situations, serious consideration needs to be given as to how to facilitate competence in their mother tongue. Can it ever really be reasonable to say that resources do not allow for the routine provision of interpreters at contact? Local authorities regularly fail to provide interpreters in such situations. When parents slip into their own language during supervised contact they too often experience admonishment from the contact supervisor and arouse suspicion as to what it was they were seeking to communicate to their children. There are some ways of speaking with affection and some terms of endearment that simply do not translate into English: it is entirely artificial to expect parents to behave otherwise in such circumstances, quite apart from the wish to ensure their children speak their language.

The important status of marriage means a stigma is still attached to divorce. As has already been mentioned, it is not a step taken lightly. Therefore when an Asian woman leaves the marital home it raises questions in the community about why she left. An inability to accept any blame for the breakdown of the marriage by the husband and his family, often gives rise to a number of common allegations levelled against the woman in order to preserve their family honour, at the wife's cost.

For example, it might be contended that she was a bad wife/mother/daughter-in-law, lacking in a sense of duty, or that she was unduly influenced by others such as family members still aggrieved over issues relating to the dowry, or by people from other communities or faiths: it might be suggested that she was acting in an involuntary manner, or even that she had been the victim of black magic. It is frequently alleged that the woman is suffering from a mental illness, or arguably most injurious of all in terms of damage to her '*izzat*', that she had formed a relationship with another man. This is an easy accusation to make and a difficult one to refute. In the rare case where this is part of the reason for leaving the home, it is extremely unusual for this to be admitted because of the serious social consequences. This should not necessarily taint credibility in other areas of the evidence.

Mental health

Statistics show that Asian women, as a demographic statistic, suffer a disproportionately high incidence of mental health problems. Research indicates that one in three Asian women suffers from problems such as depression and self-harm.

In their country of origin women's daily lives would be very different to their experience here. They would have been free to socialise, safe in the company of other women in their communities, and in rural areas they would have had access to open areas. Consider the impact on a woman of leaving family and homeland behind, moving to an inclement climate and being virtually locked up in overcrowded, poor, inadequate housing with very limited social life. The incidence of depression is not surprising and it is little wonder that the statistics are so high.

Issues of mental health arise in both public and private law proceedings. For second and third generation women the social and psychological pressures and conflicts between duty to the family, and their individual needs and desires can severely effect their functioning. Mental health problems are frequently cited as a reason to deny a mother residence of children, even where it is difficult to establish that anyone other than the mother was the primary carer, given the clearly defined gender roles within Asian households.

The implications for the family justice system, which arise out of issues relating to mental health, are that children are sometimes neglected over a lengthy period requiring the deployment of social services resources and possibly resulting in care proceedings. Expert assessments by psychiatrists/psychologists are often necessary in both private and public law proceedings.

Problems arise in representation, not just as a result of the need to interpret unfamiliar terms such as sexual abuse (there simply is no direct translation available in most Asian languages), but also in respect of concepts such as counselling and therapy. The latter are a cultural anathema. The prospect of discussing intimate personal details with third parties is commonly viewed with horror and bewilderment. In care proceedings significant emphasis is placed on the need to engage with such services before it is deemed safe for children to return to the family home, yet these are 'pre-Oprah Winfrey' societies where an intellectual link is not made between life experiences and later behaviour.

I recall a case where I represented a Sikh woman who was raised in England from a very young age and spoke English fluently with a cockney accent. During contact/residence proceedings it emerged that the mother had an older daughter aged 18 who was not the subject of proceedings. There had been no reference to this daughter in the papers. It transpired that this daughter had, literally, been taken by the paternal family and given to a paternal aunt to raise, as she had been unable to have children of her own. The mother explained to me that although unhappy about this, she had acquiesced to the arrangement as she felt she had little choice in the matter. The mother experienced other difficulties with the father and the extended paternal family, which resulted in this daughter growing up completely estranged from her mother, even though she lived only a few streets away.

Frequently the family pressures faced by young Asian men and women will result in forced marriages. I use the term forced marriage to include subtle but intense emotional, psychological and financial pressure in order to obtain 'consent' in 'arranged marriages'. (I use that term not in the legal sense, where the test is that the factors operating upon the individual must be so great that his/her will must be overborne in order to obtain nullity on the grounds of duress.) Many young people go along with the marriage out of a sense of duty, the nature of which is not readily understood by western observers who point out that these individuals may be educated here and integrated into society.

Witchcraft

Belief in witchcraft or 'black magic' is fairly widespread in Asian communities and is referred to as '*jadoo-thuna*'. This issue crops up frequently in both private and public law proceedings. I represented the guardian in contact/residence proceedings, which involved an Indian Muslim mother, 'S'. Her marriage had collapsed and she had the care of three children; two girls (aged nearly 16 and therefore considered to be of marriageable age) and a boy. The father failed to keep in contact with his children after separating from 'S'. She found the breakdown of the marriage and her efforts to bring up her three children as a single mother both stressful and highly traumatic. She suffered episodes of severe depressive illness and developed an almost paranoid fear that the authorities might separate her from her children.

She visited a Pir (an Islamic mystical seer) with her children on a visit back home. This is quite usual amongst those suffering from severe personal difficulties. It was done to obtain a diagnosis as to why she was suffering from repeated bouts of depression, and encountering so many personal difficulties. The Pir made a diagnosis that all S's troubles had come about because of the ill will of her former husband and mother-in-law, who had used black magic to bring adversity on her deliberately. A remedy was provided by way of a *taweez* (protective amulet), which S was instructed to wear at all times to keep the evil being directed at her at bay.

Thereafter she refused to allow the children to receive, even touch, any form of communication from the father by way of letters, cards and gifts believing that *jadoo-thuna* may have been inserted into anything he or his mother may have touched.

In assessing the mother's motives for opposing contact and her credibility as a witness it would have been easy to simply treat this mother as yet another parent wilfully obstructing contact unreasonably. On a subjective analysis, if those views were genuinely held and she was the children's primary carer, acting in what she considered to be her children's best interests, what would the right outcome have been? Should such beliefs be regarded as little more than examples of culturally conditioned superstitious paranoia and therefore discarded as irrelevant to the substantive issues facing the court? Or should we be looking for assistance that might be provided by other disciplines?

On behalf of the guardian, a consultant anthropologist was instructed to assist the court and to elucidate those aspects of this family's religious, social and cultural behaviour that might potentially be misread by an observer who was unfamiliar with their precise character and contents. His overall opinion was that whilst many 'rationally oriented westerner observers' might instantly dismiss the mother's ideas, actually they might have some concrete empirical substance.

Analysing the evidence he concluded that the story of *jadoo* and the defence against its consequences by the use of *taweez*, provided 'a metaphorical vehicle' for expressing the far from unrealistic fear that these proceedings had been brought by the father and encouraged by his mother, in an effort to ensure that they could gain access to the children and thereby ensure that the girls' marriages were arranged to their father's advantage rather than their mother's. He was able to confirm on the basis of his professional experience, that such manoeuvres are far from unusual in South Asian contexts. It is equally commonplace for those who fear that others are seeking to disadvantage their future, to express their fears in occult malfeasance such as witchcraft. Hence there was some accuracy in S's statement that 'all Muslims believe in a holy man and most believe in black magic'.

These ideas have direct behavioural consequences. The anthropologist said, 'Accusations of black magic are best understood not as an indication of superstition, but rather of a telling indicator of some very real and deep-seated social tensions'.

The father had alleged that during the marriage his wife 'would leave the home naked, that she would throw his clothes out of the house, and that she talked of ghosts coming to talk to her every night, telling her to do such things'.

Allowing for a degree of exaggeration on the father's part, the anthropologist explained that there was no reason to assume that such behaviour or beliefs should be regarded as a conclusive indication of psychosis on S's part. Rather than a psychological disturbance per se, such episodes of spirit possession should be viewed as a strategic means of putting the person (or persons) who have made their life difficult under severe pressure, and are not unusual amongst distressed young South Asian brides.

A psychiatrist's assessment report was made available to the court. It concluded that the mother's mental health, stabilised by her current medication, did not interfere with her care of her children. The anthropologist queried whether a diagnosis in the past of psychotic depression was accurate. His view was that 'psychiatrists can too easily make a diagnosis of psychosis when dealing with patients with whom they cannot communicate directly in their own tongue, and with whose cultural, social and religious conventions they are unfamiliar'. (This is a concern often expressed by lawyers in respect of other areas of expert assessment, such as psychometric testing of personalities). In raising this matter, the anthropologist was not seeking to contest the view that S had experienced periods of severe psychological stress, 'but only to indicate that there are good reasons to suppose that the source of her problems may well have been as much exogenous as endogenous'.

The children complained of a lack of presents from the father over the years, and this highlighted another area of cultural divergence. It was explained that this was entirely in keeping with South Asian cultural conventions in which birthdays are not a significant occasion for gift giving. By contrast, on return from travel abroad there would be an expectation of gifts and the father's failure to comply with this expectation was, in the cultural context, far more blameworthy.

SELF-REGULATING COMMUNITIES V FAMILY JUSTICE COURTS

As I have already mentioned, Asian communities are often self-regulating. This extends to arrangements in respect of loans and employment as well as models of alternative dispute resolution for family problems. It is quite usual to see community elders intervening in marriage breakdown by conducting forms of mediation, counselling and arbitration. The latter involves hearing both parties, along with their families and/or representatives, in a process to determine fault in respect of the conduct during the marriage, and may include division of assets and even custody and contact arrangements in respect of children. The only thing that binds the parties is their *izzat* in publicly expressing their consent. Frequently these processes operate in tandem with family court proceedings and inevitably impact upon them.

It is important to note that these communities are not familiar with notions of state intervention in family life. In their countries of origin there is no equivalent to child protection agencies such as social services. The welfare of children is subordinate to the rights of adults, and therefore parents have real difficulties in understanding why their children were removed at all.

Apart from neglect, a common reason for Asian children being received into care is excessive or inappropriate chastisement. Issues of control, shame and honour all play their part, together with the cultural and generational conflicts between children and their parents. On behalf of parents in care proceedings it is often conceded that the 'threshold criteria' is met because, at the very least, there is usually compelling evidence to suggest the child has experienced such chastisement in a harmful way. Hence, even if such concession is not forthcoming, it is likely that the court will find the 'threshold criteria' is met in any event.

Whether or not there should be reunification of a family causes considerable problems. For that to happen, the received wisdom is that there needs to be acknowledgment and acceptance that there have been difficulties. The capacity to change harmful parenting practices should be considered possible by the professionals involved. Although issues of denial by parents in public law cases are common to cases across all cultures, they appear to be particularly pronounced in Asian families. An extreme example was a case in which parents maintained that children (who were likely to have been their nephews) were their own, in the face of DNA evidence to the contrary.

In another case, despite overwhelming evidence and judicial findings of excessive physical chastisement confirmed by all the children, a father consistently refused to acknowledge that he had behaved inappropriately. Yet the relationship with the children had improved dramatically (so much so that two of the older children had returned home) and the quality of contact with the three younger children still in foster placement was very good. Nevertheless, the father's refusal to acknowledge past failings resulted in the court approving the final care plan for adoption. Is there not an alternative way of dealing with cases that involve such extreme denials? I do not have any answers, but given that culturally appropriate placements are hard to come by, it must be an issue worth addressing.

The quality and extent of denial in Asian families probably has multiple causes. My view is that it is a mix of issues, which include shame and honour considerations, a suspicion of authorities arising from perceptions of institutional and state corruption in the countries of origin, and an overwhelming belief that divine powers will overcome any difficulties. At the same time there is concern about a tendency to return Asian children home, despite the existence of continuing risk, because of the difficulty and cost involved of finding a home for what are often large sibling groups that require significant resources.

CONCLUSION

A fundamental principle of our legal system is that justice has to be done and seen to be done. If little or no regard is paid to matters of cultural difference we run the risk not only of failing to address the real issues in a case and thereby reaching the wrong conclusions, but also of alienating those who come before the courts expecting justice. If litigants feel they have not been afforded a fair hearing, experience teaches us that they are far less likely to accept the resulting decisions.

The Language of Law and the Nature of Families

*Katherine Gieve**

I wish to explore the way in which legal language in family law restricts and even distorts our thoughts about parents and children, and the way in which this is in contrast to our understanding of families from a psychological point of view. There is still a great gulf between our thoughts about relationships and family life in psychodynamic terms and in legal terms.

The last decade has brought a greater awareness of the importance of psychological understanding and we are moving towards a better structure for the manner in which psychological contributions are made when deciding children's futures. However, it is also a decade in which social work practice and the narrative of the court remain far distant from a psychological view.

MUTUALITY AND THE NEED OF PARENTS

My key concern is the way in which parents and children are put into two distinct categories, almost as if they were separate species; where one, the older, has responsibilities towards the younger and where the pleasure the parent takes in the child is omitted. It seems that the need the parent has for the child, rather than being an essential part of a benevolent relationship, is suspect. The formulation, 'what is in the best interests of the child', cannot allow the description of anything that might be an expression of the desire and need of the parent/s.

The courts deal with extreme cases and it may be that only by this stark differentiation between children's needs and those of the parents, that decisions can be made and disasters be avoided. But I am concerned by the narrowness of thinking which arises from this language, denuding the complex interrelationships between parents and children that are the source of parental passion and children's survival.

Children's survival is assured because they delight their parents and their parents feel passion for them. Of course children are not always delightful and parents must go beyond their own pleasure in caring for them – they must take responsibility for them and must be selfless in caring for them. But at the core, the relationship between parents and children survives because

---

* Katherine Gieve is a solicitor and head of her firm's family department. She specialises in cases concerning children, both public and private law cases, concerning medical treatment, adoption and declarations of parentage, and represents both children and parents in surrogacy cases. She takes abduction cases for the Central Authority. She is a member of the Family Justice Council and chairs the Children and Safeguarding Committee. She is a member of the Law Society Children Panel, a member (and former chair) of Resolution Children Committee, and a member of the ALC. She sits on the Nuffield Foundation committee on Child Protection and Family Justice. She lectures on children law. She published *Balancing Acts on Being a Mother* Virago 1989.

it is one of mutuality and mutual satisfaction: it is not at root a relationship of obligation and altruism. Yet the notion of mutuality, delight and passion is almost entirely missing from the language of social work and the courts.

I acknowledge the pressure and anxiety experienced by social workers, who are heavily criticised if they make the wrong decision and leave a child with dangerous parents. But I suggest that it must be possible to develop a language and ways of thinking about parents and their children, which does not leave children at risk and yet simultaneously acknowledges the connection between the child and his/her parents as though they are part of the same world. These descriptions are present in a psychological analysis of a family, but are often lost when that is translated into care planning and a social work analysis.

Why am I worried?

Decisions by social workers are made as though parents and children are separable in a way that they are not. Often, in their concern to focus on the needs of the child, they lose sight of the role of the parent in protecting and caring for the child. There is only limited recognition of the fact that the distress of the parent can endanger the well-being of the child, and decisions are referable to the needs of the child without noting the connection.

Example

A child is removed to foster care and there is an evaluation made of the extent of contact with the parent. That evaluation looks at the child's need for contact with the parent and not at the parent's need; yet the parent who suffers grief and loss also has needs. Their grief and anxiety will in turn affect their well-being and their capacity to care for their children. The bond between parents and children is one of mutuality – not just the child bonding with the parents. It goes in both directions. Winnicott's concept and description of the nursing pair is scarcely given lip service. As a consequence, decisions are made during the process of court proceedings that may damage children, paradoxically in the interests of keeping them safe.

There is sometimes a lack of compassion and a failure to appreciate the importance of support needed by the parents, in order that they can care both for their children and for themselves. Whilst I accept that the welfare of the child should be paramount, at present it seems to me that social work decisions and court orders often do not reflect the symbiotic nature of the relationship between parents and children. If children's welfare is to be served, the psychological needs of parents cannot be forgotten. It is not easy for parents to separate what they do for their children from what they do for themselves. The question 'is this mother/father capable of putting their child's needs before their own?' is a familiar and frequent one. I suggest that the answer is more complex than we generally allow for.

A mother when asked, 'why do you think your child should come back and live with you?' might answer, 'because I love to read her stories at bedtime and watch her when she goes to sleep'. The mother is reflecting on her own needs and desires and not the child's. But it is this pleasure that a parent takes in her child which provides the enduring substance in the relationship.

Example

A 17-day-old baby with fractures is removed from the family home to a foster home. There is no evidence as to the cause of the fractures and no other concerns about the care of the baby. The mother is desolate and by the time of the final hearing nine months later, which establishes that the mother has not harmed the baby, she is profoundly depressed and in need of psychological help. The baby cannot be returned to her without extensive support.

A view that is alive to both the protagonists in the mother/child relationship, would be more open to maintaining the relationship between them in supervised accommodation rather than assuming the baby should be removed. The assessment of risk needs to be subtler than it is at present in my experience, and needs to balance the psychological risks both to the parent and the child of a separation.

RECIPROCITY

Children, in the language of the courts, are the objects of adult attention and obligation; they are subjects in their own expressions of wishes and feelings and in discussion about children's rights. We are more cautious in seeing them as people with their own obligations to others. Thus again they are thought of in a separate category: adults have obligations to children but not vice versa. Yet part of the upbringing of a child in ordinary life is to help them learn about their obligations to others and to take responsibility in the proper measure for their age. Whilst it is important to protect children from having too great a responsibility and particularly from taking care of their parents rather than the other way around, we should be less afraid of children's obligations and the notion of reciprocity. It is in part the obligation for others which roots you in the world. It is an advantage in life to have a grandmother for whom you, as a child or young person, take out the rubbish or change the light bulb – it is an aspect of belonging in a community of which many children in care are deprived.

Example

A boy's parents are dead and he cannot, for good reason, be cared for by his aunts who would like to look after him. The aunts wish to maintain their relationship with him through presents and correspondence. This is not allowed on the basis that the boy should not be burdened with a relationship of obligation to his aunts – he should be free of obligations to others.

Our language of children law has developed historically in response to the exploitation of children and to a culture in which parents (fathers) had rights over their children, and in which they were seen as possessions. Nevertheless, in developing the modern law we need to be sure that we are not too narrow in the description and understanding of relationships. To lose the notion of reciprocity between children and adults is a serious deprivation.

CHILDREN WHO HARM OTHER CHILDREN

The conceptual division between adults and children in the way I have described brings with it another hazard, which is the difficulty in acknowledging when children have done something wrong. Again, in every day life we recognise that children have dark thoughts and that they can be jealous and angry and do spiteful and mean things. But in the framework of the court they have become the recipients of good and bad acts by adults rather than actors themselves, with human feelings albeit still immature. I grant that it may be more usual for parents to harm children and then blame siblings, but the way we think about adults and children restricts our understanding of what is possible.

Example

A case concerned a small baby with a bilateral skull fracture. A three-year-old was said by members of the family to have been in the room with the baby when she was found injured. However, neither the social workers nor the medical experts could contemplate an injury of this kind being caused by another child, so that the possibility was not properly investigated until shortly before the final hearing and then during the hearing itself. The evidence showed without doubt that the three-year-old had caused the injuries. The mother was reunited with the baby after considerable time apart.

CHILDREN'S RIGHTS

The development of children's rights is an important step in the protection of children and in the recognition of children as individuals, rather than the possessions of their parents. There is legal debate as to how far the recognition of children's rights has genuinely moved forward (see, for example, Jane Fortin's article 'Children's rights – substance or spin' [2006] Fam Law 759 (September)). There has been relatively little debate about how a rights-based analysis fits with the inter-relationship between parents and children and the child's right to dependency. We need a greater dialogue in this field with colleagues from the psychological professions.

Within families where parents are able to be parents together, the movement from parental authority to a young person's autonomy is a gradual and complex development that varies from culture to culture, from household to household, from parent to parent and from child to child. Parents maintain boundaries, exert control, and use their authority to protect their children in very variable ways. Children do not generally accept authority because it is backed by force; they accept authority because it is in the order of things. On the other hand parents have to be cautious in making demands of a child that they know s/he both can and will resist. From a very young age there are negotiations and compromises to be made on both sides, with toddlers and teenagers affording particularly testing times when the terms of the relationship are in a state of flux.

How do children's rights fit into this complex picture? Are there disadvantages for children in the encapsulation of their rights? How do rights fit in with the expectation that parents will provide their children with firm boundaries – which is a commonplace of good parental care?

Example

Has this 13-year-old boy seen a doctor for his 'looked after' medical? No, he does not give his consent and we must respect his wishes and feelings.

A 13-year-old boy, being well looked after by his parents, would not generally refuse a necessary visit to the doctor. He would probably go and not resist the implied authority or care – he would not consider his right to object. This is not because his parents were oppressive and did not respect him, but because they took responsibility for aspects of his care that he did not challenge. I believe that there is a risk that children in public care will not be looked after in an authoritative way out of a misplaced respect for rights. Whilst the recognition of rights is an important element of the protection of children, we need to develop parental care simultaneously so that children are not uncared for.

The language of the rights of children when set against adult authority can make it very difficult to look after children, especially if they are moved from one environment to another. Whilst I recognise the importance of that language in enabling children to protect themselves from exploitation and abuse (and this is true both in care and within families), it is difficult to match it with the subtlety and ambiguity of family relationships. A teenager who has been in care learns the language of rights and may return home to assert them. 'You cannot tell me what to do', can make the child ungovernable and thus vulnerable.

The language of children's rights has been developed out of a need to recognise the position of children and to put them on the map of independent entitlement; yet it has not come with a full discussion of the impact on inter-generational relationships or of children's reciprocal obligations.

The recognition of rights (and wishes and feelings) has a particularly important part to play for children whose parents are separated. Where there is a dispute between parents about where a child should live, or whether or when s/he should see the parent with whom s/he does not live, the welfare checklist[1] has the child's wishes and feelings at number one on the list. There is also a right for a child[2] to be 'provided the opportunity to be heard in any judicial and administrative proceedings affecting the child, either directly, or through a representative or appropriate body'. The kinds of freedoms brought to children by these measures (when they are working effectively) also bring a price. However clearly children are told that their wishes are not determinative of the decision, they often feel a great deal of responsibility. Sometimes they feel entitled and are liberated by the sense that their voice is heard, but sometimes they are burdened. The choices made by young people in their early teens often are determinative of the decision made – on the basis that otherwise they will vote with their feet. Children living in families where the parents cooperate in decision-making, by contrast, would not be expected to make such major decisions at a young age.

THE WAY FORWARD IN INTERDISCIPLINARY THINKING

During the last decade, legal practitioners have worked harder to ask the right questions, at the right time, of colleagues in the psychological professions. Through their expert evidence we have asked the courts to make decisions based on more comprehensive evidence. However, in my view that evidence is slotted in to a somewhat rigid view of adults and children in their separate categories, which does not do justice to the complexity of family relationships and in some cases leads to decisions being made that are not in the interests of children. I would like to see a greater dialogue between the legal and psychological professions concerning the way in which we talk about adults and children. I think that the entitlement to rights and the need for dependence need not compete and can work together compatibly. I hope that such a dialogue would help to protect children from the harm that is sometimes caused by the very court proceedings which are designed for their benefit.

REFERENCES

Middlemore MP *The Nursing Couple* (London, Hamish Hamilton, 1941)

Winnicott DW (1959) in *Psychoanalytic Explorations* (London, H Karnac Ltd, 1989)

---

[1] Children Act 1989, s 1.
[2] UNCRC, Art 12(2).

SECTION 3

Henry Brown, a solicitor, questions the appropriateness of the legal process for some cases and offers detailed thoughts on mediation and the possibilities it offers.

Christopher Richards, also a mediator, explains how he works and uses a solution-focused approach in an endeavour to bring couples to a state of 'reasonableness' rather than confrontation.

Michael Leadbetter, a social worker, questions the place and future role of social workers and social services in the family courts. He describes social services as being in a state of confusion as they are required to support parents and monitor and protect children, yet they lack the resources and personnel to fulfil these roles.

Visions of Excellence – Law, Healing and Humanity

*Henry Brown**

The theme of this paper, 'Visions of Excellence', relates to what we all aspire to achieve in our work as professionals; but I am not sure that 'excellence' has a clear meaning in the context of marriage breakdown and family work and that is what I would like to examine.

I will consider some random and arbitrary aspects of excellence in six propositions specifically in relation to marriage breakdown and family law and practice.

PROPOSITION NO 1: FAMILY PRACTITIONERS ARE, BY AND LARGE, NOT BRAIN SURGEONS

I realised some time ago that as a lawyer in the commercial field it was not good enough simply to say to clients 'I think you have about a 60% prospect of success' without any proper analysis or detail. Consequently, I became involved in devising a risk analysis questionnaire for commercial mediation that helps parties to assess their level of risk in litigating, not just on the basis of the legal risk, but having regard to all the wider issues that apply to each side. I am sure that something similar could be a valuable tool in family work.

Someone requiring brain surgery would not be satisfied with the surgeon saying: 'My instinct tells me that you have about a 30% prospect of survival'. They would want to have scans taken and a detailed explanation of what was involved. They would want to know how to improve their prospects of survival, what the alternative options were, and to have proper analyses of those alternatives. Apart from the difference in the life-threatening implications of brain surgery, it seems to me that another main difference from family law lies in the fact that there is a much greater element of objectivity in assessing brain function and malfunction than there is in assessing family breakdown and outcomes.

Family work is so complex and has so many uncertainties and imponderables that assessing excellence in that context is difficult to objectify in advance. We can look at something that was done and consider whether it was excellent, but it is much harder to lay down hard and fast rules as to what constitutes excellence when looking ahead generally.

---

* This paper is adapted from the Inaugural Henry Brown Lecture given in Bath on 16 September 2006.
Henry Brown qualified as a lawyer was admitted as an attorney and notary public in South Africa in 1962 and as an English solicitor in 1975. He has worked as a mediator and a mediation trainer in both the civil-commercial and family fields. He was a member of the original training faculty of CEDR (the Centre for Effective Dispute Resolution) and has trained mediators for the ADR Group. He co-founded the Family Mediators Association (of which he is a Vice-President) and co-established the mediation training programme of Resolution (formerly the Solicitors Family Law Association). He holds a Certificate in the Fundamentals of Psychotherapy and Counselling.

Excellence is rather like Lord Justice Scrutton's reference to the definition of an elephant: 'I may not be able to define an elephant, but I know one when I see it'. We may not be able to define excellence with precision, but we know it when we see it. As individuals we see through different eyes and different perspectives and we do not have scans or objective criteria to help us identify excellence in specific cases.

Some aspects of excellence can be objectively assessed. The Law Society has a 'Client Care/Practice Excellence' training package for practice management and a quality mark 'Lexcel' which aims at 'standards of excellence in areas such as client care, case management and risk management'. However, the mark does not purport to address the quality of lawyering, because here you enter a more complex and subjective area.

How does one identify excellence when one enters the area of marriage breakdown, with its range of potential issues concerning status, children, property, finance, living standards and future security, together with the complexities of adults' and children's needs, both material and emotional? Not only does every situation have its own circumstances and needs, but every client brings his or her own 'world view'.

Some years ago, I overheard a snatch of a conversation between a rather exasperated mother and her young son. The mother said to him: 'Why must you always argue about everything?' to which he replied: 'I'm not arguing, I'm only telling the truth'. That exchange encapsulates many of the issues faced by family practitioners, whether lawyers, counsellors, mediators or judges: that absolute belief in one's own truth, whether expressed in the law office, the mediation room, the court or dressed as Batman at the top of Tower Bridge.

Who is to judge what constitutes excellence? The client, or the client's partner who may have quite a contrary view? Or the children of the family if they could be consulted about the way their parents and the lawyers handled the situation? Or the lawyers themselves? Or other family professionals from a distance? The media would probably base their judgement on the level of capital settlement.

Excellence may mean no more than making the best of very difficult and challenging circumstances, and may come in many different shapes and forms. Which takes us to:

PROPOSITION NO 2: EXCELLENCE DOES NOT PRECLUDE PARADOX, UNCERTAINTY OR IMPERFECTION

This proposition is about not putting 'excellence' into some kind of ivory tower, when it is often a product of moving through uncertain and murky territory, going for the best you can even when you know that it is not absolutely right, or that, like Alice through the Looking Glass, you may have to go in the opposite direction to find what you are looking for.

Robert Benjamin, an American mediator, writes extensively about the frailties, oddities and paradoxes inherent in working as a family mediator. He refers to the paradox in negotiation that arises in that negotiators need to be authentic but sometimes also have to appear to be authentic when they are not. Consequently, he says, authenticity, while anchored in genuine integrity, might at times be part ruse.[1]

---

[1]   'The authenticity requirement and the necessity for deception in negotiation: the paradox' by Robert Benjamin, May 2002 at www.mediate.com.

This fits in with what Lax & Sebenius say in their book, *The Manager as Negotiator*.[2] They believe that even when people adopt a co-operative problem-solving approach, they may well still aim to achieve the best outcome for themselves within this different mode of negotiating, and that there is an 'essential tension' between competitive and problem-solving approaches.

Far from ivory-towering mediation, Robert Benjamin[3] has distilled four attributes of the 'natural mediator': confused, voyeuristic, compulsive and marginal.

'Confusion', he says, allows a mediator to understand that there are no easy answers, that heroes can be scoundrels, and victims can be perpetrators, and vice versa; that it is seldom easy or clear.

The second is 'voyeurism' which he defines as a fascination with how human beings engage with each other, construct their realities, and pursue their intimate relationships. This attribute allows the mediator a greater ability to resist being judgemental, knowing that 'there but for the grace of God, go I'.

The third attribute of the natural mediator he says is 'compulsiveness'; an obsessive working at the details in order to bring order out of chaos.

The fourth is to be 'marginal', on the fringe – less concerned about what is right, than with what will settle a dispute in the present circumstance. It means, he says, 'letting go of attachments to what life should be in a perfect world'.

US mediator Lenard Marlow defines mediation as 'an imperfect procedure that employs an imperfect third person to help two imperfect people reach an imperfect agreement in an imperfect world'.[4] Marlow's notion of imperfection accurately describes the conditions that we commonly work under in helping to create something reasonable if imperfect out of something that may be unclear, paradoxical, imperfect and very often messy. Excellence is carved out of this very hard stone.

I am reminded of the story of the rabbi in Eastern Europe long ago, who was asked to assist two people engaged in a dispute. One of the disputants told his side of the story, whereupon the rabbi told him: 'You're absolutely right'. The other party was upset and said 'Rabbi, that's not fair, you haven't yet heard my side of the story'. 'Oh, I'm so sorry', said the rabbi 'please tell me'; and when the other party had told his story, the rabbi said: 'You're absolutely right'. A bystander remonstrated with the rabbi: 'Rabbi, you've told the one person he's absolutely right and you've told the other person that he's absolutely right. They can't both be absolutely right'. The rabbi turned to the bystander and said: 'You know, you're absolutely right'.

PROPOSITION NO 3: RIGIDIFIED EXCELLENCE IS A CONTRADICTION IN TERMS

There is an inherent tendency in professional qualification and practice to regulate processes in order to ensure some form of quality control. I have been involved in it myself, in specifying practice and accreditation criteria for the FMA, Resolution, the UK College of Family Mediators and the Law Society.

I am now concerned that family mediation may have become over-regulated. Family lawyer mediators, for example, have to undergo training aimed at accreditation by their mediation

---

2   David A Lax and James K Sebenius *The Manager as Negotiator* (The Free Press (a Division of Macmillan Inc), 1986).

3   'The Natural Mediator', published in 'Peripheral Visions,' *Mediation News*, Summer 1998. Vol 18, No 1, pp 8–9.

4   Lenard Marlow *Divorce Mediation: A Practice in Search of a Theory* (Garden City: Harlan Press, 1997).

organisations, require professional practice consultancy and CPD, and may also have to conform to the requirements of the Law Society and the UK College of Family Mediators. To do publicly funded work they will also have to have a Legal Services Commission franchise or contract and comply with the LSC's Quality Mark standard.

Government and the courts understandably want to be sure that mediators, especially if publicly funded, are properly qualified. But once properly trained and judged as competent, I wonder whether there really is a need for such stringent regulation. Once solicitors are qualified they are left to get on with it, subject to ethical constraints and CPD requirements.

In the commercial mediation field, which is relatively unregulated, a new umbrella body, the Civil Mediation Council, is proposing a minimal form of regulation for limited purposes, for example for the National Mediation Helpline, by accrediting providers (in a relatively simple exercise) and requiring mediators to belong to an accredited provider. This indicates the relatively minimalist approach that can be taken to regulation.

While accepting the need for some regulation, I would argue against process rigidification, whether in mediation or collaborative law.

To take just one example, the UK College Code on family mediation stipulates that a mediator will not maintain separate confidences as between the parties. This is absolute, and there is no provision to allow them to agree otherwise. Similarly it provides that a mediator cannot say anything to one lawyer that will not also be said to the other.

That is based on one model of practice and does not allow for the fact that the mediator and the couple may agree to use a different model, in which the mediator shuttles between the parties to try to work out terms, maintaining separate confidences between them. This model is used in civil and commercial disputes, and I have also used it effectively in family issues.

I think, for example, of a high conflict divorce that I mediated, in which every possible issue was contentious. All the joint sessions seemed to go round in circles. Whenever we appeared to make progress, something would happen between sessions, and the police or social services would be called in, or some financial or other crisis would arise. Because there was a substantial family trust involved, financial discussions depended on one of the parties constantly reverting to the trustees.

Eventually I set up a day-long session with them and their lawyers, which the Chairman of the trustees attended. We had joint meetings and separate meetings, with each party and their lawyer in a separate room. I shuttled between them, maintaining separate confidences in each room, except as I was authorised to release, subject only to the condition that any financial disclosure would be open. This flouted all received wisdom about people not being able to stay in the process for more than one and a half hours (the usual family mediation session), about not maintaining separate confidences, and about the perceived disadvantages of having lawyers directly involved in the process. The couple coped very well with an all-day session, the separate confidences helped to cut through problems, and both parties' lawyers were consistently helpful. In the event, that meeting was a major contribution to the settlement that eventually followed, covering the divorce, all financial issues and the creation of an agreed parenting plan.

I can see no good reason for rigidifying the rules disallowing this, and every reason to allow parties freedom to agree other procedures. There also seems no reason to insist that the mediator cannot (on any model) have independent communications with the respective lawyers.

Because we tend to think about our model in a narrow way, family mediators have generally resisted using this kind of practice and trainers have resisted teaching it.

Many people feel that arbitration lost its way when it abandoned its informality and started rigidifying and mimicking the litigation process. That has been redressed in recent years, but we need to avoid that rigidification happening with mediation or collaborative practice.

When one moves beyond establishing competence into the realm of providing excellence, I believe that you can provide guidelines, but you cannot be prescriptive. Excellence in a straightjacket is a fundamental misconception.

Incidentally, why do we straightjacket ourselves by so commonly using the phrase 'best practice' which asserts categorically that nothing else is or can be as good or better? Anyone who does not follow 'best practice' is at risk of criticism (and perhaps of a negligence claim) when trying to innovate. Surely this is a near-sighted view that does not allow for the likelihood that sooner or later some other practice will develop that is as good or better. 'Best practice' inhibits innovation and creativity, without which neither mediation nor collaborative law would exist. What is wrong with 'good practice' or, if one needs to move to the superlative, 'current best' or 'best available' practice?

PROPOSITION NO 4: EXCELLENCE IN FAMILY WORK IS ARID WITHOUT HUMANITY

I have gone into legal bookshops and asked if they had books on law and humanity. They referred me to the section on human rights, but I could find nothing on law and humanity. Much has been written about human rights law, and about crimes against humanity, but what I am interested in is the more mundane question of how lawyers express their common humanity in the everyday practice of law.

There are groups, mainly in the United States, who seek something more profound in the way they practise law. The 'Project on Integrating Spirituality, Law and Politics' is one such, which aims for a more humane and compassionate view of legal practice. Another is the 'Renaissance Lawyer Society', with its humanistic approach to the law and a vision of 'a legal system based on problem-solving, healing conflicts, and supporting us all in working and living together in peace'. They search for ways of working that are compatible with these principles, for example through collaborative law, mediation, restorative justice and community lawyering. These are interesting developments, albeit involving only a tiny minority of lawyers.

I wanted to be a lawyer, originally in South Africa some 50 years ago, as it was a respected profession, and one in which I could make a reasonable living; but my main motivation was that I wanted to do something worthwhile and to be a part of creating a better society, in which law served everyone. I expect that everyone choosing to work in the family field was similarly motivated, by wanting to do something worthwhile.

That is the aspiration and attraction of family ADR: to find a better way of working with people in family crisis, a way that reduces rather than exacerbates their conflict, a way that allows them to move towards some future healing.

I chose the sub-title of this talk as 'Law, healing and humanity'. When I mention this title to others, there is commonly some surprise at the juxtaposition of these three words, which people do not necessarily associate with one another. 'Why not?' is the question I ask. Can law be a healing profession? What is the relationship between law and common humanity?

These are not just rhetorical questions. There are no easy answers, because of the infinite variety of ways that law can be practised, that humanity can be expressed and that healing can take place. We need to recognise that in addition to their pragmatic value, mediation and collaborative family law are both vehicles that allow for humanity and healing.

The legal profession is not readily perceived as having a capacity for humanity and healing. It has many faces, and representing people in contentious situations is a major part of what it holds itself out as doing well. I do not see that this needs to change. What perhaps needs to be reviewed is its ability to do whichever is needed of it: knight in shining armour or healer.

I should say that it is not just in ADR or family work that humanity can be expressed as part of the practice of law. I worked as a commercial litigator for over 25 years, and as a commercial mediator for nearly 20 years, and I believe from my personal experience that there is scope in both those fields for lawyers to practise with humanity and compassion. One would not push this any more than one would push one's priorities onto family clients. Rather, it is a frame of mind that allows for the possibility of a less hostile way of resolving the issues. In the same way that family lawyers have developed a more civilised approach to family issues, so litigation or commercial lawyers can adapt the way they work, think and communicate.

The way that we think does inevitably influence the way that we work. In 1989 I returned from a conference of the US Academy of Family Mediators in Colorado, where I spent one day with a conflict resolver called Tom Crum, who was also an Aikido instructor.[5] He showed us how to bring the practice of Aikido into conflict resolution, 'moving responsively with the flow of an attack to unsettle the attacker'.

I was not convinced about the relevance of this to the real world until I got back to London and received a hostile letter from my opposite number in a divorce case. It was one in which any allegation resulted in an immediate counter-allegation against the other. Fortified by Tom Crum and Aikido, I telephoned my opposite number and said: 'I have your letter and will take instructions, but if what you say is right then I will ask my client to remedy the position right away. I agree that my client's actions in that situation would be unacceptable.' My opposite number's silent amazement was audible. His whole tone changed. I added that by the same token I would be grateful if he would check some other allegation my client had made. In his subdued tone, he agreed to do so. That marked a shift into constructive negotiations and we were subsequently able to settle. Years later, my client told me that the process of resolving the issues as we had done had changed her life.

In my experience, healing is not about people instantly embracing one another. Rather, it is about working in a way that allows people to do that in their own time and their own way. Take for example a commercial dispute that I mediated. An elderly father and middle-aged son were involved in a High Court dispute with one another involving the rights in the father's shares in the family business. They had not spoken for 2 or 3 years. In the mediation, the father's lawyer mentioned in passing that the son was running the business reasonably well. In a private caucusing session with the son, I drew attention to this, and he said, 'Yes, I was pleased he said that. Actually I learned a lot about the business from my father ...'. I asked him if he minded if I told his father this, and he agreed. During my following private session with the father, I mentioned what the son had said, to which the father responded: 'Did he say that? He's a good boy really ...' He in turn allowed me to carry this sentiment back.

After a day's intense negotiations, involving joint and separate meetings, the matter settled. As they signed the settlement agreement, the son leaned over to the father and said 'I'm glad we've settled'. The father raised his thumb in warm agreement. Then they left separately.

---

5   See Tom Crum's *The Magic of Conflict* (Touchstone (Simon & Schuster), 1987).

I suppose that I had hoped to see them embrace and walk out together, but on reflection, that was about me and not about them. What we had done was to resolve the dispute at a practical level, end the hostility and leave the space for healing to follow. That is a pattern I have seen many times, and not just in matters involving families.

Yet it is not enough to have healing and humanity as aspirational concepts without the practical means for them to manifest themselves. If excellence is arid without humanity, then humanity and healing are inadequate without effective processes and skilled, knowledgeable application. We need to be able to combine our belief in a better way with the mechanics and skills of providing it. This may be another paradox, but we need to be hard-headed and pragmatic, highly skilled and very effective if we want our compassion and our humanity to have a practical and tangible outcome.

We need the reliable frameworks that both collaborative practice and mediation provide, and the specialist skills and understandings we learn in order to become excellent collaborative practitioners or mediators.

Which leads me to the fifth proposition:

PROPOSITION NO 5: PURE LAW IS NOT ENOUGH

When I trained as a family mediator 21 years ago, conciliation was only used by therapists, counsellors and other non-lawyer professionals in relation to children's issues. Financial issues were dealt with by the lawyers outside the conciliation process. I joined with others to run an inter-disciplinary pilot scheme in which a lawyer and non-lawyer co-mediated, to address all issues arising on separation and divorce. The pilot scheme turned into the Family Mediators Association.

In the course of developing FMA training, we worked extensively with an inter-disciplinary model. For us lawyers, it was an invaluable experience in seeing how different disciplines addressed the same issues, and I believe that the benefits were reciprocal. Even though the FMA no longer exclusively works in the co-mediation model, though it remains its primary model, and even though we developed a sole mediation model in Resolution, the benefits of inter-disciplinary co-operation have remained with us.

In creating Resolution's mediation training, we drew not only on our mediation and legal backgrounds, but also on other disciplines to understand and work with couples' issues and dynamics. Counsellors and therapists supported the training and brought richness to it. They did sessions on family systems and dynamics. Children's issues were considered from different perspectives from those that lawyers and judges tend to. We appreciated the importance of understanding and addressing emotions. We had regard to systemic thinking, and to patterns of behaviour, looking both at each individual and the family as a whole. Many of us developed a better understanding of the counselling process and the way in which inter-disciplinary networking could be better achieved.

I would say that much of the excellence of the mediation process arises from the fact that it has developed from different professional backgrounds; and collaborative practice similarly draws on a much wider base than purely legal principles. Involving the clients directly in an interest-based negotiation process, collaborative practice demands sensitive and skilled representation with a family focus and a premium on reasonable cooperation.

In collaborative practice, the availability of a family consultant with a counselling or therapeutic background, working alongside the collaborative lawyer, is an inspired idea that should help to provide each party with practical and emotional support, and enable each to address and hopefully overcome obstacles to progress. It replicates the principle of inter-disciplinary co-mediation, but with a dynamic that allows each person the benefit of an individual lawyer and counsellor.

In Resolution's mediation model, counselling or psychotherapy may precede or run parallel with mediation, or the couple may adjourn mediation to go into counselling. But there seems no reason why lawyer mediators should not work more closely with counsellors, following collaborative practice. This is something that Resolution mediators may want to explore.

The traditional legal process offers an excellent legal and procedural framework that allows both sides to express their competing views by using excellent lawyers, ensuring that issues are considered in careful detail. Resolution is achieved either in a settlement, usually negotiated between lawyers, or in the finding of a judge who will have carefully analysed the facts and the parties' different views. I do not believe that any guidelines for identifying excellence should exclude those who provide it within the traditional legal process.

But the adversarial legal system does not create the best conditions for couples working out their own solutions for themselves and their families. It is in the nature of the process that legal principles and precedent tend to dominate over wider family interests and emotional considerations.

Mediation and collaborative family law actually provide within their systemic framework for wider issues to be taken into account than the narrower legal issues that tend to dominate the traditional process. The interests, needs and wishes of the parties are more directly addressed, and those of the children as individuals are similarly kept in clear focus by mediators or collaborative lawyers and not bypassed as their parents struggle to sort out their own issues. In order to be effective, however, it is vital for the practitioners to be skilled in what they do, and have the wider knowledge, understandings and sensitivities that the processes envisage. This in turn demands specialised skills training and a wider knowledge base than they might have expected in the traditional process.

Resolution has done a great deal to provide such knowledge and skills, but there are still lawyers who take the view that 'dealing with emotions is not part of my function'. Personally, I do not understand how any family lawyer can have that belief; but whatever the beliefs may be in traditional practice, mediators and collaborative practitioners simply could not and would not function in that way. There is just so much to learn about people, their psychology, behaviour and relationships and about the dynamics of relationship breakdown, systems and patterns that can be helpful to practitioners.

PROPOSITION NO 6: BALANCE IS CRUCIAL

In mediation, even-handedness and impartiality are inherent; but there are other balances that need to be struck in working effectively in mediation and collaborative law.

I want to touch on two inter-related areas of balance. One is the balance between rights and interests, and the other is the balance between the individual and the family.

Ideally, people whose marriage has broken down will find a balance between their respective legal rights, so far as they can assess what those are, and their interests; and also between their own personal interests and those of their family as a whole. But when people are going through the trauma of a marriage breakdown, they are not always minded to act ideally.

Both mediation and collaborative law can help people look more broadly at the family as a whole. Each of the couple should make their individual decisions on a fully-informed basis, which includes having a complete financial picture and having the best possible assessment of what their legal rights and entitlement might be. However, financial data and legal rights are obviously not the only criteria for decision-making and as we know, there are better ways to negotiate than pure positional bargaining.

In any model of negotiation, parties are reassured by having their lawyers available in the process, which is a key premise of collaborative practice. This is why I hold the view that parties' lawyers need to have a greater involvement in the mediation process in appropriate cases. This does not mean having lawyers attend every mediation session, but rather that lawyers should be able to engage more directly with the mediator, and that they should have a greater role in financial disclosure and in advising their clients as the mediation develops. They should also be able to attend some sessions, especially if their client needs that support or if conflicting legal advice is affecting progress. With the benefit of hindsight, I think that the process we devised did not give the lawyers an adequate role, while leaving them with responsibility for an outcome reached without their involvement. This aspect needs further consideration, especially as it has funding implications.

Mediators and collaborative practitioners can help people establish balance in their negotiations and find an agreed solution that works for both individuals and for the family as a whole, which minimises conflict and hostility, and which saves costs. Ultimately it is the parties' call as to how they respond to that guidance.

CONCLUSION

These propositions indicate that while excellence can exist in the traditional process, it is likely to be more rewarding for the parties and the practitioners in mediation or collaborative practice, with their wider perspective and greater opportunities for humanity and healing.

They also suggest that more work remains to be done in developing and cross-pollinating models of practice and in exploring guidelines as to what currently constitutes good practice in the use of different processes and options in family breakdown (without rigidifying).

Inter-disciplinary cooperation has developed enormously over the last decade or so, and clearly there is scope to explore how this can be furthered.

Lawyers often get blamed for exacerbating difficult situations. Sometimes this is justified, but commonly the client is pressing them to act aggressively while they are trying to help the client to adopt a more reasonable approach. In fact, lawyers have been in the forefront of moves to find better and less conflictual ways of helping couples to resolve their issues, and I think that without becoming complacent, we can have some pride in our contributions to the development of all-issues mediation and collaborative practice.

In conclusion, I would like to turn to South Africa for a final word on legal practice. The Nelson Mandela School of Law at Fort Hare University in South Africa includes the following in the expression of its values: 'The management, staff and students of the School of Law will strive to be consistently guided by the values of humanity, egalitarianism, non-racialism, societal leadership, and excellence'. Now isn't that a nice way of expressing excellence in law?

Myths About Family Mediation

*Christopher Richards**

IS MEDIATION FOR REAL PEOPLE, WITH REAL DISPUTES?

An acquaintance of a family mediator asked what she could expect from her divorce settlement. She told the mediator about the arrogance and cunning of her husband, as well as his indifference to the wellbeing of their son. The mediator offered to put them in touch with a good family mediator, although not herself, for obvious reasons of conflict of interest. The acquaintance was definite that there is no question of trying mediation: 'Not with a husband like mine. It would never work with him.'

Family mediators often experience this attitude from those facing divorce or separation. These enquirers seem genuinely to believe that family mediators have valuable knowledge about marital breakdown, yet their respect for this knowledge does not extend to the mediator's working role. When it comes to settling the practicalities of their own arrangements, such as maintenance, child support, childcare, finance and property sharing, they declare these questions to be beyond the scope of a mediator's skills, because of the impossible personality of their soon-to-be ex-partner.

Fear permeates marriage break-up. This can attach to the imagined person of the mediator. The idea of meeting, together with one's ex-partner, an unpredictable, supposedly impartial third person, in a setting far less understood than the formality of a court, can be frightening.

The mediator's experience is respected enough for her or his advice to be asked, even though advice-giving is explicitly outside the role of the mediator. One family mediator urged a male acquaintance to be aware that when all was settled, he and his ex-wife would still need to have dealings with each other. He should listen seriously to what she was asking and acknowledge rather than ignore her. When the mediator suggested they work out their settlement directly with each other in mediation, his acquaintance was adamant it could not be done, due to his wife's intractable refusal to listen to any opinions other than her own. Some months later, he thanked the mediator for the pointers she had given him about accepting that there would need to be two homes, shared funding of the children's needs, and recognition that the assets and debts which had accumulated including their pension contributions, were issues for shared decisions. As a result of what she had told him, he said they had sorted everything out to their mutual satisfaction, although at arms' length and considerable cost in legal fees.

Our acquaintances seem to think we know about issues in separation and divorce, but that we must mediate only with unusually altruistic clients.

---

*   Christopher Richards has been a social worker since 1975 and a family mediator and family mediation supervisor since 1986. He had a systemic training and family therapy practice in the 1980's, and has worked in the public and not-for-profit sectors. Now he has his own family mediation business, which has the Legal Services' Commission's Quality Mark for legal aid. He is an assessor of family mediator competence.

FAMILY MEDIATION IS AN IDEA BUTTRESSED BY MYTHS

Mediation does not fit comfortably into any theoretical structure. A family mediator is not a therapist, not a legal adviser, not an arbitrator, not a healer. What then can the practice of family mediation be, this thing the mediator actually does?

Family mediation is a metaphor, which for some lacks perceptible meaning. It does not appear to be for families at all, but for separating spouses or cohabitees. The seemingly pacific but impenetrable title has led to the evolution of a mythology. The purpose of this article is to explore the mythology, to acknowledge the truths that are wrapped in it and to discover the pattern of conversation that a mediator seeks to develop.

In what follows, little if any distinction is made between cohabitation and marriage, or between separation and divorce. There are some important distinctive issues that arise about the legal, parental and financial status of separating unmarried people, but they are not addressed here.

THE MYTH OF REASONABLENESS

The term family mediation implies a process based on reasonableness, without indicating how disputing spouses can manage to be reasonable when they are feeling vengeful, scared, sad or all of these at once. This baffles enquirers as to what it is about, when speculating as to what kind of emotional environment is likely to develop in the mediation room. The typical separating spouse is certain that the other is at their most unreasonable just now.

Those who are in the throes of experiencing divorce at first-hand may see the prospect of sitting in a room together, as incongruous folly. It is easy to imagine adults and children arguing, parting, pleading, crying, shouting, fighting, etc and to feel the fear and anger associated with marital breakdown. There is a disturbing intensity implicit for all of us in marital breakdown. In 'family mediation', conversely, it may be that there is an implicit placidity that feels unworldly and that would demand exceptional self-control and objectivity on the parts of the clients.

Actually, mediation is not for people who are behaving reasonably, because they do not need mediation. Being reasonable should not be confused with displays of embarrassed politeness, or assurances that everything has already been sorted out. Every family mediator has encountered the couple who arrive in the room polite, rehearsed and determined to 'do things amicably'. The spokesperson makes the point that there is already consensus, not dispute. She, or he, calm, smiling and measured, explains all that has been decided before arriving in mediation. I have listened in discomfort as the devastating fragments of the break-up are re-packaged: the proceeds of a house sale is to be divided to please one party leaving the other with something much inferior; children are to receive 'shared care' according to a schedule which has been tailored to split them in half; loss of pension rights is ignored. All the psychological imbalances of the marriage are reflected in this last desperate deal intended to head off the frightening uncertainties of the future. This is not reasonableness; it is a coalition of desperation.

These cases often founder in mediation. The myth of reasonableness seldom persists over the two to four months of mediation sessions. It is inevitable that the truth will break out and the reality of the conflicting needs will take over. When this happens the mediator may be blamed for allegedly sowing discord, or for allowing submerged disputes to surface and for provoking arguments by exploring the cracks instead of plastering them over. The main purpose of mediation is to undermine dispute impasses, offering the parties an unexpected and enlightening response to their conflict. A coating of false reasonableness that hides differences and stifles initiative hinders this aim. The problem of reasonableness is recognised by Robert Benjamin, observing that disputes 'are not susceptible to logic' (Benjamin, 2003). The creative potential of three individuals, two of them facing a crisis concerning the most important issues of their present lives, is lost so long as the belief persists that mediation is a theatre of the reasonable, where points of view are calmly propounded and the respective merits weighed on scales of rationality.

At the time of marital break-down, the prospect of unpredictable change can awaken submerged memories of frightening past events, abandonment and loss. Part of the motivation for cohabitation or marriage is the longing for a reliable relationship, a home, a family and support both emotional and financial in times of vulnerability. After the excitement and sexual intensity of courtship and coming together have diminished or gone, the longing for security remains.

Typically, when a family mediator meets a couple facing separation, the imbalance in their respective positions is apparent. One party, more often the woman, is determined on separation. For her the marriage no longer offers security and separation appears the safer course because it frees her from a dependency relationship that has begun to feel oppressive. This party may see the mediator as a potential ally, since family mediation is principally a context for working out arrangements for the separation or divorce that is wanted. It is clearer to this party that her goals are more congruent with the prospective mediation sessions. She is ready to risk the uncertainties of the separated or divorced state, because they are more appealing than the status quo.

The other party, more often the man, resists separation despite the signs over the past months or years that the relationship has become unsustainable. Any adverse actions on his part such as affaires, possessiveness, emotional unresponsiveness, financial failures, controlling or violent behaviour he explains away. This party can be pessimistic, even derisory, about the likelihood of working out any mutual understanding in mediation. If mediation is accepted, he does so partly with the hope of arresting the move to separate. He may also be looking for an influential third party who will confirm the injustice of the spouse who wants separation. At heart he is afraid of the prospect of loneliness.

The task of the mediator to engage with the clients is of course the task at the start of any sort of therapeutic relationship, except that the mediator has the paradoxical challenge of engaging simultaneously with clients who may be expressing diametrically opposed points of view. She wants to stay in the family home; he wants it sold. She wants him to pay off the debts from his share of the settlement; he says the debts are a joint responsibility. She wants a divorce now; he just wants to separate.

If there are children involved, they are talked about in mediation, but not often seen in person. It is an exceptional parent who is consistently able to put aside the temptation to use them as a weapon against the other party. As it is usually the father who works more hours outside the home, it is natural that the mother does most of the childcare. Consequently, there is a built-in inequality of knowledge and responsibilities with the great majority of separating parents. When they lived together, their different degrees and amounts of involvement in parenting may have been complementary and positively functional. Now faced with separation, instead of a cooperative parental relationship being accepted, a bad-tempered competition for time with the children often develops. It must, however, be pointed out that dramatic disputes about the care of children are less common in separation than may be imagined: more often it is differences over property and finance that provide the focus of disputes, while severe quarrels over the children tend to be avoided. In this avoidance, separating parents can be greatly helped by other family members, who are usually desperate to ensure that the children's sense of wider family is maintained.

At the outset, the mediator faces two people who have suspended reason. John Haynes (Haynes, 1994) used to talk about the initial effort of each client to convince the mediator of the justice of his/her story. Each client prepares and polishes a story that puts them in a good light and, correspondingly, puts the other in the wrong. It is a story that has been frequently retold and gathered support before mediation. Relatives and friends, faced with one party's account, will probably agree to it more from resignation than conviction. They will have heard about the lies, the parlous financial straits with which she or he is threatened, the imminence of homelessness because of the other's determination callously to grab a disproportionate share of the house equity; and worst of all, the selfish, unfeeling expectations the other has to control the children's lives.

> Anthony says that Louise is brainwashing the children against him and wants to cut him out of their lives altogether. Louise says that Anthony is inappropriately worrying the children, telling them that mummy is forcing him to live in a tent; promising them that they will be living with him half the time.

> When the mediator first meets them, feelings between Anthony and Louise are running high. Every time Anthony starts to answer one of the mediator's questions, Louise interrupts, insisting it isn't that way at all. Every time Louise speaks, Anthony grimaces or rolls his eyes, indicating disbelief at what she is saying. His behaviour, although not verbal, has the effect of stopping her in her tracks and arousing her irritation.

> 'Anthony likes to play mind games,' says Louise.

> 'Louise doesn't care what lies she tells, as long as she gets her own way,' says Anthony.

Each person's story really is true for that client. If the mediator seems to dismiss it, the client will be lost from the mediation. Any effort by the mediator to reconcile the two stories will fail unless some careful reframing is achieved. Yet careful reframing has its limits in the face of an impatient audience.

Arguing from positions can best be resolved by the adjudication of a third party, yet the mediation setting is not a tribunal. A mediator cannot judge or arbitrate without removing the underlying impulse of mediation, which is to restore to the clients their responsibilities to manage their own family, their own property and their own money.

Mediation began in the 1980's with the imperatives set out for 'principled negotiation' (Fisher, Ury and Patton, 2006). One aim is to develop an issue-based, not position-based, conversation. The mediator has to move the clients away from the opposing stories, into the area of mutuality: the wish for self-respect, the importance of affordable solutions, the recognition of both parents and their children to have adequate homes and lifestyles, and provision for the children to have the same opportunities as children in any other family. I have met very few warring spouses that have overtly rejected these aspirations. When the separation differences are seen in the frame of issues rather than positions, the talk in the mediation room starts to move away from posturing and into conversing.

In short, it is the task of the mediator to find that reason of which each is capable. It is not an easy task and needs to be done quickly, because an excessive number of mediation sessions (more than half a dozen), becomes frustrating for the impatient clients. This is achieved, firstly, by acknowledging the hurt and fear of each client, perhaps dramatising it, then accepting each client's view as his or her truth. Thereafter the mediator must focus on solution-finding, setting out the issues and the requirements to be fulfilled.

Separating people are capable of making effective decisions, once they have entered into a conversation based on mutual recognition. Trying to get them to be friends again is not the goal. Barbara Wilson (Wilson, 2002) wrote of clients who refused to speak directly to each other, communicating at home with post-it stickers stuck on the fridge. They were able to bend their rule in the mediation sessions and communicate by looking only at the mediator. They resolved their dispute.

The core skill is the ability to balance questioning with summarising. Questioning in mediation has been developed from the concept of 'circular questioning' in systemic family therapy. Summarising, possibly the most demanding skill, involves feeding back to the client what they are saying in the hearing of the other party. The success of summarising depends on the clients' acceptance of its accuracy, while the content is reframed to mutualise and normalise the views expressed by the client. Summaries of this sort lay down a structure for negotiating. Where one party may see the other's statements as untrue, inflammatory or impossible, the mediator's summaries should provide the opportunity for a thoughtful, face-saving, or even creative response. This is the stuff of conversation.

Clients have to regain the ability to be reasonable. Without it no resolution of their disputes will be achieved. Mediators meet unreasonable clients because their essential job is to find the clients' reason, through moving into the area of mutuality.

THE MYTH OF GENDER NEUTRALITY

Family mediation is inescapably focused on issues of gender. Gender differences permeate every aspect of separation: sexual, emotional, parental, financial and even legal. The mediator adds her or his own gender to the intense maelstrom. The scope for misunderstandings to arise from male-female interactions in the mediation room is boundless.

In the past marriages probably stayed intact because, at base, husbands had their emotional and physical needs met, whilst wives had their economic needs met. It might be said that couples used to stay together for altruistic parental reasons, but the rising separation and divorce rate now makes this argument seem increasingly doubtful. Politicians and influential community leaders may expatiate on the desirability of the intact two-parent family for children, but around 40% of resident parents, the majority of them mothers, are looking after their children on their own.

Demographic and health factors have changed the context of marriage by reducing the dependence of women on marriage. Women now work, albeit usually at lower rates of remuneration, and they can control their fertility where once this was more subject to male imposition. A marital partnership that has become marked by violence, destructive criticisms, emotional distance, repeated infidelity, or simple boredom, has a high probability of being ended, most often by the woman.

Financial factors probably exert a major influence on a partner wanting separation. If one person considers the other not to be contributing adequately or fairly, or if that other partner seems unable to control the growth of debts, the advantages of financial independence will look attractive.

> Louise and Anthony had been together 8 years and had 2 young children under 7. They had recently separated: Anthony had moved out and was staying with his parents.

> Louise worked part-time as a classroom assistant. Anthony worked full-time as a police officer. She earned about one-third as much as he. The parental roles had been shared unevenly, with Louise doing the majority. When Anthony had been at home, Louise complained that he had seemed unwilling to show any initiative in the time he spent with the children. She complained that he had been morose when he came home from work. She

also complained that he had been selfish, this being a euphemism for his expectation that their sex life would continue as when they had been childless.

Anthony did not complain much, instead he responded with monosyllabic retorts. He had become preoccupied with the stress of chasing limited senior police vacancies and with the lower material standard of living which he had discovered to be an inevitable consequence of parenthood. He was as unhappy as she, yet expressed his dissatisfaction far less eloquently, possibly because he had no idea how to put his feelings into an interactional dialogue. After all, at no stage in his childhood had he been encouraged to do so.

They found their way to mediation through the solicitor whom Louise consulted about a divorce. Louise was eligible for legal aid, for both legal advice and mediation. Anthony had to pay for mediation, but he quickly realised that if he could reduce the number of hours a solicitor spent on his case, he should be able to save several thousand pounds in legal fees.

Initially the male mediator found Louise the more appealing client. She could articulate what she wanted. She seemed to be aware of Anthony's fears of loneliness, even if he would not acknowledge it. She was even optimistic about the future, describing her vision of separation in quite contented terms.

Anthony was pessimistic and thoroughly negative; he was sure he would be the loser. He predicted that his house, his children and much of his income would be taken from his control. He saw Louise as a malignant schemer who only took and gave nothing. His parents, it seemed, agreed with this opinion of her.

It was not surprising that a male mediator would find Louise the more likeable. A persuasive, socially confident woman, so obviously committed to giving most of her time to the children, she made a far better impression than an angry, bitter man with apparently no ideas as to how to resolve the wearisome impasse. Moreover, he had become disenchanted with his job and allowed this to affect the atmosphere at home.

It took two sessions for the mediator to begin to feel uneasy about the dogmatic inflexibility of Louise's expectations. She insisted on remaining in the house, although her lower income would make it impossible for her to pay the mortgage without substantial support payments from Anthony. She would not allow Anthony to have the children with him for more than half a day at weekends. Louise's justification was that they were not yet ready for longer and she would not let them see his parents, with whom she had fallen out. She was not prepared to look for a more remunerative job. She appeared to be unsympathetic to Anthony's discomfort at living with his parents, and said it would waste time to consider an independent home for him while the children were growing up.

From time to time, Louise would explode at Anthony in frustration. In the face of his repeated insistence that the house would have to be sold, she demanded: 'Why can't you think of your children just for once?' Asked to say what he understood she meant by this, he replied that Louise wanted nothing to change in her life except for getting rid of him.

It is difficult for a family mediator to be with clients without, subconsciously at least, having personal experiences recalled by such exchanges. Female mediators might feel a sharp pain at the idea of not seeing their children for more than four hours at a time. Male mediators might feel frightened by the bitterness of a man who seems to have lost the ability to feel any hope. Counter-transference holds true in mediation as in any other psychotherapy – but it may be denied in the context of the proclaimed mediation ethics of impartiality and neutrality. Adequate opportunities for reflecting on and recognising these personal responses are needed for the mediator to maintain neutrality.

Certainly impartiality and neutrality are underlying mediation values. Impartiality is more easily implemented through an explicit rule: the mediator should monitor the attention given to each client, ensuring that each gets equal time and equal weight is given to each person's views. In the mediation room, if one client talks more than the other the mediator is required to invite the other to have her or his say. The rule of equal time also applies in caucusing, a procedure whereby the mediator sees each client confidentially on their own during a session. This offers an opportunity to express feelings that were creating an impasse, and were impossible to express in the other's presence.

> Such an impasse developed with Anthony and Louise over the question of the house sale. Seeing that the argument was becoming repetitive and exasperating, the mediator asked to see each client separately for a few minutes.

> On her own, Louise wept and said that she could not understand why Anthony was so bitter that he was prepared to see her become homeless. She acknowledged that he did need independent accommodation. On his own, Anthony confessed that the feelings he still had for Louise made him speak without thinking. He realised that she could not, even if she were to get a better-paid job, afford to move out of the home at present. His real fear was that she would soon find a new partner, who he did not want to be living in his family home.

> It can be tempting for a mediator to join with one client to persuade the other. Simple common sense indicated that Louise could not afford to buy another house. If common sense were all that mediators needed, the job would be easy. Even common sense can be perceived as bias. Anthony would have complained of unfairness if he had thought the mediator was siding with Louise about anything at all.

Neutrality extends beyond impartiality. In mediation it implies that the mediator should be value-free. For instance, mediation codes of practice usually state that the mediator has no investment in the outcome of the clients' negotiation.

Mediators, of course, are far from neutral in their beliefs and attitudes about parents, children and family life. They are certainly not value-free. Furthermore, they will see family relationships, although possibly not family responsibilities, differently depending on whether they are male or female. A man's demand that the woman get a better-paid job could arguably evoke a more sympathetic response from a male than a female mediator.

Some mediation organisations have attempted to address male/female values by co-mediation, whereby a male and a female mediator work together to provide the appearance of balance. Should one mediator seem to be influenced by her or his own personal views, the other can intervene. Should a client feel that one of the mediators is in danger of being swayed by the other client's arguments, they have the other mediator to turn to.

I believe co-mediation is a recourse of highly doubtful effectiveness. The presence of a fourth person in the room considerably increases the combinations of interactions and complicates the potential variety of disputes. To have two males and two females in the room is to invite mutual gender alliances and cross-gender alliances or antagonisms. As there are many more female family mediators, in practice co-mediation usually means two female family mediators working together. Whether co-mediators are male-female, female-female, or even male-male, co-mediation reduces effectiveness by introducing unwanted potential for dispute into the room. Every supervisor has heard the anxieties that mediators express about working with their co-mediator and the difficulties of addressing those anxieties in the limited time they have to work together.

The mediator should not take up the clients' time with pronouncements such as that he has his own views but is keeping them private, or that as a man he sees things a particular way. He should not pontificate about being 'professional', for professionalism can mean denying one's humanity or gender. He should instead express genuine curiosity. He should ask the clients to explain and clarify what he does not understand. He can summarise what he believes the client means and invite the client's comment on the summary. Male or female, it is the mediator's job to ensure that all three people in the room are talking as comprehensibly as is possible; that one person's wishes are understood by the other as well as by the mediator. Curious, respectful and honest questioning together with regular summarising by the mediator is the most likely route to informed and fair decisions. This sets a good model for conversations anywhere.

> With Anthony and Louise, there is no doubt that the decision to see them separately was instrumental in breaking the impasse. When the joint session was resumed, it was possible to elicit some acknowledgement of a desire to be fair and to accept that each should be able to get on with her or his life. They went on to make proposals, drawn up in writing, that involved Louise keeping the family home and receiving a level of child support which would be reviewed when the children had both finished primary school. At that time Louise hoped to get better-paid employment, partly by increasing her working hours. There were some savings, most notably an endowment life policy, which Anthony could take for a deposit on a flat.

> Perhaps most importantly, Louise removed her 4-hour limit on the children seeing Anthony, even accepting that they could stay overnight with him, although she remained adamant that they could not stay at his parents' house. This was a crucial step in developing a joint approach to parenting. Louise abandoned her powerful control over access to the children's lives and Anthony began to talk more acceptably, or so the male mediator concluded.

THE MYTH OF THE FUTURE, NOT THE PAST

'I can't help you with what has happened in the past', John Haynes used to tell his clients. 'What I can do is help you make an agreement about the future'.

Traditionally mediators tell each other that mediation is not therapy or counselling. It is a future focused negotiation, facilitated by a neutral mediator. The mediator manages the process by ensuring that both clients have opportunities for equal time and also by preventing abusive exchanges and challenging them to explore all possible options, not merely replay their existing positions. It is based on hopefulness, and a search for a new way.

This, the longest-established mediation approach, has a remarkably successful track record in terms of achieving voluntary settlements of finances and parental responsibilities. A staged process, varying from four to nine stages, is still taught to all family mediators. In essence these stages comprise of, 'setting the scene', 'eliciting and exploring the issues', 'generating the options' and 'securing agreement'. The mediator's role in managing this future-focused process includes:

- establishing a contract with the clients for mediation

- reframing the dispute in terms of issues for resolution

- eliciting mutually accepted criteria for evaluating the acceptability of the options, such as adequate accommodation for all the parties; positive parental roles for both spouses; equitable living standards after payment of maintenance; and so on.

- encouraging both clients to put forward all the options they can think of for resolution and suggesting options which they may not have considered

- evaluating the options, together with the clients, against the stated criteria

- drawing up what the clients have agreed in writing.

Experienced family mediators who follow this progression claim successful outcomes in around 70% of their mediation cases.

Whilst this approach contributes greatly to reaching settlements without clients resorting to litigation, practitioners of this negotiation model frequently encounter clients who are intensely preoccupied with the loss and hurt of past interactions. The paradox of being asked to work out considerate settlements with the very person who is seen as the destroyer of early promises, can be too much for some clients. The mediation room is the scene of many tears, reproaches, accusations and denials. There are heated exchanges, interruptions and walkouts, emotional threats but very seldom actual violence. The mediator often struggles to regain future focus and even when the discussion is overtly restored to looking forward, the opposing memories of the clients provide more than a palpable backdrop and intrude. Couples in dispute have opposing stories that they will not abandon. Human stories cannot be dismissed.

Over the course of family mediation's 20 years or so of history, approaches have emerged which seek to manage a conversation more linked into the clients' own outlooks and awareness. Therapeutic mediation, for instance (Irving and Benjamin, 2002), aims to prepare each client for readiness to negotiate, introducing a prior stage of preparation before the negotiation. Transformative mediation (Baruch Bush, and Folger, 1994) shifts the focus of mediation away from settling and onto empowering and recognising the clients' innate abilities to define their own issues and settlement terms. The aim is partly to prevent the sense that the mediator may be seen to be invalidating the client who wants to talk about matters which the mediator sees as unsolvable or redundant.

Narrative mediation (Winslade and Monk 2001), a development from a narrative approach to family therapy (White and Epston, 1990), is a direct exploration with the clients of the past itself, in retelling the clients' stories, to draw out realisation of the clients' courage and persistence in conflict. Their conflict is framed as an external force, generated not by the clients themselves but arising as an adversary from without. This is a collaborative search for 're-storying'. Despite its potential for remaking alliances, its scope is usually limited.

Clients who come voluntarily to family mediation will often insist on the urgency of some immediate decisions. They have to make early practical decisions, however much they seem to hark back to past resentments. The declared subject matter of family mediation sessions is literally blood, bricks and money.

Other new forms of mediation may emerge which draw on some of these inspirations and reconcile the desperation and bitterness that characterise the interactions of so many people through their years of divorce and separation. One important feature of family mediation is the awareness of other stakeholders. Children are waiting for an end to the uncertainty. Solicitors are waiting for financial information. Court hearings may be timetabled with a judge awaiting proposals. A house buyer may be waiting to hear when their offer will be considered. Grandparents are waiting for news about how the arrangements for the children are going to affect them. Divorce and separation are events that disrupt the wider family and resolution depends on the ability of the couple to attain a mutual view of the future, despite their antagonistic recollections of the past.

Family mediators start their careers as therapists, lawyers, social workers, teachers or personnel managers. They discover that the impasses brought to mediation are superficially practical, yet continue to be unresolved because of deeply felt disagreements over the past. It is the dispute over the past, which fortifies impasse over the future.

> When taking the inventory of the couple's assets, Anthony tells the mediator that his father had lent £20,000 towards the deposit on their home that they bought 8 years ago, which must now be repaid. Louise insists it was a gift, not a loan.

> The debt of £8,000 to a bank is described by Anthony as a joint liability, responsibility for which should be shared because the money was used to buy a new kitchen. Louise says she had never wanted that kitchen but he had gone ahead with the loan against her wishes.

> Anthony says that Louise will now have to get a full-time job, because their existing incomes will be insufficient to cover their future spending needs as separated spouses and parents. Louise retorts that they had agreed when they decided to have children that she should be available to them at home: that was how both of them had wanted to bring up their children. He had been instrumental in persuading her to step off the career ladder and she is in no position to change that course in her life now.

> Louise says that Anthony had been no help with the children up to a few months ago. She sees no justice in his expectation that they should share equal time with their children from now on. If they were to have equal parental time, there could be financial consequences, in that he would need to buy a similar house to hers and would not be able or willing to pay her as much maintenance as she says she is going to need. Why, she demands, is he playing the role of devoted father, if he had not done so when she had wanted and needed him to do so? It is obvious to her that he is motivated by money, not by any concern for the wellbeing of the children.

In all such arguments there is a danger that while the clients parade their outrage at the betrayals and denials from the past, the mediator will respond without taking these feelings into account, intensifying efforts to focus the clients on what is needed now and is affordable. The core interactional skills of family mediation, questioning and summarising, have to include attention to feelings about the past because without such attention the clients may disengage from the mediator. Nevertheless, the mediator knows that dwelling on the past will see positions restated oppositionally and that it will not be long before one or both clients criticise the mediation as a waste of time. A delicate balance between past and future issues has to be achieved. The past should not be allowed to oppress decision-making, but it may significantly influence the resolution of the problem. Negotiating about memories is unlikely to prove successful. People in dispute seldom give up their beliefs about what was said or done by the other. It is too easy for them to see this as surrender. The reality of the separation provides a motivation to hold onto self-justifying recollections.

However, sometimes the possibility of an apology emerges (Whatling, 2004) and the mediator should always be alert to this potential. It offers recognition of the feelings of the other. When it emerges authentically, and even better, when it is accepted, the character of the conversation in the mediation room can be wonderfully transformed, although an apology is not a necessary ingredient of successful mediation. Personal grief may be sustained by a sense of having been wronged, not of having done wrong. Grief will not be ended by a few mediation sessions or by an apology, although when an apology is given, it is valuable.

> 'Louise, how do you remember the way the money from Anthony's father came to you both?' asks the mediator.

'It was all done between Anthony and his father. I was told by Anthony', replies Louise. 'He gave me the impression it had been given to us.'

'Do you suppose his father meant it as a single indivisible gift to both of you or, say £10,000 each?'

'Well, I can't obviously claim that he wanted to give me money personally', replies Louise.

'So looking back on Anthony's father's decision to help, you remember that he did it through Anthony. I guess you wouldn't have expected it to happen any other way. He wanted you both to have a house and he explained to Anthony what he intended. Anthony then told you it was a gift to the two of you as a couple. Have I got that right?'

'Yes', says Louise.

'And now that your marriage has foundered, would Anthony's father be rethinking the basis on which he let you both have the money? What do you think? If you were Anthony's father, would you still describe it as a gift?'

'Maybe not, but I'm pretty sure some of it still is a gift to Anthony. I could accept that half of it should be repaid. Anthony's half is another matter; that's between him and his father. I can't be expected to lose out now for what happened once between Anthony and his father. I'm sure that it was a gift. The most that I think Anthony and I are due to repay is half,' says Louise.

Alternating questions and summaries offers great scope for linking the separate memories of the clients into mutual decision-making. The purpose of summarising is to check that the mediator understands the client's meaning; then the summary should lead into the next question providing the opportunity to look forward. Therefore settlements for the future depend for success on respect and understanding of individual memories. Perhaps the best way to distinguish how to address past and future is not by looking for agreement on the past, but by recognition of the impact of the past on the client's readiness to resolve differences. The importance of adequate recognition should not be underestimated.

THE REALITY OF MEDIATION

The outcome of mediation is future-focused. Clients usually accept this overtly, despite the dire pessimism with which some of them view the prospect of the future. The mediator must accept that the outcome is theirs. Most mediators come from professional backgrounds where they are expected to advise on solutions. Lawyers entering mediation training often comment on how hard they find it to give up their known approach of identifying the problematic facts and then setting out the solution. Some other professionals are struck by how demanding it is to have nothing invested in the solution, but everything invested in helping the clients to find their own mutual solution. It has been described as having expertise without being an expert (Benjamin, 1995).

How, for instance, does a mediator react when the clients are proposing a parenting arrangement which would seem to split the children exhaustingly between two homes, lacking the certainty and consistent routine that children enjoy in intact two-parent families? The mediator's own childhood memories and parental experiences are likely to intrude. What comment should the mediator make to the wife who is so desperate to get out of the relationship that she is willing to give up all access to the pension built up by her husband when they were together and which she will need in the future? What kind of solution is that? Even neutrality is conditional and the limits will shift between individual mediators.

From time to time family mediators are sorely tempted to abandon the proclaimed condition of neutrality, for in reality separation and divorce are frightening and isolating events for most of us. The looming loneliness, guilt, betrayal, and final loss of hope that things could be retrieved, hang over everyone in the room, including the mediator. Mediators have recourse to defences such as professionalism, or acting as expert advisers, or characterising families and individuals as 'dysfunctional'. This may protect them from immediate pain, but everyone is psychologically affected even if s/he will not allow it on a conscious level (Bowling and Hoffman, 2003). Family mediators cannot escape entirely from the connection that exists between themselves and the people who present disputes for resolution.

The greatest challenge for family mediators is to convince our clients that we combine confidence and competence with humility and compassion. The miasma around the mythology has to be pierced, to see the possibilities of the conversation within.

REFERENCES

Baruch Bush, RA and Folger, JP *The Promise of Mediation* (Jossey-Bass, 1994)

Benjamin RD 'Managing the Natural Energy of Conflict' in (eds) D Bowling and D Hoffman *Bringing Peace into the Room* (Jossey-Bass ,2003) 89–94

Benjamin, RD 'The Mediator as Trickster: The Folkloric Figure as Professional Role Model' *Mediation Quarterly*, Fall 1995, 3–18

Bowling, D and Hoffman, D 'Bringing Peace into the Room: The Personal Qualities of the Mediator and their Impact on the Mediation' in (ed.) D Bowling and D Hoffman *Bringing Peace into the Room* (Jossey-Bass, 2003) 13–47

Fisher, R, Ury, W and Patton, B *Getting to Yes* (Houghton Mifflin Books, 2006)

Haynes, JM *The Fundamentals of Family Mediation* (Suny Press, 1994)

Irving, HH and Benjamin, M *Therapeutic Family Mediation* (Sage Publications, 2002)

Whatling, T 'Apology Matters – The Power of Apology in Family Mediation' *Mediation in Practice*, Mediation UK and UK College of Family Mediators December 2004, 7–10

White, M and Epston, D *Narrative Means to Therapeutic Ends* (WW Norton, 1990)

Wilson, B 'Learning from Virgil – a philosophy for mediators' *Family Mediation in Practice*, UK College of Family Mediators Summer 2002, 1–5

Winslade, J and Monk, G *Narrative Mediation* (Jossey-Bass, 2001)

What is the Future for Social Work with Children?

*Michael Leadbetter**

This chapter will reflect on some fundamental issues related to the role and nature of social work. I intend to highlight significant areas rather than offer a comprehensive analysis, whilst at the same time stimulate and provoke the reader to reflect on what can be done by learning from the past, without letting the past inappropriately influence the potential to do things differently in future.

I will examine:

- The history of the discipline and maturity of its concepts.

- Location: the decision taken when Social Services Departments were established to locate their activities within the family of local government, rather than within the Health Service.

- Staining and projection.

- Lack of clarity regarding the role of social workers.

- The failure to secure a universal sense that children's and social care services are valuable and offer indispensable benefits to local communities.

HISTORY AND MATURITY

The 1971 Seebohm reforms introduced the concept of the generic social work department, which was intended to be a one-stop shop for all welfare matters. The aim, to have one point of contact, led to the concept of the 'generic social worker' who was expected to cover all the complex areas of knowledge and input. It was thought that a single social worker could provide a better comprehensive service without subjecting the individual or family to contact with a number of different departments. I believe this concept to be fundamentally flawed. It was as if social workers were expected to act as GPs, but without any possibility of referral to specialist social work services, which were no longer available.

The 1970s saw a mass influx into the profession of young graduates. They were committed, bright and able to acquire the necessary range of competencies. However, this was the first generation of young people to carve a markedly separate path from that of their parents and grandparents. Liberated by much improved access to education, health services and economic

---

* Michael Leadbetter was Director of Social Services in Tameside and Essex for 17 years, and President of The Association of Directors of Social Services 2002–03. He now offers consultancy and interim management in the field of social care and health services. Former member of the President's Interdisciplinary Committee.

independence the 'baby boomers' quickly signalled divergence from 'the establishment', preferring to franchise a whole new set of personal and political values. They took these passionate and politicised beliefs into their work and sought to empower individuals and families grappling with the damaging effects of poverty and deprivation on bringing up their children, or mitigate the physical and emotional consequences of old age and impaired ability. These were and remain vital components of the social work task.

Conversely this oppositional, anti-authority pull was a downside for a nascent profession struggling to carve out an identity. Some social workers were conflicted about their role. On the one hand there was recognition that if social workers did not intervene in various situations things would go from bad to worse, but simultaneously there were feelings of discomfort about being perceived as an 'instrument of social control'. Consequently, some preferred to vest all the power with the client to the detriment of clarity about function and role. This confusion was not uncommon. During one of the first Inquiries into a child murder, the social worker spoke of not wanting to upset her relationship with the parents by insisting on actually seeing the child.

It was not unusual for an unqualified social worker in the 1970s, to have a caseload of over 100 clients, across the range, with diverse problems. Social workers, who had previously built up a particular body of knowledge, were suddenly expected to work with all of the specialisms. Obviously it was only a matter of time before their expertise was diluted and in some instances lost. Experienced practitioners left or retired, and the drain of expertise was compounded by the rapid promotion to first line and middle management of extremely inexperienced managers. Managers, perhaps from a mental welfare background, could be found trying to supervise colleagues dealing with childcare and physical disability matters. Little wonder that social work had such a shaky start given this dilution of expertise. Now, 35 years later, we have returned to specialisms comprising of children's directorates; mental health (with most mental health social workers now working in health trusts); and adult services that can be seen as a re-branded welfare department. For a thorough briefing on the history and projected future of child protection services, including a trawl through the legislation, I recommend Martin Calder's (2006) exceptionally good piece of work.

In the interim the profession lost and wasted valuable time. Subsequently, expertise has had to be rediscovered and reclaimed by giving up the organisational omnipotence contained in the concept that everyone should be able to do everything. Confidence was undermined not only within the profession but also externally. Nonetheless, social work continues to benefit from an understated but tremendous commitment from a significant part of its workforce. Despite the frequent upheavals in structure, restrictions due to financial limitations and the torrent of new information that must be mastered and adapted for the vicissitudes of practice, many social workers demonstrate considerable resilience in continuing to provide useful services of a consistently good quality for their client groups. Social work has had relatively little time to revive its reputation embedded in expertise, or to market itself effectively. By marketing I mean sending clear, universally understood signals regarding purpose and task and the principles that inform actions.

LOCATION IN LOCAL GOVERNMENT

Local government has been a force in British democratic life for over 150 years. The established professions of law, accountancy, education, architecture, and engineering traditionally held pride of place in the local democratic system. Significantly all these also held status in the 'external market'. Social work in England, (though not in the USA), has always been tied to the local state, whether that was through the Poor Law Boards or the post-war Children's Departments.

Then in 1971, the new Social Services Departments were introduced. From the outset they were perceived as being disproportionately favoured by Government. Additional responsibilities were transferred to them without general agreement; for example responsibility for what used to be called Junior Training Centres for children with learning disabilities was transferred from Education to Social Service Departments. These transfers were easily perceived as an attack on the education and health systems and inevitably this created conflicts, envy and jealousy. There was scant regard for the dynamics such changes would create amongst those working within local government. Thirty years later and prior to the recent amalgamation of children's services, many Directors of Social Services experienced extreme difficulties working with both Education and Health, riven as the situation was with distrust, competitiveness and often open resentment.

The frequent restructuring right across public services, has repeatedly fractured professional relationships and created new areas for potential mistrust; or simply created a climate where it is difficult to 'place trust'. Government and media criticisms of public services from the 1980s onwards have added to poor morale and a climate has evolved in which professionals have developed a bunker mentality and a culture of self-preservation. The turbulence caused by the introduction of Social Service Departments in the 1970s, compounded over the years by the undermining of public services and the continued restructuring every three or four years by politicians of all parties, begs the question as to whether services can thrive in such a climate? Have there been any significant improvements in the attainment of outcomes? If not, why not?

STAINING AND PROJECTION

My hypothesis is that the profession of social work attracts more than its fair share of negative projections, as a result of the people with whom we work and the circumstances in which many of them live. The views that percolate out through newspapers and television can be understood as the public's defence against the reality of the pain of others. These views are dismissive and quick to marginalise and ostracise. Judgments tend to be passed in terms of the deserving and undeserving, refracted through a truncated understanding of the impact of immigration, class and race: the complexity of these issues are avoided or dismissed. The perception is that if only the people caught in these difficulties had paid more attention to their education, looked after themselves better, looked after their families in a proper manner, or stayed in their country of origin then they would not need help. Hence the social workers involved with them can easily be categorised and dismissed as 'bleeding heart liberals and do-gooders'. It is as if, by being close to people in difficulties, professionals become 'stained' or 'tainted' by association. (It is worth reading the 2002 Reith lectures by Professor Onora O'Neill, which deal most eloquently with the placement of trust and also the role of the media. In her concluding lecture, she examines the role of a totally 'unaccountable' media and contrasts this with the attention to micro management and accountability evident in the rest of public life).

Social work, in whichever organisational structure, has always encompassed a tremendously wide and complex range of skills and responsibilities in service delivery. Our work is often synonymous with encountering pain, distress and disappointments and therefore can bring us face to face with our own disappointments, losses, mortality, and at times feelings of futility. We know from psychoanalytic theory and practice that individuals in distress use mechanisms including 'projective identification' to deal with their difficulties. 'Projective identification' involves pushing their unmanageable, often unconscious and unresolved feelings into those they come into contact with, so that the recipient (in this case the social worker and indeed the organisation itself) feels overwhelmed by unsettling and disturbing feelings at a primitive level of understanding. One way of dealing with such difficulties is to attempt to evade them. The findings of Isobel Menzies-Lyth's study of the nursing profession (1959) are equally relevant to social work and quoted in Huffington et al (2004). Menzies-Lyth identified the common 'coping' strategy of individual and organisational 'evasion', which actually exacerbates anxieties by draining emotional energy and meaning from the worker's relationships both with clients and with colleagues. The concomitant organisational recourse to over rigid procedures, further inhibits the exercise of real and potential capabilities: hence the familiar scene is set for escalating sickness patterns and staff turnover.

When representing the Association of Directors of Social Services in media interviews, I was frequently asked, 'What can you do Mr Leadbetter, to assure me this (child abuse) will never happen again?' This question is typical of the wish to embrace omnipotent solutions. I responded that we must hold two opposing constructs in our mind at the same time, (although I did not put it quite like that when appearing on the Jimmy Young show!). There have been some terrible professional failures and we must do everything possible to minimise the likelihood of future tragedies through a detailed analysis of what went wrong and straightforward, robust steps to make improvements. Simultaneously the profession must educate the public by acknowledging that inevitably, as we are dealing with frail and vulnerable human beings, tragedies will definitely occur again.

> 'Child protection is perhaps the most demanding, conflict-ridden, worrying and controversial of modern public services. That is because in exercising its responsibilities to safeguard children, the state uses its power to become involved in the most intimate and sensitive family relationships. The public is frightened of the system that has been set up to protect their children.' (Cooper, Hetherington and Katz, 2003).

In their paper for Demos, the above authors identify three particular problems inherent in the child protection system: lack of child focus, the failure of professionals to efficiently assess and then communicate adequately with each other; and, regrettably, the system's potential to further traumatise those involved. These problems of old look set to continue despite the plethora of legislation and government guidance that has come into being over the past 10 years. Certainly, there is a new vision for social care that emphasises the importance of holistic universal services for all, including children. It purports to give better access to joined-up services across the previously rather impermeable boundaries of health, education, housing and social care. Much improved multi-agency inter-professional communication is vital if the policy is to translate into reality. This is easy to articulate, yet from each and every Inquiry into a child's death, the common theme is that of failings of communication which took place both within the professional groups and between different disciplines.

Cooper et al (2003) offer an interesting perspective on why this continues to happen: 'Failures to communicate are the symptoms, not causes, of the difficulties that the system experiences.' The authors think that: 'The underlying problem is the fundamental relationship between children, families and the state.' They point out that comparative research shows child protection systems are powerfully shaped by the history, politics and legal cultures of the nation state. Factors at work in the UK system include our adversarial legal system, an absence of the potential for working together that authentic inclusive citizenship generates for individual and state alike, along with a risk adverse society. They argue that this has resulted in an over legalised child protection and welfare system, with its daunting quasi-judicial child protection conferences and child protection register. Cooper and his colleagues make the case for a revalidation of 'relationship-based practice and institutional management in which negotiation, mediation and personal judgement are fundamental'. Their overview is that public services for children are so challenging to deliver because relationships are pivotal to this work, and these relationships involve people, professionals and clients alike facing unwelcome realities.

Their vision and deconstruction of what is needed to change the practice, culture and behaviour of front line practitioners is inspirational. Eschewing new structures or processes, they maintain that three related principles will improve practice, protect children better and increase professional job satisfaction: these are trust, authority and negotiation. These are not moral but 'systemic' principles, allowing social systems to operate more effectively in dealing with child welfare related conflict. 'Space for thinking, negotiating, taking risks, or working in confidence has to be fought for and won at local level ... supported by institutions which legitimise it.'

What I find remarkable is that the identified skills are in fact the core tools of any competent social worker, although stymied by their lack in the organisations that employ them. Why have we failed to articulate and win support for this important body of knowledge? Are we reluctant to trumpet this contribution of relationship based practice, because it appears too basic and not sufficiently technical or sophisticated enough? Appearances deceive, as success in this sphere requires highly sophisticated analytic and communication skills. Social care providers have become accustomed to wave after wave of policy initiatives: but put this mass of directives, initiatives and operational drivers to one side and one is left with the reality of everyday service delivery which is universal, elemental and very simple – a few people coming from different vantage points, engaged in conversations in an attempt to cope with conflict as it arises. It is all about making, keeping and deepening productive professional relationships.

Social work has failed to get across to the general public exactly what we do and why we do it. The profession has too often been apologetic, defensive and 'on the back foot'. Since the 1980s we have been neither sufficiently political (arguing for and alongside disadvantaged people), nor sufficiently confident to explain and create understanding about the complex realities and dynamics social workers deal with. As a profession, social work has also failed badly, as have other professions, on a number of high profile occasions. The murder of the child, Victoria Climbié, is the most recent example.

In Lord Laming's otherwise first rate Inquiry Report into the above failure, there is an absence of detailed forensic analysis of why these failures in professional responsibility occurred, and why social work has failed to make itself indispensable to the communities it serves. But in discussion Lord Laming (2003) commented that he believes there is a question of courage (or its absence) at the heart of the failure: the courage needed by a worker to engage with difficult families when extremely frightened of physical and verbal abuse; the courage to query the professional opinion of a senior colleague; the courage to say something is wrong when other staff seem content. In these comments one sees that much hinges around the failure of communication and responsibility.

What was it about these situations that caused people to lose courage? It is relatively easy to pathologise individuals, but what appears to be individual pathology within an organisation can usually also tell us something important about how the organisation or system is functioning. See, 'Working Below The Surface The Emotional Life Of Contemporary Organisations' (2004 Tavistock Clinic Series).

This raises two key questions in my view:

- Why has social work failed to win credibility and value for its contribution to community life in the UK?

- Why has the profession failed to present a coherent and understandable definition of what exactly social work does?

The remainder of this chapter will seek to address these issues.

WHY HAVE WE FAILED AND WHAT CAN WE DO ABOUT IT?

At two recent lectures given to social work managers and practitioners, the audience was asked if they could agree a common definition of social work. They could not. The discussion reflected on whether we could draw on the occupational standards for social work. The general consensus was that the standards were somewhat impenetrable and inaccessible. The international definition of social work was also dismissed as too vague. Subsequently I asked the same question of friends and colleagues, many of whom have been or are social work trained and qualified, including two professors of social work. My finding, albeit not subjected to academic research, is that there is no one consensual workable definition of social work recognisable to social workers or their colleagues from other agencies. This damaging absence of a succinct definition permits a skewed and negative 'brand image' to live on in the public domain.

Professor Malcolm Payne, in a lecture to the British Association of Social Workers (2006), postulated that there are three aspects to social work and therefore one straightforward definition is not appropriate. He suggested that social workers:

- offer therapeutic advice and support; work at an individual level and focus on the individual as part of the community and the changes open to that individual to make more meaning of their life;

- have a role in providing welfare advice and support including welfare benefit advice;

- are brokers and assessors of services: providing an entry point into services via assessment of need and in-depth knowledge of the sector.

This definition has merit as it measures up to the test suggested by Dr Brenda Clare (2005) that learning and ideas need to resonate with 'lived experience', whilst at the same time having a firm basis in theoretical understanding and historical evidence.

Payne's pragmatic definition of social work presents a significant and realistic framework embracing the statutory, private, voluntary and independent sectors. It is a definition encompassing the range of activities that Alan Milburn, then Secretary of State for Health, in his keynote speech to the 2001 social services conference described as 'the glue which holds society together'.

The problem is that this definition of social work is not widely recognised or 'owned' either inside the profession or equally important, outside it. People know, or think they do, what doctors, nurses, solicitors and teachers actually do. However, the general public does not know what social workers do, hence overly stereotypical, negative and fantasised images pervade.

THE RISE IN MULTI-AGENCY WORKING – CHILDREN'S DEPARTMENTS AND CHILDREN'S TRUSTS

Recently, in theory at least, the focus has shifted to the child with the 'Every Child Matters' (2005) initiative, which sets out a vision and direction for children's services including five essential outcomes for any child/young person. These are: being healthy, feeling safe from abuse, enjoying life, experiencing achievements, and making a positive contribution as a citizen equipped with sufficient skills to achieve economic well-being. No one would dispute the intrinsic value of this projected ideal outcome. However, the specialist social work services for children will not be able to secure these targets without a renewed and increased investment in preventative work, since the reality is that most children's resources are now focused on high risk situations and crises. A direct contradiction has been created in terms of funding.

Recently there have been several major national initiatives: Every Child Matters; Change for Children; The National Service Framework for Children and Families. All herald a significant change in the direction and momentum of services for children and families. All rightly subsume the prominence of cross agency working. Nonetheless, as Calder observes, the government's proper expectation for 'joined-up working' is painfully difficult to achieve in practice and has not alas been modelled by different government departments. For example, Calder lists seven databases each warning of potential dangers to children without guidance on the legal and technical logistics of sharing data.

These initiatives arose in part as a response to the Victoria Climbié tragedy, together with Frank Dobson's concern and commitment when Secretary of State for Health. In his famous speech (1998) about the plight of children in the Looked After System, Frank Dobson was the first Secretary of State to take the situation seriously. He was genuinely appalled at the level of neglect and lack of government response to the alarming evidence about poor academic outcomes, health needs and the number of children from the care system that ended up in prison. Notwithstanding the excellent 1989 Children Act, the fact remains that the outcomes for children in the Looked After System would not be anywhere near acceptable for the children and grandchildren of people reading this chapter. We have tolerated and acquiesced to a system, which, until some recent changes, entrusted our most vulnerable, damaged and disaffected children and young people to the care of largely unqualified and under-supported residential care workers and foster parents.

The government initiatives and in particular, 'Every Child Matters' (2005) bring in significant changes. Schools and health professionals have been given additional duties and responsibilities requiring them to attend to the health and educational needs of Looked After Children. The formation of Children's Trusts will further promote multi-agency working and involvement. However, the devil is in the detail, and in this instance it is in the delivery. The Pathfinder Children's Trusts have identified both progress and difficulties. The Braintree Pathfinder CT has shown a reduction in the number of children coming into the care system, improved school attendance and there are indications of improving academic attainment. On the negative side there have been, and will continue to be in my opinion, problems regarding:

- Success that depends on individual cooperation and goodwill rather than adherence to universally agreed protocols.

- Professionals are still not accountable to the Director of Children's Services, as the Children's Directorate does not directly employ them. This means that a range of professionals integral to the success of Children's Trusts can only be made accountable for delivery through their own organisations. These include doctors, health visitors, school nurses, teachers, clinical psychologists and psychotherapists.
  Lord Laming's cornerstone aim of single accountability as a means of better protecting children, has not been realised.

- Paradoxically, the formation of Children's Directorates, whilst being generally welcomed as a positive move, has caused huge turbulence and resentment in many local authorities.

- In two separate pieces of work for different organisations, designed to bring together staff from the former education departments and the children's section of what used to be Social Services Departments, I was disheartened by the disparaging and dismissive views each group had of the other's standard of work and their fear of closer involvement with each other.

Therefore, whilst there are good intentions and a sound policy initiative there are still challenges ahead involving culture, attitude and behaviour. 'There is sustained pressure on policy-makers to introduce more procedures to reduce risk ... Our argument is that trust, rather than control, management or elimination, is the surest foundation for achieving risk reduction' (Cooper, 2003). As always, matters of professional identity and status will need to be worked through.

This will require sophisticated and elegant leadership, demanding a high level of psychodynamic understanding of group dynamics in cross-agency working, together with a sound knowledge of complex organisations.

Jim Collins, in *Good to Great* (2001), proposes ideas for the way forward that are supported by substantial research. In this and the subsequent monograph, *Good to Great and the Social Sectors* (2005), he has taken on the task of tailoring business processes to the public service sector. Collins' pivotal argument is that unless a business or service makes itself 'indispensable' by virtue of its excellence, the organisation (private or public) will fail to flourish and probably not survive. Collins suggests the following components as instrumental to good (moving towards great) functioning of public services.

- An effective match between vision and resources, including in the statutory sector. The expectation that all funding should come from central government could be viewed as creating unhelpful, infantilising dependence.

- The public should regard the services provided as an intrinsically useful and an essential feature of community life.

- Children's and social care services should be 'marketed' effectively with a 'brand image' that can stand up to public scrutiny.

In my view social work generally, and social work with children and families in particular, does not pass this test. It could and should do, but alas it does not. Collins describes successful organisations as possessing clarity of task, offering indispensable public services and having a reasonable match between expectations and resources. It seems to me that social work struggles and fails to meet these criteria.

WHAT CAN BE DONE?

The remaining section of this chapter will suggest some ideas for what individuals can do and what the profession might campaign for from government, local government and professional bodies.

We should leave the existing structures in health, education and social care intact for at least five years. Constant changes disrupt relationships on a scale not appreciated by government. Likewise service users subjected to this constant restructuring become cynical. One only has to look at what is currently happening in the National Health Service. Understandably staff focus on their personal futures at the expense of their task in the organisation. As a result of the reforms resulting from the introduction of Primary Care Trusts, 50,000 people lost or changed jobs in the health service in 2001/02. In 2005/06 these reforms were reversed and large numbers of senior managers have had to apply for their jobs: as posts have been cut, many will not be successful.

We must endeavour to make politicians aware of the impact of constant structural changes. One can always find arguments for changes in organisational boundaries. It is the balance between what might be perceived as necessary, and the huge disruption caused to services when change is instigated that needs careful consideration. Collin's view is that most organisational change is actually a red herring that produces a sense of purposeful activity without achieving real benefit. Instead what is required is to have the right people in place, working to clearly prioritised tasks with considerable leeway for decision taking, unhampered by continuous audit interruptions. Such a structure would facilitate the move to the 'relationship based authoritative professionalism' proposed by Cooper et al (2003).

Calder (2006) likewise notes that the vaunted 'Common Assessment Framework' and rallying cry for a cross professional 'common language' would not have saved Victoria Climbié. He maintains what is needed is 'the re-establishment of inquisitiveness and moral responsibility in social work'. That requires really listening to the child's and others' concerns and, crucially, speaking out and challenging colleagues. Furthermore, this moral responsibility should not be solely vested in the social work profession or their multi-agency colleagues but actively embraced as a shared responsibility by all in the community who see and hear children in serious distress, eg a relative, neighbour, postman, church warden or local shop keeper.

'Audit and Inspection' is now a powerful industry exerting great influence. Even if totally justified, a zero star rating for Children's Social Services causes staff to leave the authority, morale takes another downturn and scrutiny is increased. The auditors and inspectors making the assessments have no direct responsibility for improving the situation: this responsibility rests entirely with the local authority. The current situation is an example of the unhelpful separation of the power to make judgements with far-reaching consequences from the concomitant responsibility for grappling with the diverse operational mechanics of delivery within tight financial boundaries.

This trend of separating duties and responsibilities, functions and judgements, needs to be reconsidered. For example, recent advice from Health Authorities indicates that they will work almost exclusively with commissioning Primary Care Trusts and consequently Provider Trusts are not expected to participate at this stage of the process. The rationale is that the commissioners should deal with the Trusts on a business basis only, as strategic development is a matter for the Primary Care Trusts and Strategic Health Authorities. This means that those carrying the most knowledge about the service and its delivery are excluded from contributing to planning and development.

Local government is finally beginning to recognise the importance of both adult and children's social care services. The inspection framework requires these services to be functioning at a two or three star level in order for councils to be deemed excellent overall. Therefore, there has been a huge change in how children's and adult social services are perceived within local government circles, and by the elected members. Without adult and children's social services there would be little left for local government to manage. Schools manage more than 80% of the education budget, whilst housing has shrunk significantly and is mainly outsourced. Planning is increasingly determined by central government. Therefore whilst social care is of intrinsic value to the community, it now also holds the future of local government in its hands. This could prove to be a wake-up call for many elected members who have not previously taken an interest in social care matters.

PROFESSIONAL RESPONSIBILITY

The British Association of Social Workers must increase its visibility and impact. Social work needs a strong voice and the Directors of Social Care have spoken about its importance and values. Social workers need a credible professional voice free from directorate and local government influence, even if that influence is mostly benign. We need to improve social work training, and involve lecturers with relevant current experience. We must identify appropriate practice learning opportunities (which must be the responsibility of everyone in the profession), and manage tight quality control combined with high expectations of excellence in order to produce social workers who are confident and proud. An improvement in this area has been achieved by the implementation of the 3-year degree and input from the Practice Learning Taskforce, but there is room for still more improvement. In its final report the Taskforce highlighted a major concern about the impact of structural turbulence on learning and training.

INDIVIDUAL RESPONSIBILITY

Social work practice has a code of conduct that places personal responsibility on individuals to behave professionally, and that means to carry professional responsibility for safe, good practice. This includes following proper procedures for dealing with colleagues who are not performing, and attending social work training courses to improve personal practice. Unless social workers are able to say, 'I am a social worker, this is what I do, and I am proud of what I achieve', much of the rhetoric in the media will go unchallenged.

Service user involvement and empowerment should also be fully embraced. When I was Director in Essex, many teams and managers welcomed the idea of user representation in projects such as Direct Payments, Family Group Conferencing and involving users and carers in interviews, policy analysis and development. Yet, there were also several teams and managers who did not, with referral patterns and data analysis giving evidence of this repeatedly. Targeted management action improved the situation. However, I never got to the bottom of the question as to why there was such reluctance from certain teams and individuals to this agenda, as it offered a powerful coalition between professionals, users and carers. This area is one in which social work is already strong compared to many other professions but there is much more to be achieved.

FINAL COMMENTS

Childcare social work is at a crisis point. There are a number of reasons for this in my view:

- The court system appears to value the expertise of guardian ad litems (social workers employed by CAFCASS) and other professional experts well above the expertise offered by social workers. This runs contrary to the reality that it is the local authority social worker who, in the majority of cases, has direct knowledge and much more insight into the full psycho-social circumstances of the child and family.

- Vacancy rates of anything between 10 and 50% are common for social work posts specialising in work with children and families.

- Training targets for residential social workers, which really are not onerous, (NVQ level 3) are not being achieved. Therefore we still have a transient and partially unqualified workforce in residential childcare.

- The financial situation is volatile. There is a need to invest in long-term preventative services offering much more focused and informed support to families along with access to therapy services for children and young people. However, it is difficult for many Children's Social Services Departments to disinvest from the Looked After System. In other words, if the numbers of children in care is to reduce, then there must be an improved range of services.

- The only solution to this is for government to specifically ring fence funding for Local Authorities. Funding would then be secured for support, prevention and therapeutic services for families, children and young people before difficulties escalate to the necessity for inclusion in the Looked After system.

- Structural turbulence has resulted from the formation of Children's Directorates. Even though the reforms are generally seen as sensible, implementation is nearly always more disruptive than government appreciates. Over 70% of the new Children's Service Directors are from education. This has inevitably caused a loss of social childcare expertise at the top.

- Alliances with other professions should be pursued along with strong representation to government and local government to call a moratorium on any further restructures for the immediate future.

- Clarity of definition and confidence about role and task are absolutely essential. Stronger professional leadership and a stronger professional organisation are 'must haves'.

- Finally social workers must accept personal responsibility, not only for their own professional development and expertise, but also to 'speak up for the profession' in a proud and confident manner, by setting out what we can do, how we do it and what has been achieved.

REFERENCES

Calder M *The future of child protection: where have we come from and where are we going?* (CareKnowledge Briefing 15, 2006). Available at www.careknowledge.com (subscription required)

Clare B *Promoting Deep Learning: A Teaching, Learning and Assessment Endeavour* (Paper presented at International Conference of Social Work 09/2005 to be published in 'Social Work Education', date to be confirmed; available from bclare@cyllene.uwa.edu.au)

Collins J *Good To Great* (Random House, 2001)

Collins J *Good To Great And The Social Sectors. A Monograph* (Random House, 2006)

Cooper A, Hetherington, R and Katz, I *The Risk Factor: making the child protection system work for children* (DEMOS publication Online – available at http://www.demos.co.uk/publications/riskfactor (2003))

Huffington, C, Armstrong, A, Halton, W, Hoyle, L and Pooley, J *Working below the Surface: The Emotional Life Of Contemporary Organizations (sic)* (Tavistock Clinic Series: Karnac Books, 2004)

Menzies Lyth I *The functioning of social systems as a defence against anxiety: a report on a study of the nursing service of a general hospital* (1959). (Reprinted in Menzies Lyth I, *Containing Anxiety in Institutions* (London: Free Association Books, 1988)

Laming, Lord Herbert, An address given at the Michael Sieff Foundation meeting 4 September 2003, Cumberland Lodge Windsor Great Park

National Social Services Conference – Cardiff 2001

O'Neill O, (2002) A Question of Trust – Reith Lectures. Available at http://www.bbc.co.uk/radio4/reith2002/

SECTION 4

Here, in the last two papers we move away from the individuals and the uniqueness of each family situation with which we started this collection. These final papers are by people not directly involved with the Family Justice System, but on whose work it is nevertheless dependent.

The large scale, long term research that Professors Philip and Carolyn Pape **Cowan** undertaken gives us important guidance about where preventative funds should be directed and the approach that is likely to be helpful in creating a positive parental environment for children's healthy development. Family justice requires such researchers to inform it of the likely efficacy of possible interventions, as does Government in its policy decisions. The Cowans' research indicates that focusing on the couple relationship of the parents maximises good outcomes for the children.

Dr Stephen Cretney is the pre-eminent family law academic of his generation. *Family Law in the Twentieth Century, a History* (2003) by Stephen, is and will remain the definitive record of the curious processes that have driven the development of our family law over the past century and a half. In his paper he reviews the rules surrounding marriage and reflects on recent changes in the law, raising questions about the role of the State, religious institutions and the law in how 'marriage', 'partnerships' and the 'family' evolve. He leaves us wondering what the concepts will mean to those a few generations forward.

Beyond Mothering: Dispelling Three Myths About Family Relationships and Children's Adaptation

Professors Philip A Cowan and Carolyn Pape Cowan*

In every historical age, in every region of the world, there are passionately held beliefs that are regarded as 'accepted wisdom' about what is best for children. These beliefs shape the norms of childrearing practices when families are working reasonably well, and dominate discussions in the child welfare and legal systems about how to protect children from the unsettling vicissitudes of family disintegration – domestic violence and abuse, contested custody decisions, and placement away from their biological parents. For more than a century, social scientists studying families have attempted to evaluate accepted wisdom and contribute to public discussion about how family relationships affect children's development, adaptation, and psychopathology (see PA Cowan & Cowan, 2006; Cummings, Davies, & Campbell, 2000). Because a great many controversies within social science research on families are far from settled, we are not claiming that contemporary research on families can settle all issues and provide clear guidelines for parents, the family justice system, policy makers, or others concerned with the well-being of children. Our goal in this chapter is to show that findings from family research, especially those emerging in the past three decades, tend to challenge some of what has been accepted as wisdom. This analysis suggests that we reinterpret two widely accepted 'truths' as family myths and reconsider a third widely-held belief that is not supported by the data.

WHAT DO SOCIAL SCIENTISTS AND CLINICAL SCHOLARS KNOW, AND HOW DO THEY KNOW IT?

Let us clarify at the outset what it means when family researchers or clinicians claim to know something. The first and primary criterion is that claims by social scientists and clinical scholars that their statements represent knowledge must be based on systematic observation. This is in

* Carolyn Pape Cowan is Professor of Psychology, Emerita at the University of California, Berkeley, and co-director with Philip Cowan of three longitudinal preventive intervention projects: Becoming a Family, Schoolchildren and Their Families, and Supporting Father Involvement. Dr Cowan has published widely in the professional literature on family relationships and family transitions, is co-editor of *Fatherhood today: Men's changing role in the family* (Wiley, 1988), and consults widely on the development and evaluation of interventions for couples who are parents of young children.

Philip A Cowan is Professor of Psychology, Emeritus at the University of California, Berkeley where he has served as Director of the Clinical Psychology Program and the Institute of Human Development. In addition to authoring numerous scientific articles, he is author of *Piaget with Feeling* (Holt, Rinehart, & Winston, 1978), and co-editor of four books and monographs.

The Cowans are co-authors of *When partners become parents: The big life change for couples* (Erlbaum, 2000), and co-editors of *The family context of parenting in the child's adaptation to school* (Erlbaum, 2005), part of the series, *Parenting: Science and Practice* (Erlbaum, Editor Marc Bornstein).

contrast with claims by mathematicians, which rely on deduction, definition, and logical consistency, and moral philosophers' claims, which rely on rational analysis of what is good and just. The emphasis here is not simply on observation, but on observation that is systematic, and done according to a protocol described in enough detail that another observer could replicate it to arrive at similar (or different) conclusions. By this criterion, a claim made by an isolated researcher or clinician that does not provide a method to enable other researchers to replicate the findings cannot be used legitimately to distinguish between knowledge and belief.

A second criterion defining knowledge is that, in contrast with physical scientists of the past who claimed to have discovered absolute laws that held over time and place across our universe, empirical research on families is limited to statements about probabilities.[1] For example, a claim that divorce is harmful for children is a statement about risks and outcomes, which asserts that parents' divorce is *more likely* than parents' staying together to result in difficulties for the child. We discuss the merits of this claim below. For now, we are simply stating that *all* conclusions in the social sciences represent probability statements rather than absolute and certain truths. A faith-based belief that divorce is morally wrong does not depend on observation or on real-world facts. It may have its own legitimacy in the realm of morality and law, but it cannot be challenged on empirical grounds. By contrast, a belief that maintaining a strained marriage is more likely to benefit children than divorce is open to scientific test.

A third knotty issue in defining scientific knowledge is the need to distinguish between causation and correlation. Why is this important? An intervention into family life, such as a decision about which parent should have physical or legal custody after divorce, or about whether to remove a child from a violent home, should be based on solid evidence that the intervention is likely to have a direct effect on at least some optimal outcomes for children. A statement based on simple correlation is much less likely to lead to sensible intervention strategies. The most current egregious example in the United States is the current Administration's assertion that, because children of single mothers tend to fare less well than children in two parent families (a well established fact, Waite & Gallagher, 2000), the government ought to work toward getting single mothers married (a hypothesis about causation with no supporting evidence).

We have written elsewhere that providing evidence of causality in the study of families and children's development is a difficult task (PA Cowan & Cowan, 2002). Causal statements must be based on systematic observations that the presumed causal variable (A), precedes the effect (B), and that it provides some force or action that brings the effect into being (A → B). Furthermore, to establish causal connections, it is necessary to prove that B is not traceable to factors other than A – that there is a unique connection between cause and effect. That is, we need to know not only whether joint physical custody in divorce cases is associated with a particular outcome for the child, but also whether that same outcome also follows from other family arrangements. Studies in which family factors and child outcomes are measured at the same time can never be taken as proof of causality. In that case, we can never know whether parenting is responsible for a specific child outcome, or whether the child's problematic or cooperative behavior is the driving force behind the quality of the parent-child relationship.

The 'gold standard' for demonstrating causality is an experiment in which there is random assignment of people to two or more conditions, one with a treatment, and one serving as a control. Without random assignment, it is always possible that the people who chose the treatment are somehow better off or more motivated. Legal decisions and policies based on

---

[1]   By this definition, Freud and many other clinician/scholars are regarded as scientists because their observations are reported and their methods may be replicated by other trained clinicians.

satisfied consumer testimony – for example, that a costly family service program works – are on shaky ground, because we do not know whether people without the intervention, a much less costly alternative, also improve over time.

We need to acknowledge that some experiments are impractical or unethical. We cannot simply randomly assign children to divorced and non-divorced parents. Another way of trying to assess whether risks and outcomes are causally related is to use comparison data and statistical controls in an attempt to rule out alternative possibilities. In this case, causal interpretations of the data become more plausible, but the consumers of such research need to read very carefully to find out whether the researcher has tested the alternatives in a reasonable way.

In this chapter, most of the claims that we make about the links between family relationships and children's adaptation are based on research studies that adopt a risk-outcome paradigm, originally used to great positive effect in the field of Public Health epidemiology (Kleinbaum, Morgenstern & Kupper, 1982):

1 a risk factor is an antecedent variable or condition associated with an elevated probability of a specified outcome in a population;

2 a protective factor is a variable or condition that reduces the probability of negative outcome despite the presence of risk; and

3 a vulnerability factor is a variable or condition that increases the probability of a negative outcome associated with a given risk.

What follows is a description of three widely-held beliefs about families, along with a brief summary of the evidence concerning risks, protective factors, vulnerabilities, and outcomes. These examples force us to conclude that none of these beliefs is supported by the facts. We then discuss some of the implications of this de-mythologising for those who are attempting to enhance the well-being of children or to protect them from further harm.

MYTH 1: FATHERS ARE RELATIVELY UNINVOLVED AS PARENTS. FORTUNATELY, MOTHERS ARE MORE IMPORTANT THAN FATHERS IN SHAPING CHILDREN'S DEVELOPMENT

It is widely believed that mothers are as essential as good nutrition and non-toxic physical environments for children's healthy development and well-being. By contrast, fathers' active involvement in the life of their children is treated either as a vanishing prospect (D Blankenhorn, 1995) or as a luxury – nice to have, but not to be counted on. Reinforcement of this double-sided myth (fathers are uninvolved; mothers are key to children's development) comes from many sources at all levels of society. The general public is not alone in assuming that mothers play a much more central role in children's development than fathers do. Social service agencies reinforce this perception. A quick look at most family service agencies reveals that the rooms are decorated in feminine colours, with pictures of mothers and children on the walls, and day time appointments during hours when most fathers and many mothers are at work. Until recently, researchers also contributed to the problem. Eleven years after the publication of the first version of the *Handbook of Child Psychology* (Carmichael, 1954), Nash (1965) pointed out that 'father' had not been included in the index. Except for studies of the impact of father *absence* on children's development, the impact of father involvement was rarely investigated systematically. To this day, the fields of Developmental Psychology, Sociology, and Mental Health tend to focus on mothers and children, although research on fathers is on the rise.

If the issue is framed simply in terms of time spent, it is clear that in both single parent (Carlson & McLanahan, 2002) and married parent households (Day & Lamb, 2004), mothers spend more time with children, regardless of whether they work outside the home (CP Cowan & Cowan, 1988). Nevertheless, studies in the past two decades, summarised in a number of books and chapters (PA Cowan, Cowan, & Cohen, (in press); Lamb, 2000; Parke, 2002; Tamis-LeMonda & Cabrera, 2002), provide extensive support for two clear conclusions:

1   Married fathers are not usually as involved as mothers are in the daily care of their young children, but contemporary men are more involved with their children than men used to be (Coltrane, 1996; Pleck, 1997) – and a large proportion of fathers are substantially involved with their children even when they are divorced or separated from the mother (McKenry, McKelvey, Leigh, & Wark, 1996).

2   Of the growing number of children living with only one parent, about 23% to 25% in both the United States and the United Kingdom, the vast majority live with their mothers. Many assume that fathers are absent from the child's life in these 'lone parent' families. In fact, a 20-city study of unmarried couples having a child together in the United States, the *Fragile Families* study (Harknett, Hardman, Garfinkel, & McLanahan, 2001), finds that especially around the time of birth, about half of unmarried fathers are living with the mother, and most are romantically involved with her and involved with the baby. We assume that the figures would be similar in Great Britain. Although these fragile family relationships are at high risk for dissolution, many fathers do remain involved with the mothers and the children.

Two conclusions follow from these facts. First, many fathers in families with different structures are actively involved in the daily lives of their children. Generalisations about how contemporary fathers are unmotivated to engage with their children are simply that – generalisations. Second, it should never be assumed that a 'lone mother' is parenting a child by herself. In many cases, the biological father is living in the home and actively involved with the child, or not living in the home but involved in many ways. Family service workers who ignore the father in calls or visits could assume that he is more or less absent.

Many researchers assume that a high level of father involvement is better for children than a low level or total absence, and the results of countless studies reveal that the *quality* of fathers' involvement is associated with negative or positive outcomes for children (Florsheim, 2000; Parke, 1995; Pleck, 1997). Positive paternal involvement – fathers' warmth, closeness, and responsiveness to their children – is consistently associated with the children's advanced cognitive skills, academic achievement, and emotional adjustment (Amato, 1998; Amato & Gilbreth, 1999; Black, Dubowitz, & Starr, 1999; Zimmerman, Salem, & Notaro, 2000). Similarly, when the father-child relationship is positive, children are less likely to show maladaptive, problematic behavior or to receive DSM-IV diagnoses (Brody & Flor, 1996; Cicchetti, Toth, & Maughan, 2000; Conger & Chao, 1996; Hetherington et al, 1999; Hinshaw et al, 2000; Phares, 1996).

Although these results are based on correlational studies and open to the criticism that perhaps fathers are more likely to stay involved with more competent, well-behaved children, the findings are consistent with two hypotheses: that it is beneficial to children when their fathers are positively involved with them, and that it may be wise to encourage this kind of involvement. In writings or lectures on this topic, we have found that some readers or listeners are sceptical about any intervention that would increase father involvement. They hear the plea to pay attention to the potential contributions of fathers as a dismissal of mothers' contributions, or as an inflated claim that unless children have a father or father-figure in the home, they cannot develop in a healthy way. In fact, a few have argued that fathers are necessary for healthy development, especially of boys (DG Blankenhorn, Bayme, & Elshtain, 1990; Popenoe, 1996). Others have attempted to counter this claim by pointing to evidence that fathers are not *necessary* for children's healthy development (Silverstein & Auerbach, 1999). Still others have expressed concern about fathers who are violent and abusive to their partner and children being encouraged to spend more time with them, and we share this concern. Beyond the controversies, the conclusion we draw from systematic research is simply that fathers who have positive ongoing relationships with their children and are actively involved in their children's daily care can contribute significantly and often in unique ways to the children's development. Furthermore, since many contemporary fathers say that they want to be more involved with their children than their fathers were with them (CP Cowan & Cowan, 2000), it seems reasonable to find ways to help make this happen. We focus on the implications of this point for child custody decisions in our discussion of the second family myth.

MYTH 2: CHILDREN WILL BENEFIT FROM UNHAPPILY-MARRIED PARENTS STAYING TOGETHER FOR THEIR SAKE

There are two related assumptions contained in this myth – that parental divorce is harmful to children and that even when parents are unhappy, it is better for the children if they stay together.

Divorce

The question of how divorce affects children remains one of the most contested areas of family research. We do not have space here to describe the controversy, but the issue has been well-described elsewhere in publications in the United States and the United Kingdom (Ahrons, 2004; Amato, 2001; Hetherington & Kelly, 2002; Rodgers & Pryor, 1998; Wallerstein, Lewis, & Blakeslee, 2000). There is no doubt that at least in the short term, most children of any age are disequilibrated by the divorce of their parents, and a substantial number suffer at least temporary setbacks in social and emotional development and academic achievement. In the long-term, however, the negative effects dissipate for most children, so that 'only' about 20% of children suffer in lasting ways (Hetherington & Kelly, 2002). This means that a substantial number of children may be suffering some consequences of their parents divorce, but it is also true that the vast majority of children of divorce go on to develop healthy and productive lives. In our view, the sociologist Paul Amato (2000) has a sensible perspective on the issues surrounding divorce. He suggests that the usual framing of the question – 'Does divorce hurt children – yes or no?' – is misleading. He suggests a more differentiated approach: 'Divorce benefits some individuals, leads others to experience temporary decrements in well-being, and forces others on a downward trajectory from which they might never recover fully. Understanding the contingencies under which divorce leads to these diverse outcomes is a priority for future research.'

Staying together: the issue of marital conflict

The other side of the divorce issue is the claim that, unless there is a high level of couple violence or child abuse, children of parents who remain in unhappy marriages will ultimately be better off. Our response to this claim is that 'it all depends'. More than 25 years of research on the association between marital conflict and children's adaptation clearly suggests that when parents have high levels of *unresolved* conflict as a couple, or silent, frosty relationship struggles, their children are at risk for higher levels of internalising problems such as depression and social withdrawal, externalising problems such as fighting, stealing, and oppositional behavior, and more likely to have lower levels of academic achievement (PA Cowan, Cowan, Ablow, Johnson, & Measelle, 2005; Cummings, Davies, & Campbell, 2000; O'Connor et al, 1999). Our own research on families with children between 3 and 14 years of age indicates that it is very difficult for parents to maintain productive relationships with their children when their couple relationships is in distress. Distress in the relationship between parents, then, should be regarded as a risk factor for compromised parenting that is either too harsh or too permissive (Conger, Elder, Lorenz, Simons, & Whitbeck, 1994; Kitzmann, 2000). In contrast to more responsive and effective parenting, compromised parenting is associated with children faring less well (PA Cowan, Powell, & Cowan, 1998; Kuczynski, 2003; O'Connor, Dunn, Jenkins, Pickering, & Rasbash, 2001; Steinberg, 2001).

All of the results cited so far are based on correlations among couple relationship distress, parenting quality, and children's developmental outcomes. It is possible to argue, and some do, that the child's problematic behaviour makes him or her difficult to manage and that this difficulty has a negative impact on the couple relationship (Fincham, Grych, & Osborne, 1994). Of course, if we look at the family as a system, the impact of any major distress is likely to reverberate from parent to child and child to parent (Jenkins, Simpson, Dunn, Rasbash, & O'Connor, 2005). We have some experimental evidence, in a study of a preventive intervention, that marital distress plays a causal role in both parent-child relationships and children's adjustment (CP Cowan, Cowan, & Heming, 2005). Beginning with 100 working class and middle class families whose first child was about to enter kindergarten at age 5, the Schoolchildren and their Families Project invited the parents for an interview as a couple. During the recruitment, no mention was made of the possibility of an intervention, so we were not attracting couples in desperate need of help. Couples were randomly selected to participate in one of three study conditions: (1) Brief Consultation – a chance to consult on family issues once each year with the staff couple who interviewed them; (2) a 16-week couples group led by the staff couple interviewing them, in which parent-child relationships were emphasised; or (3) a 16-week couples group with their staff couple, in which the parents' relationship as a couple was emphasised. (The variation in emphasis was not described to the participating couples.) The group leaders were trained mental health professionals who led semi-structured groups that (a) followed a general curriculum of topics to be discussed, along with (b) open time for the couples to bring their own issues to the group. Extensive assessment including interviews, questionnaires, and family observations were completed before the intervention, and again when the child was in kindergarten, first grade, fourth grade, and ninth grade.

We have published results of the first 3 years of the study, centering on the child's transition to elementary school (PA Cowan, Cowan, Ablow, Johnson, & Measelle, 2005). In comparison with parents in the control condition (Brief Consultation), participants in the Parenting-focused couples groups conducted during the pre-school year had more effective interactions with their children a year later, as we observed them during a 45-minute interaction in a laboratory-playroom, and their children had significantly fewer adjustment problems as the children described themselves, and significantly fewer internalising problems (depressed, anxious, socially withdrawn), as their teachers described them in kindergarten, first grade, and fourth grade. In the context of the present discussion, it is noteworthy that the participants in the Couple-focused groups not only decreased their conflict as a couple when they worked and played together with their child in our project playroom, but their parenting became more responsive and effective, and their children showed higher academic achievement scores and less aggression according to their teachers in the five years after the intervention. That is, using a couples group intervention format, a focus on parenting brought improvements in the parent-child relationships, but not in the couple relationship, whereas a focus on the couple relationship improved relationships for the couple *and* between each parent and the child. Furthermore, in some complex statistical analyses, we also found that *changes* in parents after the intervention were associated with their children's higher levels of adaptation to school. Finally, very recent results reported to the Society for Research on Adolescence (Cowan, Cowan, Measelle, & Schulz, 2006) reveal that the positive intervention effects on parents and children last for 10 years – until the children, who are now adolescents, enter high school at age 14. We are gratified by the power and longevity of the couples group intervention effects. The point we want to emphasise here is that the results, obtained in a random assignment experiment, demonstrate the *causal* connection between couple relationship quality and children's outcomes, and suggest that the couple relationship, at least in this study, is more likely to affect the parent-child relationship than vice-versa.

What we have been describing about the links among couple relationship quality, parent-child relationships, and children's outcomes applies not only to families in which parents are married or cohabiting. When separated and divorced parents fight overtly, especially over the children, parent-child relationships tend to be compromised, and the children are more likely to have academic difficulties and externalising or internalising disorders than children of divorce who do not have the added risk of unresolved parental conflict (see for example Amato & Booth, 2001; Hetherington & Kelly, 2002; Pruett, Williams, Insabella, & Little, 2003).

In sum, the belief that children will benefit from their parents staying together 'no matter what' is a myth. It does matter what. If parents can overcome the difficulties between them and work together effectively in co-parenting their child, children in two-parent families can enjoy a number of psychological and economic advantages. If, however, the parents live together in a state of unresolved tension, they are not doing the child any favours, because the children are aware of and react to the tension in the family atmosphere (Ablow, 2005).

Studies that provide a more differentiated picture of the risks of divorce and the risks of couples remaining married add a new perspective on one of the essential ingredients of children's well-being. Certainly, as the raft of popular books and the volume of research on parenting would attest, how parents behave with their children and the quality of relationship mothers and fathers establish with them, constitutes one important aspect of the family environment affecting children's adjustment. The research we have cited shows that beyond parent-child relationship quality, couple relationship quality is central to children's development. The most obvious implication of these findings is that parent education and classes on parenting may not be sufficient to enhance the ability of parents to provide the most supportive environment for their children. Education and services directed toward improving the parents' relationship as a couple may be necessary to turn unrewarding parent-child relationships around.

Let us return to the issue of child custody. In our view, family research findings do not help those in the legal system to decide whether *in a specific case* custody ought to be shared or allocated to this mother or this father. Neither do research results support the practice of times past when mother custody was the default decision. Fathers can and do make important contributions to their children's development. Joint custody should be a less likely alternative when the parents cannot collaborate on their co-parenting relationship. Thus, the quality of the family relationships, not simply the *structure* of the family arrangements, is most important to consider in terms of enhancing children's well-being.

The findings associated with Myths 1 and 2 are relevant to policy issues concerning the allocation of government resources for families to benefit children. During the time we spent in London on sabbatical in the spring of 2004, a policy shift was taking place within the new Department for Education and Skills, which is responsible for supporting services for families. Funds were being withdrawn from support of help for couples (which had been given proportionately more support in England than in the United States) and reallocated to parenting education programs (Moran, Ghate, & van der Merwe, 2004), on the theory that the improvement of parenting skills was the most direct way to enhance children's adaptation. It is clear from the results we have presented that policy-makers may need to reconsider this shift.

MYTH 3: FAMILIES ARE IN A STATE OF SERIOUS DECLINE

The statement that contemporary families are not faring well seems 'obviously true'. The statistical trends being used to support this statement hold for both American (Popenoe, 1993) and British (General Household Survey, 2002) populations. There is no question that there is an increasing diversity of family forms, interpreted as a move away from the traditional two-heterosexual-parent nuclear family. Although divorce rates have leveled off in recent years, they remain at near all-time highs. Marriage rates have declined, cohabitation has increased, and couples are having fewer children. In the United States and Europe, overall rates of lone parenthood are increasing, although they are decreasing sharply among African American youth. Mothers of young children are increasingly involved in the paid workforce. Gay and lesbian couples are adopting children when the law permits, and raising children together, even when both partners have no legal parental status with the child. Pitted against what might be a sentimentalised and inaccurate view of families 50 to 100 years ago (Coontz, 1992; Skolnick, 1991), all of these changes have been described as evidence of family decline.

To many social observers, what clinches the family decline argument is the fact that these changes in the 'traditional nuclear family' have been accompanied by perceived increases in the incidence of problems in children and teenagers. We say 'perceived' because concerns with family decline have heightened over the past two decades along with a depiction of youth as troubled in the public media. Yet, both United States (Hernandez, 1996) and United Kingdom (Bradshaw & Mayhew, 2005) social trends reveal a mixed picture. Overall, physical health, life expectancy of children and youth improved dramatically over the twentieth century. There is no question that teenagers are more sexually active than they used to be but sexual risk-taking has declined over the past two decades, and, despite public concerns, so has violent crime. Teenage pregnancy increased dramatically over the past century, but in both the United Kingdom and the United States it is leveling off, with a notable decline in African American communities.

We are not Pollyannas. The incidence of diagnosed mental illness in children and youth has increased (Bradshaw & Mayhew, 2005; Eberstadt, 2004), especially Attention Deficit Behavior Disorder, Asperger's Syndrome, and conduct disorder, although it is not clear whether the increases in incidence and prevalence represent a true increase in the occurrence of psychopathology or whether the trends might reflect increased attention to the mental health of young people, increasing diagnostic skill, or more efficient reporting and data collection. Also of concern is a steep increase in the number of children in poverty toward the last half of the twentieth century, although the new century appears to have brought some decline. In sum, the public perception of increasing problems in children and youth is not always matched by systematic data. Despite some indicators of increasing distress, there is no evidence that today's youth are in a state of intellectual, emotional, and moral decline.

It is possible to argue that the trends describing family diversity and children's well-being have only recently taken a turn for the better, and that compared with a century ago, there have been significant rises in conditions of risk for families and individual family members. Our response returns to the issue of what can legitimately be inferred from social trend data. In our view, there are two serious problems with the evidence used to support the family decline interpretation, serious enough that we cannot accept it as valid. First, it is not clear that all changes away from traditional family arrangements are negative for family members. For example, some divorces do not produce long-term damage to children and adolescents, and may even protect them from the pain of unending family conflict or disengagement. Mothers who work outside the home because they want to, and have the support from their partners to do so, are less likely to be depressed, and more likely to have competent daughters (Moorehouse, 1993). The expectation that children of gay and lesbian parents would somehow suffer from this non-traditional arrangement has been substantially disproven; in fact, many studies suggest that these children are faring even better than comparable children of heterosexual parents (Golombok & Tasker, 1994; Stacey & Biblarz, 2001). These examples illustrate the fact that we can no longer assume that a traditional two-heterosexual-parent family with mum at home and dad providing the income is the ideal environment for children and youth.

Second, revisiting the general principles of correlation and causation, we find that the family decline argument rests on the correlation between two sets of statistical trends – changes over the same period of time in family structure and changes in children's well-being. Even if we accept the argument that the well-being of children has declined as family diversity has increased, it is not legitimate to conclude that family change is *causing* children's difficulties. There are too many exceptions to this generalization – too many other changes in the world, or lack of change, that could account for shifts in children's well-being – to blame negative outcomes on changes in family structure. In short, the evidence does not support the belief that families are in a state of decline and that children are paying the price. Increasing diversity, yes. Increasing risk, perhaps, especially because family members creating these new family forms have few guidelines to help them create the kinds of family environments and support that are necessary for parents and children to flourish.

What difference would it make to the justice system if the idea that families are in a state of decline were regarded as a myth? We believe that better decisions would be made for children and families if it were not assumed that every departure from traditional two-heterosexual-parent families creates a risk of increased harm for children. Decisions about divorce, custody, and other family issues need to be based on the quality of relationships in the families under discussion, not on generalisations derived from a frequently erroneous comparison between this family and a mythical ideal.

CONCLUSIONS

We have attempted to show that three widely-held beliefs about families may not be true. Contrary to the myth that mothers are essential to children's development and fathers are necessary only in a biological sense, recent research has demonstrated the important and unique contributions that fathers make to their children's development. Contrary to the myth that parents should stay together for the sake of their children no matter what, some genuine risks for children are associated with couples' decisions to remain together. We are not advocating divorce as the best solution for all couples in distress, but the research forces us to pay attention to the fact that there may be negative consequences for children of warring parents who stay together 'for the children's sake'. Finally, despite the fact that we see the significant stressors that many contemporary families face during the childrearing years (Cowan & Cowan, 2000), we are not convinced that families are in a state of psychological and moral disarray.

From the systematic research that we cited in the dispelling of these myths, we draw two important messages for those who work in family law and the family justice system. First, in attempting to determine what is best for children's developmental outcomes, the law tends to focus on how children's adaptation is related to family status – whether the parents are married, separated, divorced, or cohabiting. By contrast, family researchers and clinicians focus on how children's development and difficulties are related to the *quality* of family relationship processes. Although it may require more work to consider the circumstances of each case, the conditions supporting the well-being of children and youth depend in large part on the quality of relationships among family members, regardless of whether the parents are married, cohabiting, separated, or divorced. And those who are attempting to represent parents in adversarial divorce proceedings might realise, and inform their clients, that continued acrimony after divorce is likely to have a cumulative, debilitating impact on their children.

As our title suggests, concern for the well-being of children and youth must extend beyond mothering. Fathering is equally important to children. The co-parenting relationship between the parents, regardless of their marital or living arrangements, also plays an important role in the pathways children travel to adulthood. And, while we have not focused on larger systems here, the role of grandparents in the life of the child should not be ignored. Finally, we have focused in this chapter on the relationship interior of the family. In a more comprehensive and systemic analysis of what is best for children, it will be necessary to examine the role of government, business, and other social institutions, in terms of how they create additional stress for families or provide supportive regulations and services to help contemporary parents and children face the real challenges of modern family life.

REFERENCES

Ablow, JC 'When parents conflict or disengage: Understanding links between marital distress and children's adaptation to school' in PA Cowan, CP Cowan, J Ablow, VK Johnson & J Measelle (eds), *The family context of parenting in children's adaptation to elementary school* (Mahwah, NJ, Lawrence Erlbaum Associates, 2005)

Ahrons, CR *We're still family: What grown children have to say about their parents' divorce* (1st edn) (New York, HarperCollins, 2004)

Amato, PR 'More than money? Men's contributions to their children's lives' in A Booth & AC Crouter (eds) *Men in families: When do they get involved? What difference does it make?* (pp 241–278) (Mahwah, NJ, US, Lawrence Erlbaum Associates, Inc, Publishers, 1998)

Amato, PR 'The consequences of divorce for adults and children' (2000) *Journal of Marriage & the Family*, 62(4), 1269–1287

Amato, PR 'Children of divorce in the 1990s: An update of the amato and keith (1991) meta-analysis' (2001) *Journal of Family Psychology*, 15(3), 355–370

Amato, PR & Booth, A 'The legacy of parents' marital discord: Consequences for children's marital quality' (2001) *Journal of Personality & Social Psychology*, 81(4), 627–638

Amato, PR & Gilbreth, JG 'Nonresident fathers and children's well-being: A meta-analysis' (1999) *Journal of Marriage & the Family*, 61(3), 557–573.

Black, MM, Dubowitz, H, & Starr, RH, Jr 'African American fathers in low income, urban families: Development, behavior, and home environment of their three-year-old children' (1999) *Child Development*, 70(4), 967–978

Blankenhorn, D *Fatherless America: Confronting our most urgent social problem* (New York: Basic Books, 1995)

Blankenhorn, DG, Bayme, S & Elshtain, JB (eds) *Rebuilding the nest: A new commitment to the American family* (Milwaukee, WI, Family Service America, 1990).

Bradshaw, J, & Mayhew, E (eds) *The well-being of children in the UK* (2nd edn) (York University: Save the Children Fund, 2005)

Brody, GH, & Flor, DL 'Coparenting, family interactions, and competence among African American youths' in JP McHale & PA Cowan (eds), *Understanding how family-level dynamics affect children's development: Studies of two-parent families. New directions for child development* (Vol 74, pp 77–91) (San Francisco, CA, Jossey-Bass, 1996)

Carlson, M, & McLanahan, SS 'Father involvement, fragile families, and public policy' in C Tamis-LeMonda & N Cabrera (eds), *Handbook of father involvement: Multidisciplinary perspectives* (Mahwah, NJ, Lawrence Erlbaum Associates, 2002)

Carmichael, L (1954) *Manual of child psychology* (2nd edn) (NY, Wiley, 1954)

Cicchetti, D, Toth, SL, & Maughan, A 'An ecological-transactional model of child maltreatment' in AJ Sameroff, M Lewis & SM Miller (eds), *Handbook of developmental psychopathology* (2nd edn, pp 689–722) (New York, US, Kluwer Academic/Plenum Publishers, 2000)

Coltrane, S *Family man: Fatherhood, housework, and gender equity* (New York: Oxford University Press, 1996)

Conger, RD & Chao, W (1996). 'Adolescent depressed mood' in LS Ronald (ed) *Understanding differences between divorced and intact families: Stress, interaction, and child outcome* (pp 157–175) (Thousand Oaks, CA, US, Sage Publications, Inc, 1996)

Conger, RD, Elder, GH, Jr, Lorenz, FO, Simons, RL, & Whitbeck, LB (eds) *Families in troubled times: Adapting to change in rural America* (New York: Aldine de Gruyter, 1994)

Coontz, S *The way we never were: American families and the nostalgia trap* (New York, Basic Books, 1992)

Cowan, CP & Cowan, PA 'Who does what when partners become parents: Implications for men, women, and marriage' (1998) *Marriage & Family Review*, 12(3–4), 105–131

Cowan, CP, & Cowan, PA (2000) *When partners become parents: The big life change for couples* (Mahwah, NJ, Lawrence Erlbaum Associates, (2000)

Cowan, CP, Cowan, PA & Heming, G 'Two variations of a preventive intervention for couples: Effects on parents and children during the transition to elementary school'. in PA Cowan, CP Cowan, J Ablow, VK Johnson & J Measelle (eds) *The family context of parenting in children's adaptation to elementary school* (Mahwah, NJ, Lawrence Erlbaum Associates, 2005)

Cowan, PA & Cowan, CP 'Interventions as tests of family systems theories: Marital and family relationships in children's development, and psychopathology' (2002) *Development and Psychopatholology. Special issue on Inteventions as tests of theories*, 14, 731–760

Cowan, PA & Cowan, CP 'Developmental psychopathology from a family systems and family risk factors perspective: Implications for family research, practice, and policy' in D Cicchetti & DJ Cohen (eds), *Developmental psychopathology* (2nd edn, Vol 1, pp 530–587) (New York, Wiley, 2006).

Cowan, PA, Cowan, CP, Ablow, J, Johnson, VK, & Measelle, J *The family context of parenting in children's adaptation to elementary school* (Mahwah, NJ, Lawrence Erlbaum Associates, 2005)

Cowan, PA, Cowan, CP & Cohen, N 'Supporting fathers' involvement with kids' in JD Berrick & N Gilbert (eds) *Raising children: Emerging needs, modern risks, and social responses* (not yet published)

Cowan, PA, Powell, D & Cowan, CP 'Parenting interventions: A family systems perspective' in W Damon (ed) *Handbook of child psychology* (5th edn, Vol 4, pp 3–72) (John Wiley & Sons, Inc, 1998)

Cummings, EM, Davies, P, & Campbell, SB *Developmental psychopathology and family process: Theory, research, and clinical implications* (E. Mark Cummings, Patrick T. Davies, Susan B. Campbell; foreword by Dante Cicchetti) (New York, Guilford Press, 2000)

Day, RD, & Lamb, ME *Conceptualizing and measuring father involvement* (Mahwah, NJ, Lawrence Erlbaum, 2004)

Eberstadt, M *Home-alone America: The hidden toll of day care, behavioral drugs, and other parent substitutes* (New York, Sentinel, 2004)

Fincham, FD, Grych, JH, & Osborne, LN 'Does marital conflict cause child maladjustment? Directions and challenges for longitudinal research' (1994) *Journal of Family Psychology*, 8(2), 128–140.

Florsheim, P (2000) 'The economic and psychological dynamics of nonresident paternal involvement' in RD Taylor & MC Wang (eds) *Resilience across contexts: Family, work, culture, and community* (pp 55–87) (Mahwah, NJ, Lawrence Erlbaum Associates, Inc, Publishers, 2000)

Golombok, S & Tasker, F 'Children in lesbian and gay families: Theories and evidence' (1994) *Annual Review of Sex Research*, V, 73–100

Harknett, K, Hardman, L, Garfinkel, I & McLanahan, SS 'The fragile families study: Social policies and labor markets in seven cities' (2001) *Children & Youth Services Review*, 23(6–7), 537–555

Hernandez, DJ in *Trends in the well-being of America's children and youth: 1996* (Washington, DC: US Bureau of the Census, 1996)

Hetherington, EM, Henderson, SH, Reiss, D, Anderson, ER, Bridges, M, Chan, RW, et al 'Adolescent siblings in stepfamilies: Family functioning and adolescent adjustment' (1999) *Monographs of the Society for Research in Child Development*, 64(4), 222

Hetherington, EM, & Kelly, J *For better or for worse: Divorce reconsidered* (New York: WW Norton, 2002)

Hinshaw, SP, Owens, EB, Wells, KC, Kraemer, HC, Abikoff, HB, Arnold, LE, et al 'Family processes and treatment outcome in the MTA: Negative/ineffective parenting practices in relation to multimodal treatment' (2000) *Journal of Abnormal Child Psychology*, 28(6), 555–568

Jenkins, J, Simpson, A, Dunn, J, Rasbash, J, & O'Connor, TG 'Mutual influence of marital conflict and children's behavior problems: Shared and nonshared family risks' (2005) *Child Development*, 76(1), 24–39

Kitzmann, KM 'Effects of marital conflict on subsequent triadic family interactions and parenting' (2000) *Developmental Psychology*, 36(1), 3–13

Kleinbaum, DG, Morgenstern, H & Kupper, LL *Epidemiologic research: Principles and quantitative methods* (Belmont, CA, Lifetime Learning Publications, 1982)

Kuczynski, L *Handbook of dynamics in parent-child relations* (Thousand Oaks, CA, Sage Publications, 2003)

Lamb, ME 'The history of research on father involvement: An overview' (2000) *Marriage & Family Review*, 29(2–3), 23–42

McKenry, PC, McKelvey, MW, Leigh, D, & Wark, L 'Nonresidential father involvement: A comparison of divorced, separated, never married, and remarried fathers' (1996) *Journal of Divorce & Remarriage*, 25(3–4), 1–13

Moorehouse, MJ 'Work and family dynamics' in PA Cowan, D Field et al (eds) *Family, self, and society: Toward a new agenda for family research* (pp 265–286) (Hillsdale, NJ, Lawrence Erlbaum Associates, Inc, 1993)

Moran, P, Ghate, D & van der Merwe, A *What works in parenting support? A review of the international evidence* (No 574) (London: Department for Education and Skills, 2004)

Nash, J 'The father in contemporary culture and current psychological literature' (1965) *Child Development*, 36(1), 261–297

O'Connor, TG, Dunn, J, Jenkins, JM, Pickering, K, & Rasbash, J 'Family settings and children's adjustment: Differential adjustment within and across families' (2001) *British Journal of Psychiatry*, 179, 110–115

O'Connor, TG, Thorpe, K, Dunn, J, Golding, J, ALSPAC Study Team, 'Parental divorce and adjustment in adulthood: Findings from a community sample' (1999) *Journal of Child Psychology and Psychiatry*, 40(5), 777–789

Parke, RD 'Fathers and families' in MH Bornstein (ed), *Handbook of parenting, vol 3: Status and social conditions of parenting* (pp 27–63) (Hillsdale, NJ, Lawrence Erlbaum Associates, Inc, 1995)

Parke, RD 'Fathers and families' in MH Bornstein (ed), *Handbook of parenting: Vol. 3: Being and becoming a parent* (2nd ed, pp 27–73) (Mahwah, NJ, Lawrence Erlbaum Associates, Publishers, 2002)

Phares, V *Fathers and developmental psychopathology* (New York, John Wiley & Sons, 1996)

Pleck, JH 'Paternal involvement: Levels, sources, and consequences' in ME Lamb (ed) *The role of the father in child development* (3rd ed, pp 66–103) (New York, John Wiley & Sons, 1997)

Popenoe, D 'American family decline, 1960–1990' (1993) *Journal of Marriage and the Family* (55), 527–541.

Popenoe, D *Life without father: Compelling new evidence that fatherhood and marriage are indispensable for the good of children and society* (New York: Martin Kessler Books, 1996)

Pruett, MK, Williams, TY, Insabella, G, & Little, TD 'Family and legal indicators of child adjustment to divorce among families with young children' (2003) *Journal of Family Psychology. Special Issue: Family psychology and family law – exploring the linkages*, 17(2), 169–180

Rodgers, B, & Pryor, J *The development of children from separate families: A review of research from the United Kingdom* (York, Joseph Rowntree Foundation, 1998)

Silverstein, LB, & Auerbach, CF 'Deconstructing the essential father' (1999) *American Psychologist*, 54(6), 397–407

Skolnick, A *Embattled paradise: The American family in an age of uncertainty* (New York, Basic Books, 1991)

Stacey, J, & Biblarz, TJ '(How) does the sexual orientation of parents matter?' (2001) *American Sociological Review*, 66(2), 159–183

Steinberg, L 'We know some things: Parent-adolescent relationships in retrospect and prospect' (2001) *Journal of Research on Adolescence*, 11(1), 1–19

Tamis-LeMonda, CS & Cabrera, N (eds) *Handbook of father involvement: Multidisciplinary perspectives* (Mahwah, NJ, Lawrence Erlbaum Associates, Publishers, 2002)

Waite, LJ, & Gallagher, M *The case for marriage : Why married people are happier, healthier, and better off financially* (1st edn) (New York: Doubleday, 2000)

Wallerstein, JS, Lewis, J, & Blakeslee, S *The unexpected legacy of divorce: A 25 year landmark study* (1st edn) (New York: Hyperion, 2000)

Zimmerman, MA, Salem, DA & Notaro, PC 'Make room for daddy ii: The positive effects of fathers' role in adolescent development' in RD Taylor & MC Wang (eds), *Resilience across contexts: Family, work, culture, and community* (pp 233–253) (Mahwah, NJ, Lawrence Erlbaum Associates, Inc, Publishers, 2000)

Relationships: Law Content and Form

*Dr Stephen Cretney**

INTRODUCTION: THE LAW AND HUMAN RELATIONSHIPS

The belief that to institutionalise essentially personal relationships – and especially the love between one human being and another – is the surest way to destroy them has a long and respectable history. What has the legal system, with all its coercive trappings, to do with such sensitive and complex matters as the feelings of one person for another or the arrangements which people make to give effect to their relationship? As a (very distinguished) English judge put it, such 'promises are not sealed with seals and sealing wax. The consideration that really obtains for them is that natural love and affection which counts for so little in these cold Courts . . .'.[1] And it is certainly impossible to read the novels of writers such as Thomas Hardy or DH Lawrence without feeling that the law generally has a destructive impact on human beings. Perhaps fear of this is a factor today influencing some of the large number of men and women who live as couples but fail to 'regularise' their relationship (to use somewhat dated terminology). Yet nowadays, 'marriage support' is an acknowledged aspect of policy: the statute book asserts that the institution of marriage is to be supported, and directs courts and others to encourage a couple in a marriage which may have broken down to take 'all practicable steps' to save it.[2] It is true that those steps are today usually expressed in terms of counselling[3] and guidance. The unhappy couple may be reminded that all relationships have their 'ups and downs', but it seems improbable that this truth would today be expressed in the once conventional language of rights and duties – a duty to accept the 'ordinary wear and tear of married life'[4] and to 'endure' personal unhappiness, coupled with a denial of any 'right' of happiness.[5]

Much of the discussion about the role of the law in respect of marriage is directed to what stance should be taken if a relationship breaks down, and yet the involvement of the legal system stems from the fact that the parties have deliberately chosen to acquire a legal status from which legal rights and duties flow. This paper seeks to ask what the legal procedures for *creating* marriage (and civil partnerships) tell us about the state's view of the nature of those relationships; and it also asks how far the law provides an adequate framework within which a couple can express the mutual commitment usually today regarded as the basis for an enduring union.

---

*   Stephen Cretney QC (hon) practised as a solicitor until 1965 after which he held academic posts including Quarrell Fellow and Tutor in Law at Exeter College, Oxford, and Dean of the Faculty of Law at Bristol University. He served as a Law Commissioner advising on law reform. He was Senior Research Fellow at All Souls College, Oxford until his retirement. His many publications include *Family Law in the Twentieth Century: A History.*

[1]   Atkin LJ, *Balfour v Balfour* [1919] 2 KB 571, 580. See further SM Cretney, 'The Literature of Family Law' (2006) 40 *Irish Jurist (NS)* 17.

[2]   Family Law Act 1996, s 1.

[3]   Family Law Act 1996, s 1(b).

[4]   As Asquith LJ put it in *Buchler v Buchler* [1947] P 25.

[5]   For a remarkable expression of this view, see the speech of Lord Hugh Cecil, see *Official Report (HL)* vol 317, col 2117 comparing the duty of an unhappily married couple to that of soldiers staying in the front line perhaps to be 'wounded, mutilated and maimed for life'.

HISTORICAL BACKGROUND

In England the State was extremely slow to get into the marriage business. With the exception of a short period[6] during the Interregnum, the law left questions about marriage to the Church and to the ecclesiastical courts. It is true that a valid marriage would give rise to very important legal consequences – for example in respect of entitlement to dower, liability to support relatives under the Poor Law, and so on; and these matters would be dealt with by the ordinary courts of the land. Because of this, the State did have an interest in knowing whether or not a marriage had been contracted, and thus in the keeping of proper records. The Marriage without Banns Act of 1695 imposed penalties on clergy who failed to keep proper records of all marriages within their parish; and in 1753 the Clandestine Marriages Act underscored this traditional view of where the dividing line between Church and State should be drawn. The established church was given a virtual monopoly[7] over the right to solemnise marriages (which were to be public events) and the Act stipulated that details of the calling of the banns (the usual preliminary to a marriage) and of the solemnisation of marriages were to be recorded in a proper register, to be 'carefully preserved for public use'.[8]

1836: MARRIAGE AND REGISTRATION LAW REFORM: BUREAUCRATIC EFFICIENCY AND RELIGIOUS TOLERATION

Yet this was insufficient to meet the requirements of an increasingly complex society. Access to hard factual information about the population and especially about demographic trends became necessary not only so that government could make appropriate provision but also so that (for example) mutual life assurance could be organised on sound actuarial principles. A Whig government had sufficient Benthamite zeal to push through reform of the laws governing marriage and the registration of births marriages and deaths.[9] Radical reform of the administration of the Poor Law[10] had created a bureaucratic machine which could be pressed into service to deal with registration procedures (although the Established Church was left to a significant extent to its own devices). True, today the Registration Service and local authorities have long ago taken over the functions once administered by the Poor Law, but the fundamental principles established in 1836 remain essentially unchanged 170 years later.

The 1836 legislation was based on a very simple and entirely rational principle: the State had a proper interest in defining the basic principles of what constituted a marriage (who could marry whom? what formalities were necessary to create the legal status of marriage?) and equally in defining the legal consequences flowing from that status, and it was for the State to establish a procedure whereby it could be determined whether or not a person was married. The State was therefore entitled to insist on a universal and efficient system for the registration of marriages, and indeed to ensure that such a system was in place. But so far as the actual celebration of the marriage was concerned, the State's role was limited to ensuring that the ceremony be recognised by both parties as binding.[11]

The Marriage Act 1836 reflects another important principle: in accordance with sound Whig principles it was founded on religious toleration. The Church of England was stripped of the

---

6   From 1653 (when statutory provision was made for civil marriage contracted before Justices of the Peace) until the restoration of the monarchy in 1660.

7   The Clandestine Marriages Act 1753 did not extend to the marriages of Jews Quakers or members of the Royal Family: ss 17, 18.

8   Clandestine Marriages Act 1753, ss 14, 15.

9   Births Deaths and Marriages Registration Act 1836; Marriage Act 1836.

10   Poor Law Amendment Act 1834.

11   See SM Cretney *Family Law in the Twentieth Century, a History* (2003), p 9.

monopoly[12] which it had enjoyed since 1735 of celebrating marriages: marriages could be celebrated, not only in Anglican churches, but also in any other building certified[13] as a place for religious worship and registered as such with the Registrar-General. And there is a complete tolerance of different forms of ceremony in such religious buildings: the parties may use 'such Form and Ceremony' as they choose. The only specific legislative requirement is that at some stage they must declare that they know of no legal reason why the marriage should not take place, and they must utter statutorily prescribed 'words of contract' calling upon those present to witness that each takes the other to be his or her wedded wife or husband.[14] Finally, the 1836 Act established a purely civil form of marriage: anyone who did not want a religious ceremony could marry in the office of the Superintendent Registrar, and all that was required as 'ceremony' was that the prescribed statutory words should be uttered.

DISTINCTION BETWEEN RELIGIOUS RITE AND CIVIL CONTRACT

The result is somewhat paradoxical. On the one hand, the legislation was intended in part to promote toleration: it is today possible in England to marry in a Hindu or Sikh temple, in a Mosque, or in a Church or other place of religious worship of any denomination. Such marriages may be celebrated by a Minister of that religion according to whatever rite those involved choose.[15] The legislation also permits a secular wedding; but this is where toleration – or to put it in the language of the twenty-first century, recognition of diversity – stops. The law draws a rigid distinction between the two kinds of wedding, and statute forbids the holding of any form of religious service[16] in a civil wedding. That prohibition has been strictly interpreted. Until recently[17] not only were readings from religious texts (for example, the *Song of Songs*[18]) prohibited but so were the 'only connect' passage from EM Forster's *Howard's End* and indeed some popular songs such as Robbie Williams' *Angels* (the lyrics of which contain what was apparently regarded as being a 'religious' reference).[19] Couples are still today debarred from exchanging the time-hallowed vow 'to have and to hold . . . for better for worse, for richer for poorer, in sickness and in health, to love and cherish, till death us do part' because that is taken from the Book of Common Prayer. In contrast, those who opt for a religious option can (subject to the agreement of the celebrant) have any readings or music they choose.

There is another significant distinction between the 'religious' weddings and the 'civil' wedding. The 'religious building' wedding can be solemnised by any person authorised to do so by the

---

[12]   Jews, Quakers and members of the Royal Family continued to enjoy the exemption which had been accorded to them by the Clandestine Marriage Act 1753.

[13]   The governing provision is now the Places of Worship Registration Act 1855 (which in fact was the crucial provision making it clear that all 'religious' places of worship were on the same footing for purposes of registration).

[14]   Marriage Act 1836, s 20.

[15]   Marriage Act 1949, s 44(1).

[16]   Marriage Act 1949, s 45(2).

[17]   In November 2005, the General Register Office announced that whilst readings from sacred texts, hymns or religious chants would still be prohibited, readings and songs containing incidental references to 'god' or other religious terms would be permitted if used in an 'essentially non-religious context', and in 'certain circumstances (to be discussed further with local registrars) classical music of a religious origin' – such as *Ave Maria* or *Zadok the Priest* – might be permitted as 'part of the background at a civil ceremony': *Modernisation of civil registration* (16 November, 2005).

[18]   'My beloved is mine and I am his . . . Set me as a seal upon your heart, as a seal upon your arm; for love is strong as death, jealousy is cruel as the grave . . . Many waters cannot quench love, neither can the floods drown it . . .'

[19]   *Content of Civil Marriage Ceremonies, A Consultation Document* (2005). In the outcome of this Consultation, the Registrar General has amended the Guidance about the interpretation of the statutory provisions: see *Content of Civil Marriage Ceremonies, Outcome of Consultation* (2006) but the 'clear distinction' between civil and religious ceremonies is to be preserved: *General Register Office Press Release*, 16 November 2005.

authorities controlling the building in which the wedding takes place.[20] In contrast, the presence of a State-appointed Registrar is a pre-requisite to the civil marriage.[21]

DISCRIMINATION AGAINST THE CIVIL WEDDING

It would be difficult to deny that the 'civil wedding' has in the past been distinctly second best. In part, this was because of the poor level of amenity in many of the Register Offices provided by Local Authorities – in 1970 the Register Office in Lambeth was situated in the middle of a building site and consisted of two rooms divided by a public lavatory, the larger of which measured 20 feet by 12[22] – and it has to be admitted that in this respect vigorous efforts have been made to improve matters. But the law continues to discriminate against those who feel the need for some 'numinous' element to mark what is on any basis a hugely important rite of passage but are either debarred by the rules of their particular religion from marrying in accordance with its rituals[23] or do not wish to accept the ministry of any recognised religion. In an increasingly secular age, when religious belief has also become much more varied and flexible, it is questionable whether such discrimination can be justified. Moreover, the validity of the rigid distinction between 'religious' on the one hand and 'civil' on the other is blurred by doubt about what exactly is required to satisfy the requirement that a building registered for the solemnisation of 'religious' weddings must be one in which *worship* associated with a *religion* takes place. There is, of course, no doubt that all the major faith groups qualify. But the Court of Appeal has held that scientology does not.[24] And the reality is that religious belief has become so diverse that it is virtually impossible to find any wholly satisfactory way of defining what is and what is not within the definition. Moreover Humanist groups believe that the refusal to allow trained Humanist officiants accredited by the British Humanist Association to officiate at Humanist weddings in the same way as can Ministers of Religion offends against the 'freedom of thought, conscience and religion' guarantee contained in Article 9 of the European Convention on Human Rights.[25]

It is true that Statute recognises the right of those married in a civil ceremony subsequently to have a religious service – as was, for example, done in the case of the wedding of the Prince of Wales and the Duchess of Cornwall. But the legislation makes it quite clear that such a ceremony has no legal effect: in no way does it 'supersede or invalidate' the civil ceremony nor is it to be recorded as a 'Marriage' in the Parish Register.[26] Whatever significance such a service of blessing may have for the parties, legally it is entirely irrelevant.

---

[20]   Marriage Act 1949, s 43.

[21]   Marriage Act, 1949, s 49(f)–(h). This account glosses over many refinements: for example, marriages in the Church of England must be conducted according to a form of service authorised according to the law which governs the Church as the established church of the land and a Church of England marriage must be celebrated by an ordained Anglican priest (or deacon): see generally SM Cretney *Family Law in the Twentieth Century, a History* (2003), pp 8–37.

[22]   Cretney, *op cit* p 27, note 157.

[23]   For example, although in principle everyone has a legal right to be married in their parish church statute has been careful to exclude those whose marriage would be contrary to Anglican canon law: hence, a person whose former spouse is still alive may be denied a wedding in an Anglican church (Matrimonial Causes Act 1965, s 8(2)) whilst the church is not required to permit the marriage of persons within the prohibited degrees of relationship as they were before the relaxations effected by the Marriage (Prohibited Degrees of Relationship) Act 1986.

[24]   *R v Registrar-General, ex parte Segerdal* [1970] 1 QB 430; and see *Re South Place Ethical Society* [1980] 1 WLR 1565.

[25]   As embodied in English law by the Human Rights Act, 1998: see the letter dated 6 August 2002 from the British Humanist Association to the Registrar General posted on www.humanism.org.uk/.

[26]   Marriage and Registration Amendment Act 1856, s 12; see now Marriage Act 1949, s 46.

THE MARRIAGE ACT 1994: 'CONSUMER CHOICE'

In the years following World War II civil wedding increasingly became the preferred option:[27] by 1981 civil marriages accounted for approximately half of all the weddings in England and Wales. But complaints about the starkness of the procedure and the poor facilities provided in some areas for civil marriage, coupled with the Thatcher government's ideological commitment to increasing consumer choice through competition and the operation of market forces, led to what is in some ways the most radical change in the laws governing marriage since the nineteenth century: a civil marriage can now take place in any premises approved by the local authority in accordance with very detailed regulations made by Central Government.[28] Those regulations are in part intended to ensure that the venue is 'seemly and dignified' and there are detailed provisions intended (amongst other things) to allay fears about the consequences of excessive consumption of alcohol at certain venues. But the rules also reflect the long standing distinction between the civil and the religious marriage: premises to be approved must have no recent or continuing connection with any religion, religious practice or religious persuasion; and it is specifically provided that no religious service is to be used, and that any reading, music, words of performance forming part of the ceremony must be secular in character.[29] Moreover a Registrar must be present to ensure that the prescribed declaration and words of contract are pronounced, and that the registration details are properly completed.

This legislation thus allows civil marriages to be celebrated with degree of solemnity and perhaps pomp which had been difficult to attain in the stark facilities at one time provided for civil marriage in the facilities originally provided by Poor Law Unions[30] and latterly by local authorities. It is now possible to have a wedding in a hotel (Claridges or the Dorchester, for example) a stately home (Blenheim Palace or Caerphilly Castle) or even at a sporting venue (Cheltenham Racecourse or Newcastle United Football ground). Moreover, local authorities have also been encouraged to embrace the consumerist approach, providing 'enhanced facilities' for those who want them (and are prepared to pay additional charges). The legislation seems to have met a real demand: at the turn of the century nearly 15% of all marriages and a quarter of all civil marriages took place in approved premises.[31] But one principle remains constant: you cannot have a friendly clergyman (or anyone else, for that matter) pronounce a blessing or say a prayer, nor can you make your vows in the way sanctioned by 300 years of history. To do so would blur the boundary between the civil and the religious, and that is something against which the law still sets its face.

COMMITMENT – BUT TO WHAT?

It is a fundamental principle of English law that the 'civil marriage' has exactly the same legal consequences as the religious marriage.[32] But the prescribed formalities give no indication of

---

[27] See J Haskey, (2002) *Population Trends* 35; and *Social Trends*, No 37 (2007) Table 2.10 and p 18.

[28] See now the Marriages and Civil Partnerships (Approved Premises) Regulations 2005 (replacing the Marriages (Approved Premises) Regulations 1995 in order to provide a uniform system for the approval of premises in which civil marriages and the formation of civil partnerships may take place). In addition to providing a Register Office, local authorities may provide additional rooms (even in the same building) which can be approved for civil marriages and civil partnerships.

[29] Ibid.

[30] The 1836 legislation deliberately made use of the administrative machinery established under the Poor Law Amendment Act 1834: for example, the Clerk to the Poor Law Guardians would normally double as Superintendent Registrar: see Cretney, *op cit* p 13. Even the Earl of Rosebery (1847–1929, Prime Minister 1894–1895) had to go to the Poor Law Office (albeit in Mayfair) for his wedding with Hannah de Rothschild in 1878: see L McKinstry, *Rosebery, Statesman in Turmoil* (2005).

[31] See J Haskey, 'Marriages in Approved Premises . . .', *Population Trends* 107, Spring 2002, p 35.

[32] The Deceased Wife's Sister's Marriage Act 1907 (presumably in an attempt to allay opposition on the part of the Church to relaxation of the law) permitted marriage (formerly prohibited) between a man and his deceased wife's

what this means; and from time to time, this omission has given rise to concern. In 1947, for example, the Denning Committee on Procedure in Matrimonial Causes,[33] believing that 'false ideas and unsound emotional attitudes' had led to a decline in respect for marriage, criticised the fact that civil marriages commonly gave the parties 'no guidance at all as to the obligations which they are undertaking'. The form of marriage should (the Committee believed) be revised 'so as to emphasise the solemnity of the occasion and clearly to express the principle that marriage is the personal union, for better or for worse, of one man with one woman, exclusive of all others on either side so long as both shall live'. Instructions were accordingly given to Registrars to remind couples of the 'solemn and binding character of the vows you are about to take' and of the fact that 'marriage, according to the law of this country is the union of one man with one woman, voluntarily entered into, for life, to the exclusion of all others',[34] and for a time the prescribed form of notice for marriage[35] was endorsed with a similar statement. But the fact that a significant number of civil marriages 'for life' involved people who had already been parties to an earlier marriage 'for life' ended perhaps because it had not been to the exclusion of all others led to the requirement being quietly dropped. Even so, 40 years on, the newly elected Blair government enthusiastically adopted[36] the 'marriage support' policies of its Conservative predecessor:[37] these were to include giving an 'enhanced role for marriage registrars'[38] who would not only provide couples intending to marry with a clear statement of what their new status meant in terms of extra rights and also extra responsibilities but also give better support to couples contemplating marriage.[39] Whether such a 'statement' would be more effective than

---

sister and declared that such marriage should be valid 'as a civil contract'. In *R v Dibdin, ex parte Thompson* [1910] P 57 the Court of Appeal held that this classification did not affect the principle stated in the text. And in *Weatherley v Weatherley* [1947] AC 628, the House of Lords denied that the civil consequences of marriage were necessarily identical with its consequences as a matter of religious doctrine: 'What marriage means to different persons will depend on their upbringing, their outlook and their religious belief' and the answer to questions about the obligations of married persons which came before the courts was to depend 'not on a consideration of the Christian doctrine of marriage . . . but on the true construction of the relevant Acts of Parliament'.

33   Final Report of the Committee on Procedure in Matrimonial Causes (1947, Cmd 7024) paras 5, 29.

34   This oft-repeated and oft-approved statement (see e g *Corbett v Corbett* [1971] P 83; *S-T (formerly J) v J* [1998] Fam 103, 141, 146 *per* Ward and Potter LJJ) which is taken from Lord Penzance's judgment in *Hyde v Hyde* (1866) LR 1 P&M 130, 133, was never intended to constitute a *definition* of marriage. The issue was whether the English divorce court could properly entertain a divorce petition in respect of a marriage which was potentially (albeit not actually) polygamous. The answer to that question was that 'the matrimonial law of this country is adapted to the Christian marriage [as described in the citation], and is wholly inapplicable to polygamy' with the result that the parties to a relationship actually or potentially polygamous were 'not entitled to the remedies, the adjudication, or the relief of the matrimonial law of England'. The court did not decide that a polygamous 'marriage' had no legal consequences as between the parties, and the courts have indeed subsequently accorded a substantial measure of recognition to such relationships provided that the parties have the legal capacity by their personal law – the law of the domicile – to contract such a marriage.

35   See e g SI 1968, 2049, forms 15 and 16. The forms currently prescribed no longer include these words.

36   See *Supporting Families, a Consultation Document* (1998) paras 4.3 and 4.6.

37   As embodied, for example, in Part 1 of the Family Law Act 1996.

38   *op cit* para 4.4. This enhanced role could extend to providing 'naming ceremonies' to celebrate a child's birth and 'renewal of vows' ceremonies to celebrate a marriage at special moments in the couple's lives or to renew, in the company of friends and family, their commitment.

39   The cynic may notice that the only specific proposals given legislative effect were included in the Immigration and Asylum Act 1999 and required couples to give a longer period of notice than had previously been prescribed and stipulated that they should both attend the Register Office to make the necessary arrangements. It should be mentioned that considerable anxiety developed at this period about the potential impact of 'sham' marriages on immigration control: eventually, the Government responded with legislation, the Asylum and Immigration (Treatment of Claimants) Act 2004. This prohibited superintendent registrars from acting on a notice of an intended civil (or non-Anglican religious) marriage to which a person subject to immigration control was a party (unless he or she belonged to a class specified by the Secretary of State) if that person did not have an entry clearance granted expressly for the purpose of enabling the marriage to take place or had the Secretary of State's Certificate of Approval (only issued on payment of a substantial fee). However, reflecting the traditional approach of the marriage laws allowing the Church of England a separate regime (including the right to celebrate a marriage after the publication of Banns of marriage without any reference to the Registration authorities) these rules were not to apply to Anglican weddings. In *R (on the application of Baiai and another) v Secretary of State for the Home Department* [2006] EWHC 823 (Admin), [2006] 3 All ER 608 Silber J held that this special treatment constituted discrimination on grounds of religion and nationality contrary to the rights guaranteed in Human Rights Act 1998, Sch 1, Articles 12

allowing the couple to pledge themselves to one another 'for better or worse, in sickness and in health, till death us do part' is a matter on which opinions may differ.

THE IMPACT OF THE CIVIL PARTNERSHIP ACT 2004

Whatever else may be said about the lack of a clear definition of marriage and its consequences the view was that marriage could, in this country, take place only between a man and a woman. But in the last decade of the twentieth century there was increasing pressure to give people of homosexual orientation the right to enter into a union recognised by law and attaching to the relationship many of the legal consequences attached to marriage. In some parts of the world (for example, the Netherlands,[40] Canada,[41] and South Africa[42]) this led to acceptance that marriage should no longer be legally confined to a relationship between a man and a woman but should be equally open to two persons of either sex. In the United Kingdom, in contrast, it was decided that same sex couples should not be allowed to marry,[43] but should instead be permitted to enter into a 'civil partnership', a relationship said to be 'parallel' to marriage but different from it, and designed both to acknowledge the legitimacy of the claim of those in same-sex relationships to recognition and to attach to such relationships many of the legal consequences of marriage.[44]

Some were apparently unsympathetic towards these linguistic and conceptual subtleties: one Government Minister[45] launching a campaign intended to promote awareness of the legislation declared that there would henceforth be 'no legal difference' between a civil partnership and marriage; whilst a Lord of Appeal in Ordinary[46] wrote in a Law Review article on 'Homosexual Rights'[47] that civil partnership would be 'marriage in almost all but name'. But the denial of the description 'marriage' to same sex relationships is of great importance to some, as became very clear in the long struggle for 'gay rights' perhaps most powerfully expressed in the United States. In this view marriage was a civil right which gays and lesbians were not to be denied: they were not to be fobbed off with some kind of 'separate but equal' institution like 'partnership' any more than the civil rights movement had allowed blacks and other victims of racial discrimination to be fobbed off with 'separate but equal' facilities in schools, public transport or indeed at lunch counters. In March 2004 the Supreme Judicial Court of Massachusetts upheld the view that to confine same sex couples to a legal regime – like civil partnership – which would allow them to acquire most of the rights and duties of marriage whilst denying them the legal status of marriage (an institution 'specially recognised in society' with 'significant social and other advantages') would be to 'maintain and foster' a 'stigma of

---

and 14. The Home Secretary apparently did not seek to lead evidence justifying the distinctive position of the Church of England on historical grounds, but preferred to rely on the belief (unsupported by evidence) that the procedures of the Church sufficed as an effective deterrent against sham marriages whereas the procedures applicable to other forms of religious marriage did not.

[40] Netherlands Civil Code, Article 30; and for a comprehensive account of developments in the European Union, K Boele-Woelki and A Fuchs, *Legal Recognition of Same-Sex Couples in Europe* (2003).

[41] The Civil Marriage Act, Statutes of Canada 2005, chapter 33.

[42] *Minister of Home Affairs v Fourie and Bonthuys* (2005) 1 December.

[43] According to a Government spokesman (Lord Filkin, at the time a Minister of State in the Department for Constitutional Affairs) same-sex marriage was 'a contradiction in terms') and the Government's position was 'utterly clear': 'we are against it, and do not intend to promote it or allow it to take place': *Official Report* (HL) 11 February 2004, vol 657, cols 1094–1095.

[44] Mrs Jacqui Smith, Deputy Minister for Women and Equality: *Official Report* (HC) 12 October 2004, vol 425, col 174, 1095.

[45] Ms Meg Nunn, Deputy Equality Minister, at Westminster Register Office, as reported in *The Daily Telegraph*, 15 September 2005.

[46] Baroness Hale of Richmond.

[47] [2004] CFLQ 125, 132.

exclusion' incompatible with constitutional human rights guarantees.[48] Decisions of the courts in Canada,[49] South Africa[50] and elsewhere have been to the same effect.[51] But English law, in contrast, remains clear: civil partnership is not 'marriage'.

CIVIL PARTNERSHIP: LEGAL TRANSACTION OR COMMITMENT TO A RELATIONSHIP?

Whether any further attempt will be made to test in the courts of this country the continued denial to gay and lesbian couples of the right to marry remains to be seen,[52] and this is not the place to attempt to rehearse the arguments which might be advanced on either side. The creation of a civil partnership is at one level a legal transaction: civil partners have the same property, pension, and support rights, the same taxation and welfare advantages (and disadvantages), and the same rights to be treated as legally related, as do married couples. But there is much more to it than that. As one West London couple were quoted as saying,[53] 'the legal and financial reasons for registering [as Civil Partners] are very important. But what's important to us is that it will be a symbolic marking of our relationship in front of our friends and family'. As the Massachusetts Supreme Judicial Court eloquently put it, marriage fulfills 'yearnings for security, safe haven, and connection that express our common humanity' embodying not only a 'deeply personal commitment to another human being' but also a 'highly public celebration of the ideals of mutuality, companionship, intimacy, fidelity, and family'. In this view, it follows that the law should give gay and lesbian couples exactly the same right to make a legal commitment to an intimate and lasting human relationship as different sex couples have traditionally enjoyed.

British Government Ministers, whilst firmly holding out against formally accepting that civil partnership was *the same* as marriage (rather than a 'separate but equal' institution) would (it seems) not disagree with the view that the partnership involved a commitment: they repeatedly asserted that the Civil Partnership Act would allow couples to make a formal and public commitment to one another, which would be reflected in the legal consequences attached to such a relationship. Yet anyone turning to the statute book will not find it easy to see any manifestation of such (or indeed any) 'commitment' in the procedures laid down in the Civil Partnership Act. In a *religious wedding* you are allowed to use any form of service you wish; and a service in the Christian tradition will invariably include vows of fidelity and exclusivity. In a civil *wedding*, you are (as we have seen[54]) prohibited from using the vows hallowed by religious tradition, but statute does require you to say that you are taking your partner as your wife or husband – nouns which will be almost universally recognised as connoting a relationship intended to be enduring and (at least in the Western tradition) exclusive. In contrast, a couple wishing to contract a *civil partnership*, are denied any possibility[55] that the partnership can be

---

[48]   *Opinions of the Justices to the Senate*, Supreme Judicial Court of Massachusetts, 802 NE 2d 565; and see *Hillary Goodridge & others v Department of Health and Others*, Supreme Judicial Court of Massachusetts, November 18 2003, 798 NE 2d 941.

[49]   *In the matter of s 5 of the Supreme Court Act* [2004] 3 SCR 698. (The issues of principle were first addressed in the individual Provinces: see notably *Halpern v Canada (Attorney General)* (2003), 65 OR (3d) 161, June 10, 2003.)

[50]   *Minister of Home Affairs v Fourie and Bonthuys* (2005) 1 December.

[51]   Legislation in several countries of the European Union has simply redefined marriage as a union between two persons: see eg the Netherlands Civil Code, Article 30; and for a comprehensive account of developments in the European Union, K Boele-Woelki and A Fuchs, *Legal Recognition of Same-Sex Couples in Europe* (2003).

[52]   The full and incisive judgment of Sir Mark Potter P, in *Wilkinson v Kitzinger (No 2)* [2007] 1 FLR 295, [2006] EWHC 2022 (Fam) would not seem likely to encourage such an attempt at the present time.

[53]   By Patrick Collinson, *The Guardian*, July 2 2005.

[54]   See p 163, above.

[55]   The Act provides that the registration is not to take place in 'religious premises' (ie 'premises used solely or mainly for religious purposes' or which 'have been so used and have not subsequently been used solely or mainly for other purposes': Civil Partnership Act 2004, s 6(2)); and that 'no religious service is to be used while the civil partnership registrar is officiating at the signing of a civil partnership document': Civil Partnership Act 2004, s 2(5).

created in the context of a religious service;[56] and there is no provision for expressions of 'commitment' in the Civil Partnership Act or in any of the (numerous and voluminous) regulations made under that Act.[57] Indeed, (in contrast to a civil *wedding*) it seems that a civil partnership can be created in complete silence. The prescribed statutory procedure is entirely one of completing 'paperwork': the parties have to give notice of their intention, and once the prescribed period of notice has expired, either party applies to the registrar for the district where the registration is to be effected,[58] the Registrar issues a 'civil partnership schedule',[59] the parties then, at the place stated in the notice and at the invitation of a Registrar,[60] sign that document in the presence of the Registrar, two witnesses, and each other;[61] the witnesses and Registrar then sign the schedule.[62] As 'soon as is practicable'[63] thereafter the authorities record the fact of registration in the Register. The crucial element in the process is simply the signature by the parties in the presence of the witnesses; and the Civil Partnership Act 2004 makes it plain that the civil partnership comes into existence when (and only when) the two parties have signed.[64] It all seems rather like making a will, or visiting a notary in France or elsewhere in continental Europe in order to conclude a property deal. Nor is there any definition of what the partnership is about in the legislation: the Act tells us that civil partnership is a 'relationship' between two people of the same sex, but nowhere is the content of the relationship explored. Specifically it seems that Parliament has not been prepared to ordain that the relationship should necessarily be a sexual relationship.[65]

EXPRESSION OF COMMITMENT: AN OPTIONAL EXTRA?

The Government's explanatory leaflet about civil partnership[66] does state that 'Getting Registered is a serious decision. As well as being an important commitment, there are significant consequences, bringing both rights and responsibilities' and the leaflet summarises the legal consequences of the civil partnership, as well as explaining how registration has to be organised. It correctly points out that the partnership is formed by the parties signing a document. The couple are told that if 'you want a ceremony around these formalities, you should discuss it with the Register Office and the venue';[67] and it is by that elliptical formula that an indication is given

---

[56] There is no legislative prohibition on their having the relationship blessed (whether before or after the statutory procedures for creating a civil partnership have taken place) but that service will have no legal significance.

[57] It is true that some idea of what is involved can be gathered from the terms of the Act, especially those dealing with what is to happen if the relationship breaks down. For example, civil partnership can only be created if both parties are unmarried and not already civil partners, and once created the partnership can only be ended by death or a judicial dissolution (or nullity) order. These procedures generally mirror the rules governing the formation and dissolution of marriage. But there are some (perhaps significant) differences: in particular, the fact that ability and willingness to consummate the relationship by sexual intercourse are not to be grounds on which the partnership can be annulled (whereas they are grounds for annulling a marriage) and that sexual unfaithfulness (in contrast to adultery as a fact sufficient to found a divorce) is not as such a basis for dissolving a civil partnership seems to indicate that civil partnership is not (as the *Pastoral statement from the House of Bishops of the Church of England, Civil Partnerships*, 25 July 2005 put it) 'predicated on a sexual relationship'. See further, SM Cretney *Same Sex Relationships* (2006) pp 32–34.

[58] And this must have been agreed with the registration authority and specified in the notice of proposed civil partnership: Civil Partnership Act 2004, s 6(3)(b), s 6(1)(c).

[59] Civil Partnership Act 2004, s 14(1).

[60] Civil Partnership Act 2004, s 2(1).

[61] Civil Partnership Act 2004, s 2(1).

[62] Civil Partnership Act 2004, s 2(3).

[63] Civil Partnership Act 2004, s 2(4).

[64] Civil Partnership Act 2004, s 2(1) and (2).

[65] See note 58 above.

[66] Published by the Department of Trade and Industry, Women and Equality Unit, September 2005.

[67] A reference to the hotels and other places approved for the registration of civil partnerships: Civil Partnership Act 2004, s 6; The Marriages and Civil Partnerships (Approved Premises) Regulations 2005, SI 2005/3168.

that the registration may take place to the accompaniment of music and readings and that it may – subject to the bar on 'religious services'[68] – include the exchange of vows or other pledges of commitment.

It appears that, at least in some areas, the Registration Service is prepared to meet the demand for ceremonial. One county council has a pro-forma intended to allow the ceremony to be personalised to a high degree of detail: the couple are invited to choose readings and music, to opt for the giving of rings (the pro-forma suggests) or other gifts and to make pledges of commitment, and to decide whether or not the ceremony will conclude with a kiss. Helpful suggestions are made. For example, the one may promise to respect the other 'as an individual, support you through difficult times, be loyal to you always, and above all love you as my partner and friend'. Rings may be exchanged to the words 'I give you this ring as a sign of our friendship and trust, wear it with happiness and pride now and always'. The suggested readings seek to meet many tastes, ranging from Sir Phillip Sidney's *Arcadia*[69] to AA Milne's 'Winnie the Pooh'.[70] Yet a same-sex couple who wish to have a reading of David's great lament on the death of Jonathan[71] – 'thy love to me was wonderful, passing the love of women' – will have to be told that (even applying the recent relaxations[72]) the bar on 'religious services' does not permit this. It is true that a same sex couple can have whatever religious[73] or other rite they wish before or after the civil partnership has been legally created. But that rite (unlike a church or other religious marriage) will be legally ineffective.

CONCLUSION

The Civil Partnership Act is in many ways a remarkable achievement: it will certainly allow same sex couples to achieve by the simple process of registration legal security for themselves and their families, and it will no doubt in practice give civil partners recognition of their factual status as a family unit. Whatever the precise legal details, it is difficult to believe that one civil partner should ever be denied recognition of his or her relationship in the many everyday situations in which that is called for. But it is regrettable that the historical development of the marriage law effectively prevents same-sex couples from expressing their commitment in the way open to different-sex couples. That in turn may lead one to question the utility of the rigid distinction between civil and religious weddings. There are no easy solutions;[74] but it is

---

[68]   See note [54] above.

[69]   'My true love has my heart and I have his
By just exchange one for another given
I hold his dear, and mine he cannot miss
There never was a better bargain driven.
My true love has my heart and I have his.' (1590. The spelling is modernised).

[70]   'Piglet sidled up to Pooh from behind
"Pooh" he whispered. "Yes Piglet?"
"Nothing" said Piglet, taking Pooh's paw.
"I just wanted to be sure of you."

[71]   Samuel II, 15–27.

[72]   See p 167, above.

[73]   It is true that many churches (notably the Roman Catholic church) regard homosexual relationships as sinful and would not be prepared to bless, much less celebrate, a same sex union. But there are churches (some with a special commitment to minister to the gay and lesbian communities) which do not accept this approach and would be willing to accept and celebrate the partnership or marriage of same sex couples.

[74]   The sorry history of attempts at reform and rationalisation is traced in SM Cretney *Family Law in the Twentieth Century, a History* (2003), pp 20–37. Progress remains slow. In 2004 it became clear that there would be difficulties in dealing with reform of the law dealing with registration of births, marriages, civil partnerships and deaths by the 'fast-track' procedure of the Regulatory Reform Act 2004. On 25 May 2006 the Government announced that it intended to 'push ahead with ... new governance arrangements foreshadowed in its consultation paper *Registration Modernisation* (2005) so far as this could be taken forward under existing legislation, and that 'the need for legislation on other aspects of civil registration' would be 'kept under review ...'. So far as the Church of England is concerned, it is proposed to legislate to allow couples to marry according to the Church's rites in parishes with which they have

suggested that the principle[75] that the State should be primarily concerned with whether eligible parties have done what is effective to bind their consciences is a sound one. It seems difficult to justify the requirement that the procedures available should be confined either (on the one hand) to the rites of a particular and officially recognised religion or (on the other) to a ceremony from which any mention of religion is rigorously excluded. This seems hardly to reflect the diversity increasingly recognised in human relationships and the way in which those relationships may be expressed.

---

a 'qualifying connection' without the need to obtain a Special Licence from the Archbishop of Canterbury. In March 2007 a draft *Church of England Marriage Measure* was debated by General Synod and committed for further revision in Committee.

[75]   See p 162 and note 18 above.

References

Ablow, JC 'When parents conflict or disengage: Understanding links between marital distress and children's adaptation to school' in PA Cowan, CP Cowan, J Ablow, VK Johnson & J Measelle (eds), *The family context of parenting in children's adaptation to elementary school* (Mahwah, NJ, Lawrence Erlbaum Associates, 2005)

Ahrons, CR *We're still family: What grown children have to say about their parents' divorce* (1st edn) (New York, HarperCollins, 2004)

Amato, PR 'Children of divorce in the 1990s: An update of the Amato and Keith (1991) meta-analysis' (2001) *Journal of Family Psychology*, 15(3), 355–370

Amato, PR 'More than money? Men's contributions to their children's lives' in A Booth & AC Crouter (eds) *Men in families: When do they get involved? What difference does it make?* (pp 241–278) (Mahwah, NJ, US, Lawrence Erlbaum Associates, Inc, Publishers, 1998)

Amato, PR 'The consequences of divorce for adults and children' (2000) *Journal of Marriage & the Family*, 62(4), 1269–1287

Amato, PR & Booth, A 'The legacy of parents' marital discord: Consequences for children's marital quality' (2001) *Journal of Personality & Social Psychology*, 81(4), 627–638

Amato, PR & Gilbreth, JG 'Nonresident fathers and children's well-being: A meta-analysis' (1999) *Journal of Marriage & the Family*, 61(3), 557-573.

Asen, E and Schuff, H 'Disturbed parents and disturbed families: assessment and treatment issues' in M Goepfert, J Webster & MV Seeman (eds) *Disturbed and Mentally Ill Parents and their Children* (Cambridge, Cambridge University Press, 2004)

Asen, E, Dawson, N & McHugh, B *Multiple Family Therapy – the Marlborough model and its wider applications* (New York and London, Karnac, 2001)

Asen, KE et al 'A Systems Approach to Child Abuse: Management and Treatment Issues' *Child Abuse and Neglect*, Vol 13, 45–57 (1989)

Baruch Bush, RA and Folger, JP *The Promise of Mediation* (Jossey-Bass, 1994)

Bateman, A & Fonagy, P *Psychotherapy for Borderline Personality Disorder* (Oxford University Press, 2004)

Benjamin RD 'Managing the Natural Energy of Conflict' in (ed.) D Bowling and D Hoffman *Bringing Peace into the Room* (Jossey-Bass, 2003) 89–94

Benjamin, RD 'The Mediator as Trickster: The Folkloric Figure as Professional Role Model' *Mediation Quarterly*, Fall 1995, 3–18

Bentovim, A and Bingley Miller L *The Family Assessment – The Assessment of Family Competence Strengths and Difficulties* (London, Pavilion, 2000)

Black, MM, Dubowitz, H, & Starr, RH, Jr 'African American fathers in low income, urban families: Development, behavior, and home environment of their three-year-old children' (1999) *Child Development*, 70(4), 967–978

Blankenhorn, D *Fatherless America: Confronting our most urgent social problem* (New York: Basic Books, 1995)

Blankenhorn, DG, Bayme, S & Elshtain, JB (eds) *Rebuilding the nest: A new commitment to the American family* (Milwaukee, WI, Family Service America, 1990)

Bowlby, J *Attachment and Loss: Volume 1 Attachment* (London, The Hogarth Press & The Institute of Psychoanalysis, London, 1969)

Bowlby, J *Attachment and Loss: Volume 2 Separation* (London, The Hogarth Press & The Institute of Psychoanalysis, 1973)

Bowling, D and Hoffman, D 'Bringing Peace into the Room: The Personal Qualities of the Mediator and their Impact on the Mediation' in D Bowling and D Hoffman (ed) *Bringing Peace into the Room* (Jossey-Bass, 2003) 13–47

Bradshaw, J, & Mayhew, E (eds) *The well-being of children in the UK* (2nd edn) (York University: Save the Children Fund, 2005)

Britton, R (2005) 'Re-enactment as an unwitting professional response to family dynamics' in M Bower (ed) *Psychoanalytic Theory for Social Work Practice: Thinking Under Fire* (London, Routledge, 2005)

Brody, GH, & Flor, DL 'Coparenting, family interactions, and competence among African American youths' in JP McHale & PA Cowan (eds), *Understanding how family-level dynamics affect children's development: Studies of two-parent families. New directions for child development* (Vol 74, pp 77–91) (San Francisco, CA, Jossey-Bass, 1996)

Calder M *The future of child protection: where have we come from and where are we going?* (CareKnowledge Briefing 15, 2006). Available at www.careknowledge.com (subscription required)

Canham, H 'Group and gang states of mind' *Journal of Child Psychotherapy*, 28:2, 113–128 (2002)

Carlson, M, & McLanahan, SS 'Father involvement, fragile families, and public policy' in C Tamis-LeMonda & N Cabrera (eds), *Handbook of father involvement: Multidisciplinary perspectives* (Mahwah, NJ, Lawrence Erlbaum Associates, 2002)

Carmichael, L (1954). *Manual of child psychology* (2nd edn) (NY, Wiley, 1954)

Chadwick DL 'The evidence base in child protection litigation' (BMJ 2006; 333: 160-161)

Chief Medical Officer (2006) *Bearing Good Witness: proposals for reforming the delivery of medical evidence in family law cases* (Consultation, DoH)

Cicchetti, D, Toth, SL, & Maughan, A 'An ecological-transactional model of child maltreatment' in AJ Sameroff, M Lewis & SM Miller (eds), *Handbook of developmental psychopathology* (2nd edn, pp 689–722) (New York, NY, US, Kluwer Academic/Plenum Publishers, 2000)

Clare B *Promoting Deep Learning: A Teaching, Learning and Assessment Endeavour* (Paper presented at International Conference of Social Work 09/2005 to be published in 'Social Work Education', date to be confirmed; available from bclare@cyllene.uwa.edu.au)

Collins J *Good To Great* (Random House, 2001)

Collins J *Good To Great And The Social Sectors A Monograph* (Random House, 2006)

Coles, P *The importance of sibling relationships in psychoanalysis* (London, Karnac, 2003)

Coles, P, (ed) *Sibling relationships* (London, Karnac, 2006)

Colonna, AB and Newman, LM 'The psychoanalytic literature on siblings' in *The psychoanalytic study of the child,* 38: 285-339 (1983)

Coltart, N *How to survive as a Psychotherapist* (London, Sheldon Press, 1993)

Coltrane, S *Family man: Fatherhood, housework, and gender equity* (New York: Oxford University Press, 1996)

Conger, RD & Chao, W (1996). 'Adolescent depressed mood' in LS Ronald (ed) *Understanding differences between divorced and intact families: Stress, interaction, and child outcome* (pp 157–175) (Thousand Oaks, CA, US, Sage Publications, Inc, 1996)

Conger, RD, Elder, GH, Jr, Lorenz, FO, Simons, RL, & Whitbeck, LB (eds) *Families in troubled times: Adapting to change in rural America* (New York: Aldine de Gruyter, 1994)

Coontz, S *The way we never were: American families and the nostalgia trap* (New York, NY, Basic Books, 1992).

Cooper A, Hetherington, R and Katz, I *The Risk Factor: making the child protection system work for children* (DEMOS publication Online – available at http://www.demos.co.uk/publications/ riskfactor (2003))

Cowan, CP & Cowan, PA 'Who does what when partners become parents: Implications for men, women, and marriage' (1998) *Marriage & Family Review*, 12(3-4), 105–131

Cowan, CP, & Cowan, PA (2000). *When partners become parents: The big life change for couples* (Mahwah, NJ, Lawrence Erlbaum Associates, (2000)

Cowan, CP, Cowan, PA & Heming, G 'Two variations of a preventive intervention for couples: Effects on parents and children during the transition to elementary school' in PA Cowan, CP Cowan, J Ablow, VK Johnson & J Measelle (eds) *The family context of parenting in children's adaptation to elementary school* (Mahwah, NJ, Lawrence Erlbaum Associates, 2005)

Cowan, PA & Cowan, CP 'Interventions as tests of family systems theories: Marital and family relationships in children's development, and psychopathology' (2002) *Development and Psychopathololgy. Special issue on Inteventions as tests of theories*, 14, 731–760

Cowan, PA & Cowan, CP 'Developmental psychopathology from a family systems and family risk factors perspective: Implications for family research, practice, and policy' in D Cicchetti & DJ Cohen (eds), *Developmental psychopathology* (2nd edn, Vol 1, pp 530–587) (New York, Wiley, 2006).

Cowan, PA, Cowan, CP, Ablow, J, Johnson, VK, & Measelle, J *The family context of parenting in children's adaptation to elementary school* (Mahwah, NJ, Lawrence Erlbaum Associates, 2005)

Cowan, PA, Cowan, CP & Cohen, N 'Supporting fathers' involvement with kids' in JD Berrick & N Gilbert (eds) *Raising children: Emerging needs, modern risks, and social responses* (not yet published)

Cowan, PA, Powell, D & Cowan, CP Parenting interventions: A family systems perspective. In W Damon (ed) *Handbook of child psychology* (5th edn, Vol 4, pp 3–72) (John Wiley & Sons, Inc, 1998)

Cummings, EM, Davies, P, & Campbell, SB *Developmental psychopathology and family process: Theory, research, and clinical implications* (E Mark Cummings, Patrick T Davies, Susan B Campbell ; foreword by Dante Cicchetti) (New York, Guilford Press, 2000)

Davies, R (1992) *Psychodynamic aspects of the professional network with forensic patients.* (Unpublished) 1st International conference on forensic psychotherapy

Day, RD, & Lamb, ME *Conceptualizing and measuring father involvement* (Mahwah, NJ, Lawrence Erlbaum, 2004).

DoH *Framework for the assessment of children in need and their families* (2000)

Dunn, J and Kendrick, C *Siblings. Love, envy and understanding* (London, Grant McIntyre, 1982)

Eberstadt, M *Home-alone America: The hidden toll of day care, behavioral drugs, and other parent substitutes* (New York, Sentinel, 2004)

Every Child Matters: change for children (2004) (London, DfES. http://www.everychildmatters.gov.uk)

Fincham, FD, Grych, JH, & Osborne, LN 'Does marital conflict cause child maladjustment? Directions and challenges for longitudinal research' (1994) *Journal of Family Psychology*, 8(2), 128-140

Fisher, R, Ury, W and Patton, B *Getting to Yes* (Houghton Mifflin Books, 2006)

Florsheim, P (2000) 'The economic and psychological dynamics of nonresident paternal involvement' in RD Taylor & MC Wang (eds) *Resilience across contexts: Family, work, culture, and community* (p. 55-87) (Mahwah, NJ, Lawrence Erlbaum Associates, Inc, Publishers, 2000)

Fraiberg, SH (1975) 'Ghosts in the nursery: a psychoanalytic approach to the problems of impaired infant-mother relationships' in Fraiberg (ed) *Clinical Studies in infant mental health. The first year of life* (London, Tavistock Publications, 1980)

Freud, A, et al *Beyond the best interests of the child* (London, Burnett Books, 1980)

Freud, A *The Ego and the Mechanisms of Defence* (London, Hogarth Press, 1937)

Goepfert, M, Webster, J & Seeman, MV (eds) *Disturbed and Mentally Ill Parents and their Children* (Cambridge, Cambridge University Press, 2004)

Goldstein *The Emotional Needs of Infants and Young Children: Implications for Policy and Practice* (1986)

Golombok, S & Tasker, F 'Children in lesbian and gay families: Theories and evidence' (1994) *Annual Review of Sex Research*, V, 73-100

Greenson, R *The Technique & Practice of Psychoanalysis. Vol 1* (London, The Hogarth Press & The Institute of Psychoanalysis, 1974)

Harknett, K, Hardman, L, Garfinkel, I & McLanahan, SS 'The fragile families study: Social policies and labor markets in seven cities' (2001) *Children & Youth Services Review*, 23(6-7), 537-555

Haynes, JM *The Fundamentals of Family Mediation* (Suny Press, 1994)

Heimann, P 'On Counter-transference' [1950] *Int J of Psycho-Anal 31*. Also in Tonnesmann M (ed) (1989) 'About children & children-No-Longer' in *Collected Papers of Paula Heimann* (London, NY, Tavistock/Routledge, 1989)

Hernandez, DJ in *Trends in the well-being of America's children and youth: 1996* (Washington, DC: US Bureau of the Census, 1996).

Hetherington, EM, & Kelly, J *For better or for worse: Divorce reconsidered* (New York: WW Norton, 2002).

Hetherington, EM, Henderson, SH, Reiss, D, Anderson, ER, Bridges, M, Chan, RW, et al 'Adolescent siblings in stepfamilies: Family functioning and adolescent adjustment' (1999) *Monographs of the Society for Research in Child Development*, 64(4), 222

Hindle, D. 'Thinking about siblings who are seen together' *Adoption and Fostering*, 19:1, 14–19 (1995)

Hindle, D (2000) *An intensive assessment of a small sample of siblings placed together in foster care* (Unpublished D.Phil. Thesis, 2000)

Hinshaw, SP, Owens, EB, Wells, KC, Kraemer, HC, Abikoff, HB, Arnold, LE, et al 'Family processes and treatment outcome in the MTA: Negative/ineffective parenting practices in relation to multimodal treatment' (2000) *Journal of Abnormal Child Psychology*, 28(6), 555–568

Huffington, C, Armstrong, A, Halton, W, Hoyle, L and Pooley, J *Working below the Surface: The Emotional Life Of Contemporary Organizations* (sic) (Tavistock Clinic Series: Karnac Books, 2004)

Irving, HH and Benjamin, M *Therapeutic Family Mediation* (Sage Publications, 2002)

Izard, CE 'On the ontogenesis of emotion and emotion-cognition relationships in infancy' in M Lewis and LA Rosenblum (eds) *The development of affect* (New York, Plenum Press, 1977) quoted in Dunn and Kenrick, 1982, p 212.

Jacobs, B *Rooted Sorrows* (Family Law, 1997)

Jenkins, J, Simpson, A, Dunn, J, Rasbash, J, & O'Connor, TG 'Mutual influence of marital conflict and children's behavior problems: Shared and nonshared family risks' (2005) *Child Development*, 76(1), 24–39

Kemp AM, Butler A, Morris A, Mann M, Kemp KW, Rolfe K, Sibert JR, Maguire S 'Which radiological investigations should be performed to identify fractures in suspected child abuse?' (*Clinical Radiology 2006*; 61: 723-736)

Kennedy H *Sudden Unexpected Death in Infancy* (The Royal College of Pathologists and The Royal College of Paediatrics and Child Health, 2004)

Kennedy, R *Psychotherapists as Expert Witnesses* (London, Karnac, 2005)

Kitzmann, KM 'Effects of marital conflict on subsequent triadic family interactions and parenting' (2000) *Developmental Psychology*, 36(1), 3–13

Klauber, T *Rooted Sorrows* (Family Law, 1997)

Klein, M (1940) 'Mourning and its relation to manic depressive states' in *Love Guilt and Reparation, The Writings of Melanie Klein Vol 1* (London, The Hogarth Press, 1975)

Klein, M 'Notes on some schizoid mechanisms' (1926), in *Envy and Gratitude* (London, Hogarth Press, 1946)

Klein, M *The Psycho-Analysis of children* (London, Hogarth Press, 1932)

Kleinbaum, DG, Morgenstern, H & Kupper, LL *Epidemiologic research: Principles and quantitative methods.* (Belmont, CA, Lifetime Learning Publications, 1982)

Kmietowicz Z 'Complaints against doctors in child protection work have increased fivefold' (*BMJ*, 2004; 328: 601)

Kuczynski, L *Handbook of dynamics in parent-child relations* (Thousand Oaks, CA, Sage Publications, 2003)

Lamb, ME 'The history of research on father involvement: An overview' (2000) *Marriage & Family Review*, 29(2–3), 23–42

Laming, Lord Herbert, *An address given at the Michael Sieff Foundation meeting 4 September 2003,* Cumberland Lodge Windsor Great Park

Langs, R *The Technique of Psychoanalytic Psychotherapy* Vol 1 (New York, Jason Aronson, 1973)

Lord, J & Borthwick, S *Together or Apart? Assessing brothers and sisters for permanent placement* (London, BAAF, 2001)

Maguire S, Mann M, John N, Ellaway B, Sibert J R, Kemp AM 'Does cardiopulmonary resuscitation cause rib fractures in children? A systematic review' (*Child Abuse and Neglect 2006*; 30: 739-751)

Maguire S, Mann MK, Sibert JR, Kemp AM (2005(b)) 'Are there patterns of bruising in childhood, which are diagnostic or suggestive of abuse? A Systematic Review' (*Archives of Disease in Childhood 2005*; 90: 186–189)

Maguire S, Mann MK, Sibert JR, Kemp AM 'Can you age bruises accurately in children? A systematic review' (*Archives of Disease in Childhood 2005*; 90: 182–186, 186–189)

McKenry, PC, McKelvey, MW, Leigh, D, & Wark, L 'Nonresidential father involvement: A comparison of divorced, separated, never married, and remarried fathers' (1996) *Journal of Divorce & Remarriage*, 25(3–4), 1–13

Menzies-Lyth, I 'The development of the self in children in institutions' in *Containing Anxiety in Institutions* (Free Association Books, 1985)

Menzies Lyth I *The functioning of social systems as a defence against anxiety: a report on a study of the nursing service of a general hospital* (1959). (Reprinted in Menzies Lyth I, *Containing Anxiety in Institutions* (London, Free Association Books, 1988)

Middlemore MP *The Nursing Couple* (London, Hamish Hamilton, 1941)

Minuchin, S *Families and Family Therapy* (Tavistock Publications, London, 1974)

Mitchell, J 'Sibling trauma: a theoretical consideration' in Coles, P (ed) *Sibling relationships* (London, Karnac, 2006)

Moorehouse, MJ 'Work and family dynamics' in PA Cowan, D Field et al (eds) *Family, self, and society: Toward a new agenda for family research* (pp 265–286) (Hillsdale, NJ, Lawrence Erlbaum Associates, Inc, 1993)

Moran, P, Ghate, D & van der Merwe, A *What works in parenting support? A review of the international evidence* (No 574) (London: Department for Education and Skills, 2004).

Nash, J 'The father in contemporary culture and current psychological literature' (1965) *Child Development*, 36(1), 261–297

National Service Framework for Children, Young People and Maternity Services: (2004) *Standards 9. The mental health and psychological well being of Children and Young People, and 11* (DoH and DfES. http://www.dh.gov.uk)

Nelson-Jones, R *The Theory and Practice Of Counselling Psychology* (London, Cassell, 1982).

O'Connor, TG, Dunn, J, Jenkins, JM, Pickering, K, & Rasbash, J 'Family settings and children's adjustment: Differential adjustment within and across families' (2001) *British Journal of Psychiatry*, 179, 110-115

O'Connor, TG, Thorpe, K, Dunn, J, Golding, J, ALSPAC Study Team, 'Parental divorce and adjustment in adulthood: Findings from a community sample' (1999) *Journal of Child Psychology and Psychiatry*, 40(5), 777-789

Ogden, T *Projective identification: psychoanalytic technique* (Aronson, New York, 1982)

O'Neill O, (2002) *A Question of Trust – Reith Lectures*. Available at http://www.bbc.co.uk/radio4/reith2002/

Parke, RD 'Fathers and families' in MH Bornstein (ed), *Handbook of parenting, Vol 3: Status and social conditions of parenting* (pp 27–63) (Hillsdale, NJ, Lawrence Erlbaum Associates, Inc, 1995)

Parke, RD 'Fathers and families' in MH Bornstein (ed), *Handbook of parenting: Vol 3: Being and becoming a parent* (2nd ed, pp 27–73) (Mahwah, NJ, Lawrence Erlbaum Associates, Publishers, 2002)

Phares, V *Fathers and developmental psychopathology* (New York, John Wiley & Sons, 1996)

Pleck, JH 'Paternal involvement: Levels, sources, and consequences' in ME Lamb (ed) *The role of the father in child development* (3rd ed, pp 66–103) (New York, NY, John Wiley & Sons, Inc, 1997)

Popenoe, D American family decline, 1960–1990 (1993) *Journal of Marriage and the Family* (55), 527–541.

Popenoe, D *Life without father: Compelling new evidence that fatherhood and marriage are indispensable for the good of children and society* (New York: Martin Kessler Books, 1996)

Prosser I, Maguire S, Harrison SK, Mann M, Sibert JR, Kemp AM Welsh Child Protection Systematic Review Group 'How Old Is This Fracture? Radiologic Dating of Fractures in Children: A Systematic Review' (Am J Roentgenol, Apr 2005; 184: 1282–1286)

Pruett, MK, Williams, TY, Insabella, G, & Little, TD 'Family and legal indicators of child adjustment to divorce among families with young children' (2003) *Journal of Family Psychology. Special Issue: Family psychology and family law – exploring the linkages*, 17(2), 169–180

Rayner, E *The Independent Mind in British Psychoanalysis* (London, Free Association Books, 1991)

Rodgers, B, & Pryor, J *The development of children from separate families: A review of research from the United Kingdom* (York, Joseph Rowntree Foundation, 1998)

Rushton, A et al (2001) *Siblings in late permanent placements* (London, BAAF, 2001)

Sandler, J, Dare C, Holder A *The patient and the analyst* (Karnac Books, 1982).

Schafer, R *The Analytic Attitude* (London, The Hogarth Press, 1983)

Schofield, G and Beek, M *Attachment handbook for foster care and adoption* (London, BAAF, 2006)

Schore, A *Affect Regulation and the Repair of the Self* (WW Norton, New York & London, 2003)

Searles, H *Collected papers on schizophrenia and related subjects* (Int Univ Press, New York, 1963)

Searles, H *Tactics and techniques in psychoanalytic psychotherapy* (Aronson, New York, 1975)

Segal, H *Introduction to the work of Melanie Klein* (Hogarth Press, 1973)

Sherwin-White, S (in press) 'Freud on Brothers and Sisters: A Neglected Topic' *Journal of Child Psychotherapy*, 2007

Silverstein, LB, & Auerbach, CF 'Deconstructing the essential father' (1999) *American Psychologist*, 54(6), 397-407

Silverstone (2006) 'Siblings' in Coles, P (ed) *Sibling relationships* (London, Karnac, 2006).

Skolnick, A *Embattled paradise: The American family in an age of uncertainty* (New York, Basic Books, 1991)

Stacey, J, & Biblarz, TJ '(how) does the sexual orientation of parents matter?' (2001) *American Sociological Review*, 66(2), 159-183

Steinberg, L 'We know some things: Parent-adolescent relationships in retrospect and prospect' (2001) *Journal of Research on Adolescence*, 11(1), 1–19

Tamis-LeMonda, CS & Cabrera, N (eds) *Handbook of father involvement: Multidisciplinary perspectives* (Mahwah, NJ, Lawrence Erlbaum Associates, Publishers, 2002)

Timberlake, E and Hamlin, E 'The sibling group: a neglected dimensions of placement' *Child Welfare* LXI 8 (1982)

Trowell, J & Huffington, C 'Daring to take the Risks: setting up a Young Family Centre' *Bulletin ACPP 14(3)* May pp 114–118 (1992)

Waddell, M (1998) 'The Scapegoat' in R Anderson & A Dartington (eds) *Facing it out. Clinical perspectives on adolescent disturbance* (London, Duckworth, 1998)

Waite, LJ, & Gallagher, M *The case for marriage : Why married people are happier, healthier, and better off financially* (1st edn) (New York: Doubleday, 2000)

Wall, N (ed) *Rooted Sorrows* (Family Law, 1997)

Wallerstein, JS, Lewis, J, & Blakeslee, S The unexpected legacy of divorce: A 25 year landmark study (1st edn) (New York: Hyperion, 2000)

Whatling, T 'Apology Matters – The Power of Apology in Family Mediation' *Mediation in Practice*, Mediation UK and UK College of Family Mediators December 2004, 7-10

White, M and Epston, D *Narrative Means to Therapeutic Ends* (WW Norton, 1990)

Williams, R (1992) *A concise guide to the Children Act 1989* (The Royal College of Psychiatrists, Gaskell, 1992)

Wilson, B 'Learning from Virgil – a philosophy for mediators' *Family Mediation in Practice*, UK College of Family Mediators Summer 2002, 1–5

Winnicott DW (1959) in *Psychoanalytic Explorations* (London, H Karnac Ltd, 1989)

Winslade, J and Monk, G *Narrative Mediation* (Jossey-Bass, 2001)

Youell, B (2002) 'The relevance of infant and young child observation in multidisciplinary assessments for the family courts' in A Briggs(ed) *Surviving Space, Papers on infant observation* (London, Karnac, 2002)

Zachary, A *Rooted Sorrows* (Family Law, 1997)

Zimmerman, MA, Salem, DA & Notaro, PC 'Make room for daddy ii: The positive effects of fathers' role in adolescent development' in RD Taylor & MC Wang (eds), *Resilience across contexts: Family, work, culture, and community.* (pp 233–253) (Mahwah, NJ, Lawrence Erlbaum Associates, Inc, Publishers, 2000)

INDEX

References are to paragraph numbers.